RESIDENTIAL
BROADBAND NETWORKS

ISBN 0-13-956442-X

90000

9 780139 564420

Prentice Hall Series In
Advanced Communications Technologies

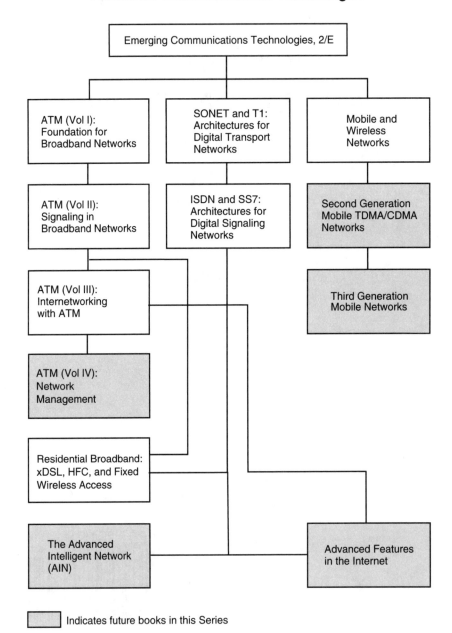

Emerging Communications Technologies, 2/E

ATM (Vol I): Foundation for Broadband Networks

SONET and T1: Architectures for Digital Transport Networks

Mobile and Wireless Networks

ATM (Vol II): Signaling in Broadband Networks

ISDN and SS7: Architectures for Digital Signaling Networks

Second Generation Mobile TDMA/CDMA Networks

ATM (Vol III): Internetworking with ATM

Third Generation Mobile Networks

ATM (Vol IV): Network Management

Residential Broadband: xDSL, HFC, and Fixed Wireless Access

The Advanced Intelligent Network (AIN)

Advanced Features in the Internet

Indicates future books in this Series

RESIDENTIAL BROADBAND NETWORKS
xDSL, HFC, AND
FIXED WIRELESS ACCESS

UYLESS BLACK

To join a Prentice Hall PTR Internet mailing list, point to:
http://www.prenhall.com/mail_lists/

Prentice Hall PTR
Upper Saddle River, New Jersey 07458

Library of Congress Cataloging-in-Publication Data

Black, Uyless D.
    Residential broadband networks : xDSL, HFC, and fixed wireless
access / Uyless Black.
      p. cm.
    Includes bibliographical references and index.
    ISBN 0-13-956442-X
    1. Broadband communication systems. 2. Telephone switching
systems, Electronic. 3. Wireless communication systems. I. Title.
TK5103.4.B54 1998
621.382′16—dc21   97–47106
                                                    CIP

Acquisitions editor: Mary Franz
Cover designer: Scott Weiss
Cover design director: Jerry Votta
Manufacturing manager: Alexis R. Heydt
Marketing manager: Miles Williams
Compositor/Production services: Pine Tree Composition, Inc.

 Published by Prentice Hall PTR
Prentice-Hall, Inc.
A Simon & Schuster Company
Upper Saddle River, New Jersey 07458

Prentice Hall books are widely used by corporations and government agencies for training,
marketing, and resale.

The publisher offers discounts on this book when ordered in bulk quantities. For more
information contact:

            Corporate Sales Department
            Phone: 800–382–3419
            Fax: 201–236–7141
            E-mail: corpsales@prenhall.com

            Or write:

            Prentice Hall PTR
            Corp. Sales Dept.
            One Lake Street
            Upper Saddle River, New Jersey 07458

Printed in the United States of America
10 9 8 7 6 5 4 3 2 1

ISBN: 0-13-956442-x

Prentice-Hall International (UK) Limited, *London*
Prentice-Hall of Australia Pty. Limited, *Sydney*
Prentice-Hall Canada Inc., *Toronto*
Prentice-Hall Hispanoamericana, S.A., *Mexico*
Prentice-Hall of India Private Limited, *New Delhi*
Prentice-Hall of Japan, Inc., *Tokyo*
Simon & Schuster Asia Pte. Ltd., *Singapore*
Editora Prentice-Hall do Brasil, Ltda., *Rio de Janeiro*

Not long ago, I read an article about how bees establish and maintain their residence, the bee hive. Since my business is communications, and I was in the middle of doing research on residential broadband technologies, I became curious about how the bee communicates with other bees in its hive. I was especially interested in the scout and field bees that fly-off from the hive—one searching for nectar, and the other bringing it back.

My curiosity was heightened by watching bees forage beds of flowers; it seemed that there would be one bee initially involved in the excursion, but before long, a group of bees would be at the same flower bed. After more reading, I discovered that the bee possesses a remarkable signaling capability, one that allows the bee to inform other bees about the location and type of the nectar.

I found also that the bee culture is similar in some aspects to the culture found in modern businesses.

Before I describe this communications skill, as well as the bee hive's organizational behavior, let me digress a moment and say that (from an anthropomorphic view), the field bee must have the best job in the hive (except for the queen bee, if one likes couch potatoes). The role of the field bee represents the last in a series of "promotions" within the hive.

Most of the bees in the hive are worker bees, and these bees must server 'lesser' jobs when they are younger, such as feeding the larvae, and guarding the hive. But the last job is that of the field bee, the one that fetches the nectar.

Like humans in organizations, worker bees get promoted. An interesting aspect of this part of the story is that, like many organizations in which I worked earlier in my career, the worker bees are promoted based on tenure (sound familiar?). In fact, bees have no notion of meritocracy. Everything is done according to the Peter Principle, and promotion rests on age alone.

Worker bees start as custodians by cleaning the hive. On the third day of their lives, they move to a new job as larvae feeders, which must be a demanding one, since each larvae must be fed 1300 times a day during a nine day period.

Their next job is to receive the food brought in by the field bees, and during this time they enter a job-training program, practicing to become field bees. And no distinction is made to merit: put in the time, and any worker bee can be a field bee.

But before assuming the field bee job, the worker bees must move to the position of a security guard. During days 17–21 of their lives, the bees must guard their home from intruders and predators.

Finally, on day 22, they become field bees, responsible for carrying the nectar to the hive. They keep this job until they are too old, at which time they usually just scout around for nectar (no heavy lifting in their senior days).

At the risk of stretching this analogy, the bees' organizational behavior resembles the way some modern organizations promote their employees. (For an authoritative study on this phenomenon, as well as a scientific comparison of worker bees to company employees, see Dilbert.)

But regarding their communications skills, bees engage in an amazing routine called a dance language, or honey dance (the Schwanzeltanze). When the scout bees return from their reconnoitering, they inform other bees about the distance and location of the nectar sources by elaborate, arobatic flying movements. Flights with figure-eights indicate the nectar is more than 100 yards away. Circular flights indicate a closer location. Sickle shaped flights are also used as part of this location process. The speed of the promenade plays a part, as does the nature of how the bee wags its tail.

This promenade (in computer network terms, a communications protocol) is executed by the bee within the dark hive, and part of the procedure is based on the position of the sun outside the hive. Some scientists believe that the bees use their antennae to follow the scout's motions; others think that the sound of the wings plays a role as well.

How do the other bees know what kind of nectar to search for? The scout bee brings back a sample. How does the scout bee know about the nectar stored in a particular flower in the first place? Some scientists tell us that the bees have an innate ability (which is not understood by these researchers) to go to the right flower (when the nectar is at its best) at the right time, without wasting time browsing at unproductive sites (a capability sorely needed in the Internet).

Earlier in this preface, I used the term anthropomorphism, which according to Webster, is ascribing human form or being to a being or thing not human. And in some circles, the term anthropomorphism is not to be used, because it may equate "lesser forms of life" to us humans. After all, bees can't think.

Fair enough, but my view is that most aspects of human behavior (and the elaborate residential communications network discussed in this book) mimic the natural world. Indeed, the communications skills of insects, fishes, and animals have long predated ours, and our methods resemble theirs, not vice-versa. The bee is just one more example. After all, the bee hive doesn't behave like corporation x—corporation x behaves like the bee hive.

Contents

CHAPTER 2 Coding and Modulation   **30**

CHAPTER 3 GR-303: Current RBB Architecture   **51**

CHAPTER 5   ATM Networks in Two-Way Access Systems   124

Preface

This book examines the emerging communications technology called Residential Broadband. While the term "residential" is in the book's title, the focus is also on the business sector. The major topic of the book is on the "local loop," that is, the link (communications channel) between a residential or business dwelling and a service provider, such as the telephone company, the cable TV operator, or an Internet service provider.

The subject matter of the book revolves around three major topics: (a) wiring or wireless schemes for the local loop, (b) coding and modulation techniques for the traffic, and (c) protocols to manage the bandwidth and control the access to/from the residential broadband system.

There are many issues pertaining to local loop access that are not yet resolved. However, the pieces are starting to come together, especially with the emergence of standards for coding/modulation, and protocols to manage the bandwidth. These issues, both resolved and unresolved, are examined in this book.

I hope the reader finds the information in this book useful. You can reach me at 102732.3535@compuserve.com.

1

Introduction

This chapter introduces the concepts behind residential broadband (RBB) and describes the problems that are leading to the deployment of residential broadband technology. As a prelude to subsequent chapters, a general review of RBB operations is provided with an emphasis on coding/modulation schemes and wiring strategies.

PROBLEMS AT THE LOCAL LOOP

For today's voice transport systems, the present structure of the local loop[1] provides adequate capacity, but that capacity is insufficient for other applications, such as data and video. Voice has a modest bandwidth requirement, with 3.5 kHz of frequency spectrum for analog voice and about 13 to 64 kbit/s for the digitized voice traffic. The local loop (the distribution plant) was designed to support voice bandwidths, with no consideration to data and video requirements.

---

[1]The local loop includes all the components (wiring, taps, connections to the customer's dwelling, etc.) between the customer premises equipment (CPE) and the service provider's equipment (i.e., the telephone company's equipment).

One of the problems we address in this book deals with local loop limitations. Many applications that are now in the marketplace, or are being developed, are significantly handicapped by local loop bottlenecks. As one example, large files often take several minutes to transfer with the current technology. Indeed, some transfers can tie up resources for hours. As another example, Internet access and browsing is often a chore, due (partially) to the limited bandwidth of the local loop. I add the word "partially" because local loop limitations are not the entire problem, as explained shortly.

Another problem deals with the capacity at the service provider's facilities to support user traffic; for example, the lack of adequate routing capacity to process the growing volume of Internet traffic. The rapid growth of the Internet, and the commensurate growth of Internet traffic, is taxing the facilities of the Internet Service Providers (ISPs). This issue is also covered in this book.

Simply stated, the present structure is not conducive to building multiapplication (multiservice) networks, because voice, video, and data applications are difficult to run concurrently on the local loop.[2]

In addition, most of the present telephone-based systems retain the practice of using 64 kbit/s DS0 (digital signaling, level 0) slots that are allocated with fixed, symmetrical bandwidth. With this approach, which has been the prevalent technology since the early 1960s, a voice call is allocated a 64 kbit/s channel in each direction of the connection. The bandwidth for this call does not change; it is "nailed up" until one of the parties hangs up the telephone handset, after which the bandwidth is made available for another call. If the two parties do not speak for a while, the bandwidth (the DS0 64 kbit/s slots) is still reserved for the call. This approach is at variance with many applications, such as data and video, that need dynamic, variable, and asymmetrical bandwidth.

Bandwidth Requirements Beyond Voice

To illustrate the differences between voice, data, and video traffic, Bell Labs has published a study of a profile of Internet traffic.[3] The study

---

[2]The term "multimedia" is the most common term used to describe a multiapplication capability. This book uses the terms multimedia, multiapplication, and multiservice synonymously.

[3]For more information, see Rodriquez-Moral, Antonio, "LIBRA", *Bell Labs Technical Journal*, 2 (2), Spring, 1997, 42–67.

reveals that much of the traffic on the Internet is asymmetrical: more traffic is sent in one direction than the other. The results are not surprising, and the symmetrical aspect of present technology does not lend itself to the support of Internet traffic.

Table 1–1 provides a summary of this study. The column labeled *Flow Type* refers to the type of traffic flowing through the Internet. The five rows in the table are entries describing five types of traffic flows. The first two entries are WEB traffic: S to C for server to client, and C to S for client to server. The third row contains information about the Mbone (multicasting backbone) application. Mbone is a video-multicasting application. It is not a backbone network per se, but operates as an application on the Internet.

The fourth row provides information on the Domain Name Service (DNS) operations. DNS is a name server procedure that correlates Internet domain names to addresses (for example, the DNS name of acme.com to an IP address of 172.16.3.4). Finally, the fifth row aggregates the other applications that were running on the Internet during this study.

The four columns in the table describe:

% of flows:	What percentage of the total Internet sessions (flows) did this flow type contribute
% of bytes:	What percentage of the Internet traffic did this flow type contribute
Average number of units:	The average number of protocol data units (PDUs) exchanged during the flow
Average number of bytes:	The average number of bytes exchanged during the flow

Table 1–1   Profile of Internet Traffic

Flow Type	% of Flows	% of Bytes	Average Number of Units	Average Number of Bytes
Web S to C	20.0	34.0	16.5	8270
Web C to S	23.3	3.3	12.5	710
Mbone	0.01	20.0	10,088	6,344,202
DNS	31.0	3.2	—	—
Others	25.7	35.4	—	—

PROBLEMS BEYOND THE LOCAL LOOP

The bandwidth problem is more than the limited capacity on the local loop media and the nature of current carrier technology. Lack of capacity can also be found in the local exchange offices, either at the called or calling side.[4] The Internet Service Providers (ISPs) have bottlenecks at their facilities as well.

Regarding the ISPs' problem, consider the decision of America Online (AOL) to offer a flat rate of $19.95 per month for unlimited Internet access. While this decision lead to a sudden surge of subscribers, AOL was already experiencing a connection time of 30 million hours per month. This usage was being experienced in the fall of 1996. By November, before the implementation of the flat rate service, AOL usage had increased to almost 60 million hours per month (for more information on this aspect of the problem see Puttre, John, "What AOL's troubles say about the 'Net'," *Business Communication Review,* March 1997, from which this data was sourced.). AOL's facilities were not designed to handle this amount of traffic. As a consequence, customers started experiencing busy signals or receiving messages indicating that service was not available. This situation reached the point where some subscribers stopped using the service.

The second problem pertains to the local telephone companies' limited capacity to handle data connections. It is well known that telephone facilities are designed to handle voice calls that are relatively short in duration, typically on the order of a few minutes. Data calls are typically longer than voice calls. Indeed, the connect time of some data calls may run into hours. Consequently, users trying to dial into the telephone network continue to receive busy signals while at the same time consuming resources at the telephone switch for detecting dial signals, returning busy tones, and so on.

The telephone network capacity problem stems from a basic fact that the holding times for Internet calls significantly reduce the capacity of the telephone switch to handle other subscribers.

The situation we find ourselves in today is a "catch-22" scenario. Once Internet customers obtain a connection, they keep it. They do not log off for fear of not getting another connection when they wish to log back on. This practice leads to a tremendous waste of bandwidth and resources at the customer site and in the network.

---

[4]While the local telephone companies have complained about the burden data places on the central office facilities, they have done a commendable job in supporting data traffic.

GROWTH IN VOICE, DATA AND VIDEO USE

Network providers, as well as the hardware and software vendors, must move swiftly to take advantage of a fundamental market reality: Data and video services as well as the markets to support these services are growing at a much faster rate than the voice market.

The statistics for the growth of voice, data, and video are shown in Figures 1–1, 1–2, and 1–3. As the figures illustrate, the voice market grew 8% in 1992, 11% in 1994, and 20% in 1996. The data market grew by 15% in 1992, 40% in 1994, and an astounding 95% in 1996. The video market has also experienced rapid growth. For example, this market grew by 5% in 1992, 25% in 1994, and 85% in 1996.

It is well recognized today that traditional voice providers and voice equipment manufacturers can no longer stay only in the voice market and expect to survive. Indeed, these figures represent a paradigm shift that has occurred only in the last few years.

There is yet another reality that operators and manufacturers must recognize. Data networking managers are migrating away from private lines toward public facilities. Perhaps nowhere is this more evident than in the success of public Frame Relay networks. The focus on public facilities will intensify with the continued growth of the Internet, which is now considered a public network.

One point is obvious: With the move toward increasing the bandwidth in the local loop, more attention is being paid to equipment and

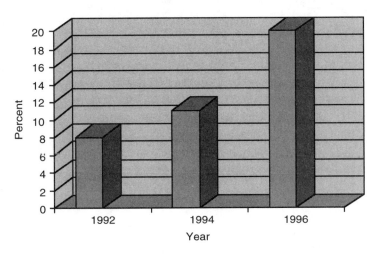

Figure 1–1   Percent growth in voice traffic.

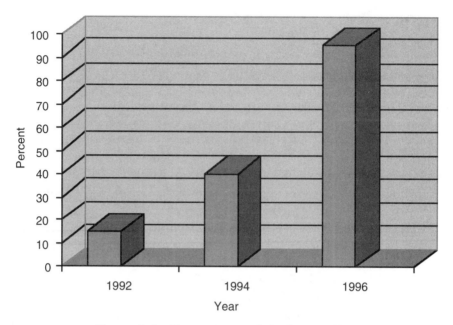

Figure 1–2   Percent growth in data traffic.

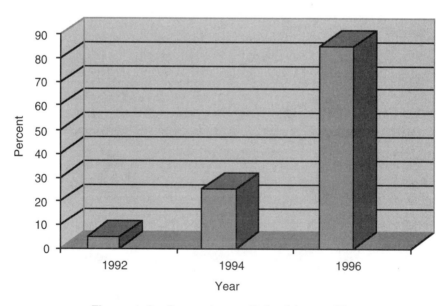

Figure 1–3   Percent growth in video traffic.

software that provide fast access from the customer premises site to an Internet service provider, or some other public carrier.

Consequently, considerable attention is focused on adding what is known as *transparent line interconnections* to service providers' current offerings. This situation means that the service providers are working to offer high-speed LAN/WAN applications entailing extending the speed of the LAN through the local loop into the WANs.

THE INCREASED NEED FOR MORE CAPACITY

In the early days of computing, a network or communications link that operated in the range of 300 to 600 bit/s was considered adequate to handle user applications. These "early" days were less than thirty years ago. But if we consider the industry only ten years ago, a 9.6 kbit/s channel and attached modems were considered rather high-capacity communications tools.

Yet, the 9.6 kbit/s speed is woefully inadequate for most applications. As an example, the reader might logon to a network to retrieve a weather map. At this speed, it takes about 40 seconds to fill the screen with a low-quality black-and-white map. A terminal user must wait several minutes for a high resolution color map to be transmitted completely. Even a relatively high-speed 28.8 Kbit/s modem cannot meet the needs of many applications. As examples, the download time through a 28.8 kbit/s modem for a single JPEG (Joint Photographic Experts Group) image is 120 seconds, and for one second of uncompressed video, 14 minutes. (1)

Technology is changing rapidly, and communications channels and computers are adapting to the increased need for higher capacity. With the increased interest in color images, voice and video, a multi-megabit communications infrastructure becomes essential. Otherwise, many of the productive and exciting applications will come to naught.

CIRCUIT AND PACKET SWITCHING

Circuit switching has been employed for a number of years to provide users with fast switching features and high-capacity transmission facilities. The technology is so named because a "continuous circuit" is provided between the two user devices. This circuit is "virtual" in the sense that it is shared by multiple users by dividing the bandwidth into time slots. Each user device is provided with reservations for these time slots. This technique is called *time division multiplexing (TDM)* and is best illustrated by the T1 system. The fabric of the T1 circuit switch uses the well-known time-slot interchange (TSI), wherein a DS0 slot on the incoming link is switched to a DS0 slot on the outgoing link.

TDM and circuit switching work well enough for applications that need continuous slots on the channel, such as voice and video. However, for bursty transmissions, the slots are not used efficiently because the slots are preassigned on a fixed basis for each user application. Therefore, the circuit switching technology is not well suited to many data communications applications that exhibit bursty-transmission characteristics.

One solution to this problem is to allow multiple users to share a network and the communications lines on an as-needed basis. Therefore, statistical *time division multiplexing (STDM)* technology has been employed for the last 25 years to meet this need. It provides a more dynamic approach to the sharing of the bandwidth. The architecture of popular X.25 uses this approach.

The attractive aspect of X.25 (and its children, Frame Relay and ATM) is that it allows multiple users to dynamically share an individual channel. It allocates the use of these channels based on STDM techniques. The allocation of the resources is based on user demand and bandwidth availability. X.25 has proven to be a very valuable resource to address the problem of dynamic bandwidth sharing, as well as providing a standard network interface that allows users to share a wide area network.

A compromise between circuit switching (with its time division multiplexing capabilities) and X.25 (with its statistical multiplexing capabilities) would be to combine the best features of the two. This approach means that an RBB technology should be able to combine the channel-sharing aspects of X.25 through statistical multiplexing and the high-speed capabilities of time division multiplexing and circuit switching. This book explains several RBB technologies that are designed to support this requirement.

APPROACHES TO SOLVING THE PROBLEMS

The bandwidth bottleneck problem can certainly be solved. Granted, it is a difficult problem, but instituting three operations will improve matters. These operations change how the local loop is viewed. I describe them sequentially here, but their implementation need not be sequential; they should be viewed as separate but mutually reinforcing operations.

Operation 1 is to increase the bandwidth of the local loop. Many efforts are underway to provide increased capacity of the media in the distribution plant. The efforts fall into two categories. The first category deals with enhanced modulation and coding schemes to make more effective use of the existing media. An example of this approach is the use of enhanced quadrature amplitude modulation (QAM) techniques that support transmission rates on the local loop in the megabit-per-second (Mbit/s) range, exemplified by the asymmetrical digital subscriber line (ADSL) approach.

The second category deals with reevaluating what the appropriate media should be in the local loop. The plain old telephone service (POTS) twisted pair remains a viable alternative. As we shall see later, other alternatives are (1) optical fiber cable, (2) coaxial cable, and (3) wireless (radio frequency [RF]) access, and combinations of the alternatives that constitute a hybrid arrangement.

Operation 2 is to develop protocols that better utilize the local loop capacity. Historically, bandwidth utilization in telephony-based networks has relied on the tried-and-true T1 technology. This technology has served the industry well, but as stated earlier, it does not meet the requirements of applications that require (1) asymmetrical bandwidth, (2) bandwidth-on-demand, and (3) variable bandwidth. Nor does the technology allow bandwidth to be borrowed from connections that are not using the bandwidth at a particular time.

Operation 3 is to expand the capacity of the service providers' facilities. These service providers are broadly classified as local exchange carriers (LECs), interexchange carriers (ICs or IXCs), and the Internet service providers (ISPs). Clearly, operations 1 and 2 will come to naught if the service providers cannot support the increased capacity of the local loop.

PRESENT RESIDENTIAL LOCAL LOOP CONFIGURATION

We have defined the problems and have laid the groundwork for solving them. Let us change pace and examine some methods that address some of these problems and, at the same time, introduce the components in a residential broadband system. This discussion will be at a general level, followed by more detailed discussions in subsequent chapters.

Figure 1–4 shows a configuration for digital two-way access services on the local loop. The telephone switch is located at the central office, generally known as a local digital switch (LDS). It communicates with an residential broadband access node through a Bellcore specification known as GR-303, more commonly known as the integrated digital loop carrier (IDLC). This node is labeled the fiber central office terminal (FCOT) in Figure 1–4.

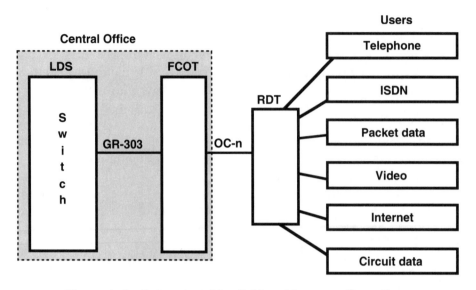

Figure 1–4   Present residential local loop configuration.

The remote digital terminal (RDT) communicates with the end user stations through the distribution plant. It is connected to an access node (a FCOT) at the central office with conventional DS1 signaling, ABCD signaling,[5] or in the more advanced RDTs, GR-303.

A common scenario for network providers is to implement a diversity of interfaces and transport options across a geographic area. Some parts of the area may need wide-area Centrex, others may need ISDN, while others at the periphery of population areas may not need sophisticated services. The point is that many of these services are not uniformly distributed and the services can vary widely in the 30 to 40 mile area covered by the serving central office (CO).

One approach is to use DS1 feeds on T1 lines (i.e., existing facilities that provide the physical media to the customer premises); then, based on the customer needs, deploy various types of services over the DS1 lines. The RDT can connect to the central office and the central office switch through GR-303 and the IDLC technology using SONET optical carrier (OC) transmission rates.

---

[5]ABCD signaling is discussed on a general level in later parts of this book and in detail in a companion book to this series, *T1 and SONET: Architecture for Digital Carrier Systems*. For the present discussion, this operation uses the robbed bits of a T1 frame. The bits are called the ABCD bits.

Full Service Terminal

Small businesses represent one of the fastest growing markets for telecommunications providers. The problem is that many of these customers are located in suburban areas, strip malls, and other geographically dispersed areas away from the central offices that provide the sophisticated services. A typical RDT is too expensive for these customers. Consequently, some manufacturers have deployed yet another piece of equipment, which is called the Full Services Terminal (FST). This configuration is designed for customers who cannot justify an RDT support of several hundred lines. Typically, this configuration is cost-effective for extending 48 to 96 lines to residential communities, university campuses, industrial parks, strip malls, and small office buildings. The configuration is shown in Figure 1–5.

One of the concepts of the FST is to allow fast response to ongoing customer requirements, which includes changing, activating, or deleting services. This type of service is very important in some locations (leased offices) where tenant turnover is high. The traffic at the FST flows to-and-from the central office through the RDT through (typically) OC-3 or OC-12 lines. From there, the traffic is sent through DS1 links between the RDT and the FST.

This brief discussion has introduced the present technology employed on the local loop, exemplified by GR-303. This technology is described in more detail in Chapter 3 and Appendix F.

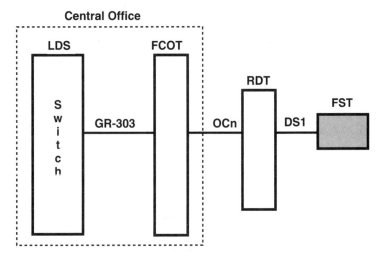

Figure 1–5 Full services terminal (FST) for small businesses.

AN OVERVIEW OF THE LOCAL LOOP

The next part of this chapter provides an overview of the local loop. The reader who is familiar with this subject can skip to the section entitled, "Digital Subscriber Line (DSL)."

LATAs

As a result of the 1984 divestiture, and the Modification of Final Judgment (MFJ), the United States was divided into geographical areas called Local Access and Transport Areas (LATAs, also called service areas) (see Figure 1–6). Divestiture separated the former Bell System into exchange and interexchange functions. Exchange services with the end user (customer) are performed by the local exchange carriers (LECs), and interchange services between LECs (across LATAs) are performed by the interchange carriers (IXCs). The LATA defines the area within which the LEC offers services, with the IXC offering services between these LATAs. The MFJ requires each LEC to offer equal and fair access to all IXCs.

The connection location between the LEC and IXC is called a *point of presence (POP)*. It is situated within the LATA, typically at a location that houses the IXC node—which could be at the LEC central office or an IXC site. An IXC may have more than one POP within a LATA. The actual connection at a POP is usually at a piece of equipment called the distributing frame, and defined as the *point of termination (POT)*. This physical termination defines the demarcation between the LEC and IXC functions, and the competitive access provider (CAP) is offered the same services as the IXC.

As Figure 1–6 shows, interLATA connections occur as

- Direct interLATA connecting (DIC) trunk: Trunks connect directly to end office
- Tandem interLATA connecting (TIC) trunk: Trunks connect through access tandem switches to end office

The Outside Plant

The line connecting the customer premises equipment (CPE) to the CO consists of the two wire configuration (see Figure 1–7). The connecting point between the CPE and CO is called the point of demarcation and is usually found in a box (the protection block or station block) on the outside of a house. The outside plant facilities include the wires and supporting hardware to the CO.

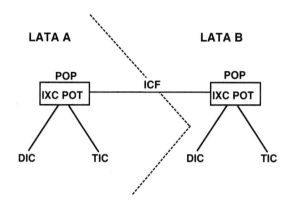

where:

DIC   Direct interLATA connecting trunk (connects directly to end office)
ICF   Interexchange carrier facility (trunks, and switching systems)
IXC   Interexchange carrier
POT   Point of termination (physical connection)
TIC   Tandem InterLATA connecting trunk (connects through access
       tandem to end office)

Figure 1–6   Local access and transport areas (LATAs).

At the CO, the lines enter through a cable room (aerial lines) or a cable vault (buried lines). The lines are then spliced to tip cables and directed to the main distribution frame (MDF); each wire is attached to a connector at the MDF.[6] From the MDF, the wires are directed to other equipment, such as a switch.

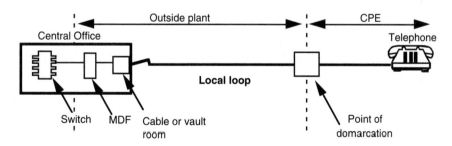

Figure 1–7   Outside plant and the local loop.

---

[6]Even though the MDF is at the CO, it is usually considered part of the outside plant and CO performance is usually measured between the MDFs.

Subscriber Loop Systems

Figure 1–8 depicts several aspects of the subscriber loop. As shown in Figure 1–8a, the system consists of feeder plant, distribution plant, and the feeder-distribution interface. The feeder plant consists of the large number of physical wires and digital repeaters, usually located based on geography constraints and customer locations. They often run parallel to roads and highways.

The distribution plant consists of a smaller number of cables and connects to the customer's network interface (NI), which is usually located in a box attached to the customer's building. The serving area interface (interface plant) is the term used to describe the manual cross-connections between the feeder and distribution plants. This interface is designed to allow any feeder unit to be connected to any distribution pair.

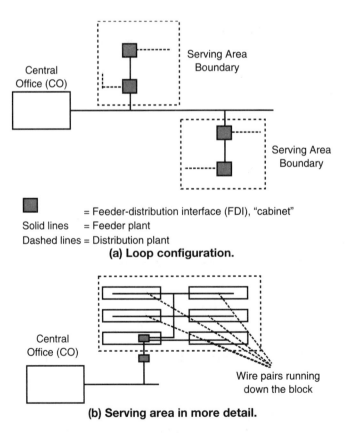

= Feeder-distribution interface (FDI), "cabinet"
Solid lines   = Feeder plant
Dashed lines = Distribution plant
(a) Loop configuration.

(b) Serving area in more detail.

Figure 1–8   Subscriber loop systems.

The subscriber loop consists of sections of copper pairs (usually about 500 feet long). These sections are joined together with electrical joints, called splices, at the telephone poles for aerial cables and at a manhole for underground cables. The cable pairs are bundled together in a cable binder group.

Figure 1–8b shows the serving area boundary in more detail. This term describes the geographical division of the outside plant into discrete parts. All wires in a serving area are connected to a single serving area interface to the feeder plant, which simplifies ongoing maintenance and record keeping.

As depicted in Figure 1–9, the feeder cables provide the links from the central office to the local subscriber area, and then the distribution cables carry on from there to the customer sites. Since the subscriber loop system is usually installed before all the customers are connected, there will be unused distribution cables. The common practice is to connect a twisted pair from a feeder cable to more than one distribution cable, and these unused distribution cables are called bridged taps. The bridged taps must be set up within the loop plant rules to minimize adverse effects on the system, such as signal loss, radiation, and spectrum distortions.

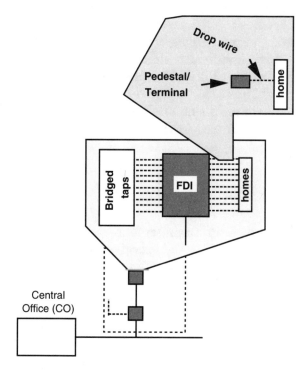

Figure 1–9   Connecting the residence.

The connection points in the distribution cables are in pedestals for underground cables and in terminals for aerial cables. The connection into the customer site is called the drop wire. It is short and can (potentially) pick up other frequency radiations. It might also radiate signals to other devices.

POTS Design Goals

In building the modern distribution system for the "plain-old telephone service" (POTS), the telephone companies established three goals. First, there had to be sufficient direct current flow to operate station sets. It was decided that all power requirements would be the responsibility of the service provider, and not the customer—a decision that millions of customers take for granted, but that provides an invaluable service.

The second goal was to support dc/low-frequency call process signaling (dialing, ringing) and to keep the signaling as simple as possible at the customer's terminal.

The third goal was to limit signal loss to acceptable levels such that the voice conversation between the customers would appear as natural as possible.

These goals have been met for POTS operations. For high-bandwidth applications, it becomes a bigger challenge. One problem is that the telephone cables use different gauges (different cable sizes), and this media difference means high-bandwidth signals must fit onto different types of media—media that exhibit different transmission characteristics.

The second problem is that twisted pair is designed for 3000 Hz telephony and not the kHz requirements for multiapplication traffic, such as video and data. For example, ADSL signals extend frequency spectrum to over 1 MHz.

DIGITAL LOOP CARRIER (DLC) SYSTEMS

Figure 1–10a shows an arrangement at the central office, where a central office terminal (COT) sends/receives 64 kbit/s signals to/from a remote terminal (RT). In this configuration, the COT is connected through a DSX-1 to a DS1–to-fiber multiplexer in order to use optical fiber on the feeder plant.[7] The RT terminates the fiber and (on the sub-

---

[7]The digital signal cross-connect (DSX, also called a digital cross-connect) is an equipment frame containing jack panels that serve as channel bank and multiplexer

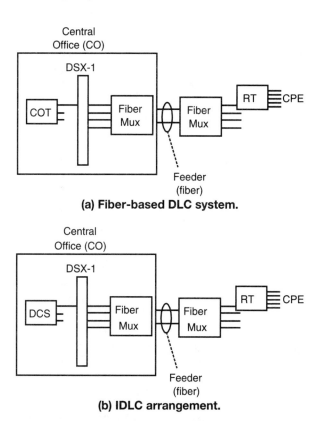

(a) Fiber-based DLC system.

(b) IDLC arrangement.

Figure 1–10   Digital loop carrier (DLC) systems.

scriber side) distributes the signals to the subscriber through copper pairs.

Figure 1–10b shows an arrangement where the COT is eliminated. This system is called an *integrated digital loop carrier (IDLC)* system because it absorbs the functions of the COT. The IDLC does not need to do analog-to-digital conversions, which are performed in the COT operation. This approach is possible because IDLC systems terminate directly into the network in a digital CO. In effect, the COT is integrated into the digital cross-connect (DCS) switch.

---

cross-connect interfaces in the telco office. The frames are named DSX-0, DSX-1, DSX-1C, DSX-3, and DSX-4 for each of the six DS rates. Each frame connects equipment that operates at the respective DSn rate. For example, the DSX-0 is employed for connecting and terminating Digital Data System (DDS) equipment.

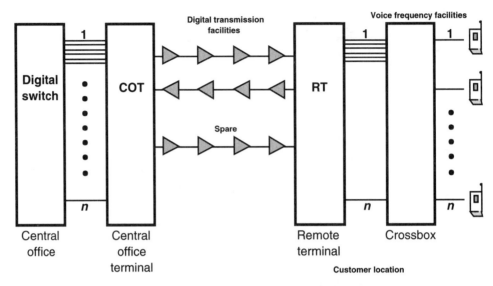

Figure 1–11   Basic subscriber system arrangement.

BASIC SUBSCRIBER SYSTEM ARRANGEMENT

Subscriber-type *pulse code modulation (PCM)* systems are available that use the same quantizing and encoding processes as the T1 systems. These systems are also software programmable for voice and data circuits just as the T1 D4 and D5 channel banks are. They are capable of advanced T1 operations[8] (see Figure 1–11). The main difference is that one terminal is located in the central office, while the other is in the field near or at the customer's location. They may be referred to also as a pair gain system, a digital loop carrier, or a subscriber loop carrier. Some of these systems can also extend a leased DS1 and/or DS3 to the customer premise for the customer's own use.

Subscriber-type systems support a wide variety of applications by various operating companies. One of the more popular uses is providing service to developing areas for new subdivisions where an existing cable plant is insufficient. A system can provide the service immediately and permanently, or it can be moved to another location (if growth in the area eventually justifies a central office). Regardless of whether the service is permanent or temporary, a subscriber system is easy to engineer and install on short notice. An example would be a new industrial park experi-

---

[8]These operations are superframe, advanced superframe, binary 8 zero suppression, etc. that are explained in the T1 and SONET book in this series.

encing sudden and unexpected growth, resulting in demands for service exceeding available loop plant. The system can be installed and operating within a few weeks. Also, many companies use these systems to provide for temporary service to large functions such as business conventions or sporting events.

Other reasons also justify the placement of a subscriber loop carrier in the loop plant. First, the copper pairs serving the subscribers will be much shorter, thus overcoming distance limitations in providing the newer services. Second, shortening the customer loop decreases the exposure to power-line interference with its resultant degradation and noise impact on these circuits. Flexibility is further enhanced by the 1200 ohm loop capability of the remote terminal. Third, electronics allow the ability to provide new services quickly. The distance from the central office to the remote terminal is limited only by the copper DS1 span line performance. Today, most of these systems employ fiber optics, so there is little distance limitation. Subscriber loop carriers provide applications for video conferencing and local area networks (LANs) links.

Subscriber carrier systems provide several functions that channel banks do not because they are in the local loop. These functions are as follows: ringing, coin collection, party lines, remote terminals, and subscriber line testing, as well as batteries for back-up power and fan units for equipment not installed in a controlled environment.

DIGITAL SUBSCRIBER LINE (DSL)

Digital Subscriber Line (DSL) distribution systems refer to a variety of systems that are designed to provide more capacity on the current embedded copper loop plant. The Asymmetric Digital Subscriber Line (ADSL), Very-high-bit DSL (VDSL), and High Bit-rate DSL (HDSL) are examples of DSL technologies. They are often grouped under the term "xDSL." Table 1–2 provides a summary of the xDSL technologies, including their bandwidth capacities and their intended deployment. We examine DSL systems in considerable detail in later chapters.

CODING/MODULATION AND WIRING SCHEMES

A number of new coding and/or modulation specifications have been published to standardize the operations across the communications link for high bandwidth performance. In addition, several subscriber loop options are under development or implementation, some of which use the

Table 1–2 Digital Subscriber Line (DSL)

xDSL Technology	Capacity	Deployment
Symmetrical Digital Subscriber Line (SDSL)	Ranges from 64 kbit/s to 2,048 Mbit/s	Conventional T1/E1 symmetrical systems
High Bit-rate Digital Subscriber Line (HDSL)	1/2 of T1/E1 in each direction	T1 lines, with ISDN line coding
ISDN Digital Subscriber Line (IDSL)	128 kbit/s in each direction	Proprietary xDSL
Asymmetrical Digital Subscriber Line (ADSL)	*Downstream:* 6.144 Mbit/s 384 kbit/s 160 kbit/s 64 kbit/s *Upstream:* 384 kbit/s 160 kbit/s 64 kbit/s	QAM techniques on twisted-pair
Very-high-bit Digital Subscriber Line (VDSL)	Variation of ADSL	Variation of ADSL

coding and modulation schemes. The organization of these schemes is depicted in Figure 1–12. This section introduces these topics and several chapters in the book are devoted to the subjects.

The more prominent coding and modulation techniques that are examined are as follows (subscriber loop options are discussed in the next section of this chapter):

- High-bit-rate Digital Subscriber Line (HDSL)
- Asymmetrical Digital Subscriber Line (ADSL) and Very-high-bit ADSL (VADSL)
  - Quadrature Amplitude Modulation (QAM)
  - Carrierless Amplitude Modulation (CAP)
  - Discrete Multi-tone Modulation (DMT)

High-bit-rate Digital Subscriber Line (HDSL)

The past several years have witnessed several new technologies in the local loop. One of these technologies is called the *High-bit-rate Digital Subscriber Line (HDSL)*. It is based on the ISDN 2B+D line coding

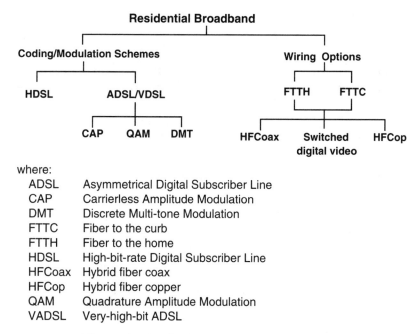

where:
ADSL   Asymmetrical Digital Subscriber Line
CAP   Carrierless Amplitude Modulation
DMT   Discrete Multi-tone Modulation
FTTC   Fiber to the curb
FTTH   Fiber to the home
HDSL   High-bit-rate Digital Subscriber Line
HFCoax   Hybrid fiber coax
HFCop   Hybrid fiber copper
QAM   Quadrature Amplitude Modulation
VADSL   Very-high-bit ADSL

Figure 1–12   Coding and wiring schemes.

(2B1Q) and will be discussed later. It operates up to 12 kft on 24 gauge copper wire, or up to 9 kft on 26 gauge. The lines are two full-duplex pairs that support bit rates of 784 kbit/s.

ADSL/VADSL

ADSL was first conceived by Bellcore in 1989. The idea is to provide different downstream speeds (network to user) and upstream speeds (user to network) to take advantage of the asymmetrical nature of many applications' transmission properties. The technology started at 1.544 Mbit/s downstream, but has now evolved to 9 Mbit/s for VADSL. At the same time, upstream technology improved from 64 kbit/s to 640 kbit/s.

Coding and Modulation Schemes with CAP, QAM, and DMT. These terms refer to several coding and modulation techniques. They are placed under ADSL/VDSL in the taxonomy because ADSL/VADSL use them in one form or another. Chapter 2 explores CAP, QAM, and DMT in more detail.

ACCESS TECHNOLOGIES (WIRING PLANS)

Figure 1–13 provides a summary of the wiring plans (also called access technologies) that are used for RBB. The RBB access is defined by six components and is discussed in more detail in subsequent chapters.

1. **Distribution:** How the media are distributed from the network provider to the area where the dwelling is located
2. **Connection of final drop:** The type of media used to connect to the customer at the curb, intermediate node, etc. (not in the dwelling)
3. **Final drop architecture:** Method of utilizing the bandwidth on the final drop

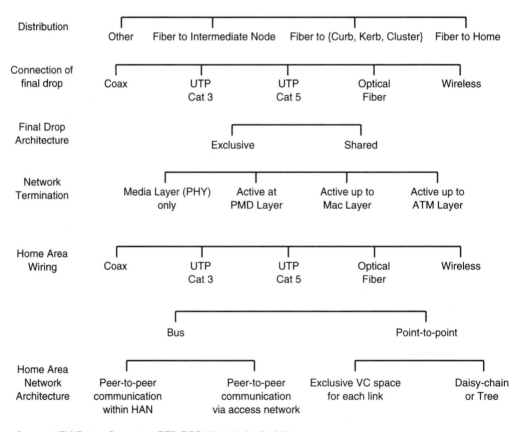

Source: ATM Forum Document BTD-RBB-001.02, April 1997

Figure 1–13   RBB access technologies.

4. Network termination: RBB layer in which network termination is/is not active

5. Home area wiring: Type of media used within customer's dwelling

6. Home area network architecture (HAN): Topology of the HAN.

Given this general taxonomy, the following discussion provides more detailed information on the more prominent wiring plans.

FTTC, FTTH: FITL

Two technologies under consideration to upgrade the local loop are fiber to the curb (FTTC) and fiber to the home (FTTH) (see Figure 1–14), also called fiber in the loop (FITL). FTTC entails the running of fiber close to the subscriber, but not to the user dwelling. The run is to a pedestal that serves the dwelling.

FTTH entails running the fiber all the way into the dwelling. While this technology provides for the most bandwidth, it is quite expensive at this stage of the local loop evolution. Each subscriber must be fitted with its own optical fiber transceiver, and the analog signals emanating from the TV must be converted to optical, digital signals. In comparison to FTTC, there is little interest in FTTH. And the FTTC proponents do not

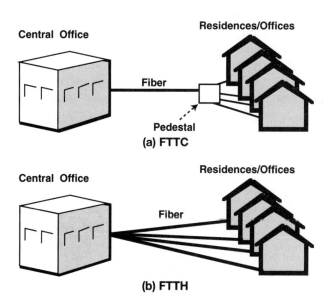

Figure 1–14 Fiber to the curb (FTTC) and fiber to the home (FTTH).

think FTTH solutions will prove as cost-effective as FTTC. Chapter 4 provides more information on FTTC, FTTH, and FITL.

Hybrid Fiber Coax (HFC)

Hybrid fiber coax (HFC) systems are being deployed in local loops in several countries. The supporters of this approach believe that the conventional twisted pair does not provide enough bandwidth in relation to its costs. The HFC technology exploits the bandwidth capacity of fiber and CATV coaxial cable.

As shown in Figure 1–15, the HFC network employs an optical fiber facility running from the central office (the headend) to a neighborhood node. The fiber has forward and return paths, and separate fibers or the deployment of wave division multiplexing are discussed in Chapter 4. At this node, users are connected by coaxial cable. The coaxial cable is shared with frequency division multiplexing (FDM) and contention resolution protocols (discussed in Chapter 7).

Switched Digital Video (SDV)

Switched digital video is yet another configuration option for the local loop. The term is confusing because it implies that it is application-specific (video). It is actually an HFC configuration, but does not use shared coaxial median. Rather, as shown in Figure 1–16, the fiber and coax are connected through a switch and each dwelling is connected by a point-to-point coaxial cable to the switch. The switch contains an optical network unit (ONU) that connects the service provider with from 8 to 40 homes.

Unlike HFC, SDV uses baseband signaling. In addition, ATM is employed to support connection management and multiapplication services.

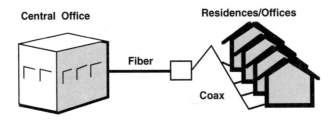

Figure 1–15   The hybrid fiber-coax scheme.

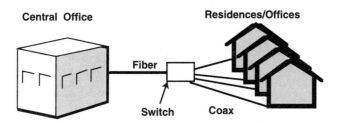

Figure 1–16   Switched digital video.

SONET IN RESIDENTIAL BROADBAND

The *Synchronous Optical Network (SONET)* was originally implemented within a service provider's backbone network. But it quickly
proved itself as a cost-effective digital transport technology for the local
access loop as well, and SONET plays a big role in residential broadband.
It provides a robust, relatively inexpensive mechanism for deploying
fiber into the distribution plant. Its extensive operations, administration,

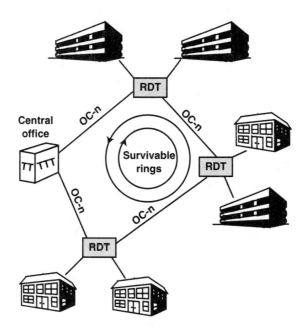

Figure 1–17   SONET in residential broadband.

and maintenance (OAM) capabilities make it an attractive technology for the service providers.

Figure 1–17 shows how SONET is being deployed to support the residential broadband technology. The most common approach is to employ SONET rings. These rings tie the customers to the central office (CO) with SONET-based remote digital terminals (RDTs). SONET payload can be added or dropped off at the customer sites through conventional SONET operations. The SONET optical carrier-n (OC-n) signals are provisionable, allowing rates (typically) in the OC-3 to OC-12 range. These "typical" rates are a function of the bandwidth requirements of the users attached to the ring.

As we shall see, SONET provides a variety of options to allow the service provider to adapt the residential broadband media to specific requirements. As suggested earlier, one of these requirements is for the use of rings. But other requirements may dictate other solutions, such as point-to-point or multipoint topologies. The use of SONET and fiber in RBB technology is explained in more detail in Chapter 4.

ATM IN RESIDENTIAL BROADBAND

While SONET has found its way into two-way, local-loop access systems, the Asynchronous Transfer Mode (ATM) technology is just beginning to emerge in this arena. One might ask why ATM would be chosen for residential broadband, when SONET and other technologies that were introduced in this chapter are available.

In some quarters, ATM is viewed as an able partner to SONET because it offers services not defined in SONET. As one example, SONET has no mechanism for setting up and tearing down connections between users and networks. ATM provides these services. As another example, SONET does not provide a means to negotiate the services (such as delay, throughput, etc.) associated with a connection. ATM provides a mechanism to negotiate these services. As yet another example, SONET is not designed to handle network congestion problems with flow control mechanisms. Once again, ATM provides a mechanism to perform flow control.

Figure 1–18 shows four user applications running on a SONET ring and utilizing ATM services, labeled A, B, C, D. SONET's responsibility is to provide a robust, relatively error-free transport system for this user traffic. It is capable of adding and dropping traffic to and from the applications' nodes as shown in Figure 1–18, but it is not capable of support-

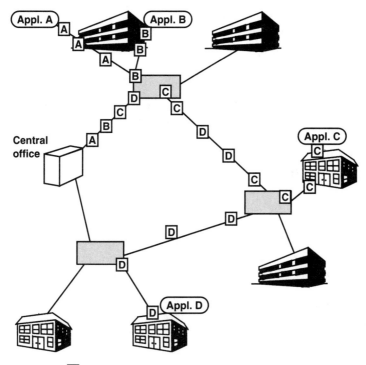

N = ATM cells with VCIs for applications (Appl.)

Figure 1–18   ATM in residential broadband.

ing a wide array of application-specific functions. In this example, traffic for application A might be a video-on-demand program and application B might be Internet traffic. Each application has different delay and throughput requirements, and ATM is able to make these requirements known to the service provider.

WIRELESS TOPOLOGY FOR RESIDENTIAL BROADBAND

Service providers, such as Cable TV (CATV) and local exchange carriers (LECs), are considering the deployment of local multipoint distribution service (LMDS), and multipoint multichannel distribution service (MMDS) in a manner shown in Figure 1–19.

MMDS operates between 2.150 GHz and 2.682 GHz and provides for 33 analog video channels. MMDS extends a cell to about 25 to 35 miles, depending on the geographical region. It is a one-way technology, and requires a separate channel (copper wire, for example) to communicate with the network provider.

The LMDS technology uses smaller cells (up to five miles for the cell radii). It supports two-way broadcast video, video-on-demand, data, and telephony services. The proposed bandwidth spectrum for LMDS is between 27.5 and 28.35 GHz. This frequency band provides much bandwidth, but at these high frequencies, the radio wavelengths are very short and more susceptible to attenuation than waveforms operating at lower frequencies. Therefore, many LMDS systems will employ digital repeaters to expand the distance of the cell. Line-of-sight is required for LMDS.

Both LMDS and MMDS are attractive for their bandwidths and their ease of installation. However their deployment is dependent upon how extensive co-channel interference will occur. To help solve this problem, some operators are looking to spread spectrum and code division multiple access (CDMA), which allows adjacent cells to share the same spectrum space.

Direct TV (DTV) via satellite is yet another option, and it is gaining in popularity. Currently, DTV can deliver 150 channels, but it is de-

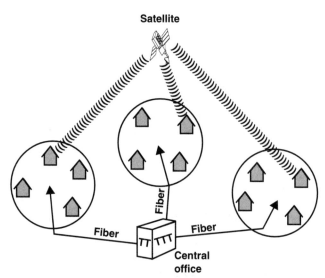

Note: Cell radius for LMDS = 5 miles and MMDS = 35 miles.
where:
    LMDS   Local multipoint distribution service
    MMDS   Multipoint multichannel distribution service

Figure 1–19   Wireless topology for residential broadband.

signed as a one-way system. Some new systems recently deployed connect the subscriber to an Internet Service Provider (ISP) with a two-way capability. The downstream channel uses the DTV media, and the upstream channel uses the conventional telephone local loop. Chapter 8 covers this subject in more detail.

SUMMARY

In order to support real-time multiservice traffic, broadband technology must be implemented on the local loop. While bandwidth allocation schemes are not yet standardized, improved coding and wiring schemes are coming into place to support residential broadband applications, and work is nearing completion on protocols designed specifically for RBB.

2

Coding and Modulation

This chapter examines the current and proposed schemes for the coding and modulation of the signals that traverse the residential broadband media and focuses in more detail on the DSL technology introduced in Chapter 1. The first part of the chapter is an introduction to modulation and coding. Next, a description is provided on modulation, with emphasis on multilevel modulation, and quadrature amplitude modulation (QAM). The next discussion focuses on the QAM-based schemes, Carrierless Amplitude/Modulation (CAP), and Discrete Multitone Modulation (DMT), the underlying technologies for ADSL. The last part of the chapter examines other aspects of ADSL.

HIGH-DATA-RATE DIGITAL SUBSCRIBER LINE (HDSL) MODULATION

In order to use the analog signal for the transmission of digital bits, the industry has developed a device called a modem. The term *modem* is a derivative of the words *mo*dulator and *dem*odulator.

Three basic methods of digital-to-analog modulation are employed by modems, and some modems use more than one of the methods. Each method impresses the data on an analog carrier signal, which is altered to carry the properties of the digital data stream. The three methods are called *amplitude modulation, frequency modulation,* and *phase modulation.*

- Amplitude modulation alters the amplitude of the signal in accordance with the digital bitstream.
- Frequency modulation alters the frequency of the signal in accordance with the digital bitstream.
- Phase modulation alters the phase of the signal in accordance with the digital bitstream.

Multilevel Coding

Multilevel coding has been employed for many years in modems and microwave and satellite transmission systems; it is the basic scheme used in ADSL and VADSL. It is found in conventional modems, such as V.32 and V.34, that operate in workstations and personal computers. Multilevel coding is used in QAM, which is depicted in Figure 2–1. On the left side of the figure, two possible signals are coded (and interpreted) as 1 or 0. Therefore, the signal is allowed to take on only two states. In the middle of the figure, the signal can take on any one of four possible states. Consequently, a single voltage (pulse value), or the phase of the signal, can be altered to represent two bits (00, 01, 10, or 11). On the right side of the figure, eight possible states can represent any one of eight 3-bit codes, ranging from 000 to 111.

Several terms are used to describe the signaling in Figure 2–1. The oldest term is *baud.* It is also called the *signaling interval, symbol rate,* or *pulse rate,* with symbol rate being the current preferred term. Thus, with multilevel coding, the actual rate (measured in bit/s) is less than the symbol rate. In this example, it is two bits per symbol rate in the middle

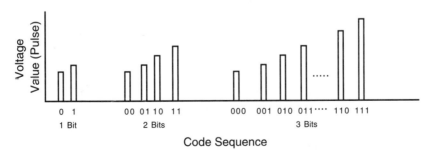

Figure 2–1   Multi-level coding.

of the figure and three bits per symbol rate in the example on the right side of the figure.

The symbol rate and bit rate are only equal if one bit is represented with each symbol. Such is the case with the older lower-speed modems, typically in the range of 1200 bit/s and less. Simple digital encoding schemes, such as non-return to zero (NRZ), explained later in Figure 2–8, is another example of encoding in which the bit rate equals the symbol rate. Higher speed modems use multilevel modulation in which more than one bit is represented with each symbol.

A signal can be modulated with the multilevel technique based on the following general definition:

$$R = D/N$$

where: R = Signaling or modulation rate; D = data rate in bit/s; N = number of bits per signaling element.

Another way to view the process is illustrated in Figure 2–2. This example shows the use of the 3-bit, 8-level coding scheme. Each of the eight possible codes is shown on the left side of the figure (I carrier) and on the right side (Q carrier). These signals differ in that they are 90° out-of-phase with each other. The I carrier is called the *in-phase carrier,* and the Q carrier is called the *out-of-phase carrier.*

In the modulation operation, the transmitter modulates two parts of the data stream onto a pair of orthogonal carriers for transmission over

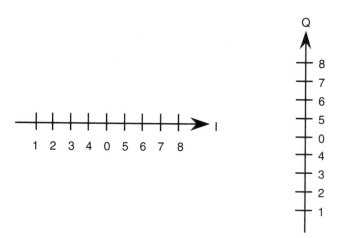

Figure 2–2   The Q and I carriers.

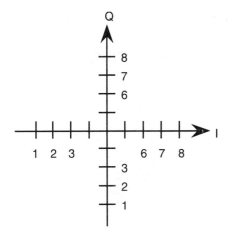

Figure 2–3 Combining the carriers.

the communications channel.[1] The relationship of the two signals is shown in Figure 2–3. The quadrature signal representations are provided by the following function, which represents orthogonality by the use of a sine and cosine mixing process. This operation can be implemented in digital coding schemes:

$$\cos (2P f_c t + Q) = \cos Q (\cos 2P f_c t - \sin Q) \sin 2P f_c t$$

The phase diagram (also called a constellation pattern) is used to represent quadrature modulation. The $\cos 2P f_c t$ signal is referred to as the in-phase or I signal; the $\sin 2P f_c t$ signal is referred to as the out-of-

---

[1] The QAM method is a form of phase modulation, or shift key (PSK). A common approach to PSK is to compare the phase of the current signal state to the previous signal state, which is known as differential PSK (DPSK). The PSK signal is represented as:

$$S(t) = A \cos (2 P f_c t + P) \quad 1$$
$$S(t) = A \cos (2 P f_c t) \quad 0$$

Phase shift key unto itself can be used to provide multilevel modulation. The technique is called quadrature signal modulation. For example, a dibit modem (two bits per symbol) typically encodes the binary data stream as follows:

$$11: = 45°$$
$$10: = 135°$$
$$01: = 225°$$
$$00: = 315°$$

phase or Q signal. QAM systems do not require that the I and Q signals coincide in any way; they are independent.

For bandwidth-limited channels, multilevel transmission is achieved by applying the following formula:

$$R = \log_2 L(1/T)$$

where: R = the data rate in bit/s; L = number of encoding levels (bits per symbol); T = length of signaling interval.

By using the I and Q signals described earlier, the receiver can detect and separate eight values on each carrier. This approach means that 64 separate states (8 × 8) can be discerned, as depicted in Figure 2–4. As a result, the symbol rate on the channel is one-sixteenth of the bit rate. As we shall see shortly, it may be less because of the use of forward error correction (FEC) operations.

The points represent the states that can be represented by the I and Q carriers. These states are called *constellation points*. The calculation for the distance between adjacent points in a PSK system is:

$$d = 2 \sin (P/N)$$

where: N = number of phases.

As the value of N increases, an increase in the bit rate results, but the closely located points are more difficult to distinguish from each other by the receiver.

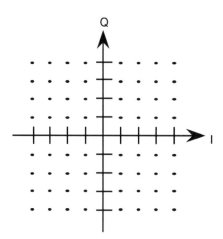

Figure 2–4   QAM constellation pattern.

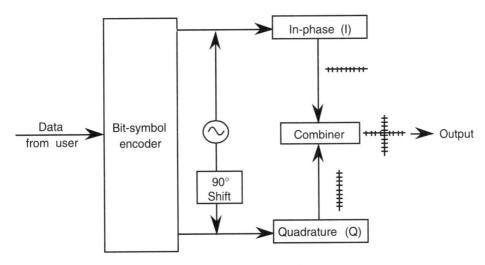

Figure 2–5   A functional view of QAM.

Figure 2–5 is a general diagram of the QAM process at the transmitter. The data bitstream from the user is placed into a bit-symbol encoder. The user bits may emanate directly from a user application to this process in one machine; for example, the user application and the QAM process coexist in a workstation. If so, they are passed to the QAM process through a buffer exchange. Alternately, the user bits may be sent from the user workstation across an interchange circuit to a modem. The interchange circuit is likely to be based on EIA-232, V.35, or other common interfaces.

The bit-symbol encoder splits the data into two half-rate streams. As explained earlier, these streams are modulated onto a pair of orthogonal carriers. Each carrier obtains its reference from the same source, as depicted by the ~ in the figure, but one bitstream is subject to the 90° phase shift (cosine function). The results of these operations are I and Q signals, which are combined for transmission onto the channel.

SYMBOL RATES AND BIT RATES

With multilevel coding, the bit rate is increased by increasing the bits encoded per symbol. To provide an example, we will use one of the physical layer specifications in the IEEE 802.14 RBB draft document, discussed in more detail in Chapter 7.

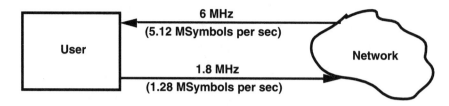

Figure 2–6   A proposed QPSK scheme in IEEE 802.14.

One of the 802.14 physical layer (PHY) options is quaternary phase shift key (QPSK), with a 2 bit-per-symbol coding scheme. As shown in Figure 2–6, the QPSK signals operate on a 6 MHz downstream spectrum and a 1.8 MHz upstream spectrum.

For the downstream direction the bit rate on each 6 MHz channel is 10.24 Mbit/s (2 bits per symbol × 5.12 Msymbols per second). For the upstream direction, the bit rate on each 1.8 MHz channel is 2.56 Mbit/s (2 bits per symbol × 1.28 MSymbols per second).

The rationale for these schemes is explained further in Chapter 7 (see "The Adaptive Digital Access Protocol (ADAPt+)"). Additional options in the IEEE 802.14 draft specification for QAM signaling are also explained in this section.

CARRIERLESS AMPLITUDE MODULATION (CAP)

Carrierless amplitude/phase modulation (CAP) is similar to QAM in that it is a 2-D transmission scheme. However, it does not use orthogonal carriers generated by a sine and cosine mixer. The modulation of the two half-rate bitstreams is performed by two digital transversal bandpass filters. Analog-type signals are used in addition to multilevel coding to represent a bitstream. The idea is for a *pair* of analog signals to represent a symbol, just as the multilevel scheme of 2B1Q accomplishes, for example. A CAP scheme for these signals is shown in Figure 2–7 for 51.84 Mbit/s 16-CAP systems. (2)

The CAP parameters for this arrangement are:

- Bits per symbol: M = 4
- Symbol rate: 1/Ts = 12.96 Msymbols/s
- Center frequency: fc = 16.2 MHz
- Lowest frequency: fl = 6.48 MHz

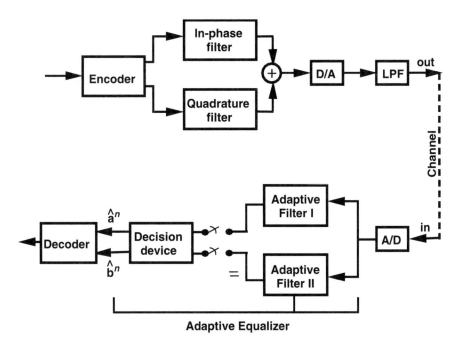

Figure 2–7   CAP transmitter and receiver.

- Highest frequency: ffh = 25.92 MHz
- Bandwidth: W = 19.44 MHz

In a manner similar to the process discussed earlier in this chapter, four bits at a time are encoded into a symbol and passed to the filters, which produce in-phase and quadrature representations of the symbol. The signals are summed, passed to the A/D converter, presented to a low pass filter (LPF), and onto the medium.

At the receiver, the signal is recovered, processed through the A/D converter, the filters, the decision devices (also called a slicer), and the decoder. The receiver's filters and slicer is part of the components of an adaptive equalizer. The equalizer compensates for the distortion in the incoming signal (3).

CAP is designed to operate at an approximate bandwidth of 6.48 to 25.92 MHz. This bandwidth means the signal does not operate in the lower frequencies where channel impairments (notches, noise) appear. In addition, a design goal is to limit the power spectrum to frequencies below 30 MHz, due to the marked increase in propagation loss at these higher frequencies. The FCC in the United States has places restrictions on using the frequency spectrum above 30 MHz, as do some other countries.

Analysis of CAP Performance

Given that the signal should not occupy the lower and upper frequencies of the available spectrum, the decision to use CAP is based partially on its frequency spectrum characteristics. Figure 2–8 compares the

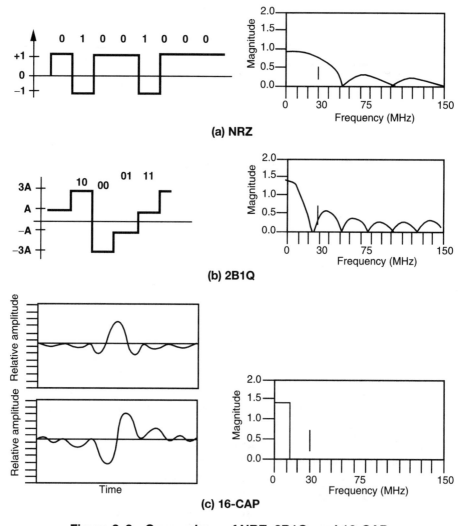

Figure 2–8   Comparison of NRZ, 2B1Q, and 16-CAP.

frequency spectrum of three schemes: (1) non-return to zero (NRZ), (2) 2B1Q, and (3) 16-CAP.[2]

NRZ uses a simple plus or minus voltage to represent binary 1s and 0s. The V.28 and EIA-232 digital coding schemes are based on this technique. As Figure 2–8a shows, the NRZ spectrum extends well beyond 30 MHz.[3]

The 2B1Q uses multilevel coding, with each digital pulse representing two binary values. The ISDN coding scheme is based on this technique. As Figure 2–8b illustrates, 2B1Q emits most of its energy at the lower frequencies, but still exhibits significant spill-over at the higher frequencies.

As mentioned earlier, CAP employs analog signals, and multilevel coding. Like 2B1Q, the analog pair represent binary values. Figure 2–8c demonstrates that the frequency spectrum produced by CAP is below 30 Hz.[4]

THE ATM FORUM CAP SPECIFICATION

The ATM Forum has published specifications for running ATM over Category 3 unshielded twisted-pair cabling. Figure 2–7 provides a summary of these specifications.

The bit rate of 51.84 Mbit/s is the SONET STS-1 rate as defined in ANSI T1.105. The physical medium dependent sublayer PMD uses CAP for bit transmission and timing. The constellation map is almost identical to V.22 bis, a widely used modem in personal computers. Of course, the symbol rate for V.22 bis is only 1200 symbols per second.

The symbol rate for the 51.84 Mbit/s interface is 12.96 symbols per second, and 4 bits are mapped into a 16-CAP constellation diagram, as shown in Figure 2–9. The lower rates of 25.92 Mbit/s and 12.96 Mbit/s use a 4-CAP code and 2–CAP code respectively. The approach is to use

---

[2]An excellent description of CAP (and crosstalk) is provided by Townsend, Werner, and Nguyen in "Using Technology to Bring ATM to the Desk Top," *AT&T Technical Journal,* July/August, 1995, from which this figure was derived.

[3]NRZ spectrum is sin x/x with the lobes (shown in Figure 2–8) extended out to 150 MHz.

[4]The spectrum shown in Figure 2–8 is not as square as shown. With the use of adaptive equalization, the spectrum is spread further out, but it is still within the 30 MHz limit.

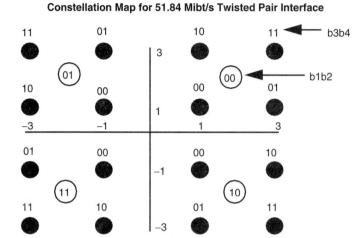

Figure 2–9   ATM forum specifications on twisted pair using CAP.

in-phase and quadrature components with four levels of coding. In Figure 2–9, the amplitudes of the in-phase and quadrature components are plotted on the vertical and horizontal axes.

DISCRETE MULTI-TONE (DMT) MODULATION

Discrete multi-tone (DMT) modulation is a multicarrier modulation technology. The unique aspect of DMT is the division of the frequency spectrum into symbol periods. Each symbol period can carry a certain number of bits. The bits are then assigned to FDM signaling tones, each operating at different frequencies as shown in the upper part of Figure 2–10. The 26 kHz to 1.1 MHz spectrum is divided into 4 kHz FDM channels, and DMT coding and modulation is applied to each 4 kHz subchannel.

If the full bandwidth operates consistently across all frequencies (which will not be the case) then the same number of bits could be transmitted in each signal period as suggested in the lower portion of Figure 2–10. However, as we shall see shortly, line capacity varies with frequency. Consequently, the subchannels operating on frequency domains

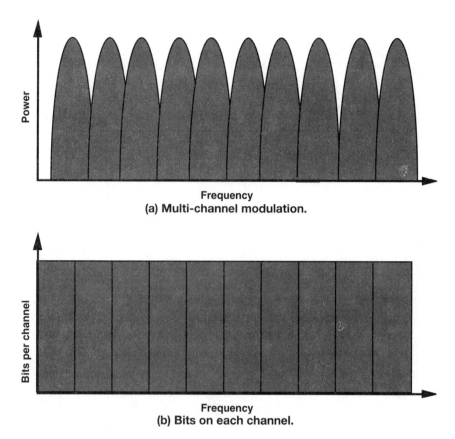

Frequency
(a) Multi-channel modulation.

Frequency
(b) Bits on each channel.

Figure 2–10   Discrete multi-tone (DMT) modulation.

of higher quality will carry more bits than the more poorly performing frequencies.

The bits for each subchannel (tone) are modulated with QAM techniques and placed onto each FDM carrier. Consequently, DMT is actually a set of multiplexed QAM systems operating in parallel with each subchannel corresponding to the DMT frequency tone. The DMT transmitter modulates the data stream by forming tone bursts and adding the bursts together and sending them onto the line in what is known as a DMT symbol.

Figures 2–11 and 2–12 depict how DMT can be programmed to adjust to the conditions across the different frequencies in a channel. The number of bits sent over each of the subchannels can be adapted to the quality of the frequencies in the channel. Figure 2–11a shows that certain frequencies are performing better than others as shown by the power gain axis. Consequently, the DMT transmitter is programmed to bear the number of bits sent in each subchannel, as depicted in Figure 2–11b.

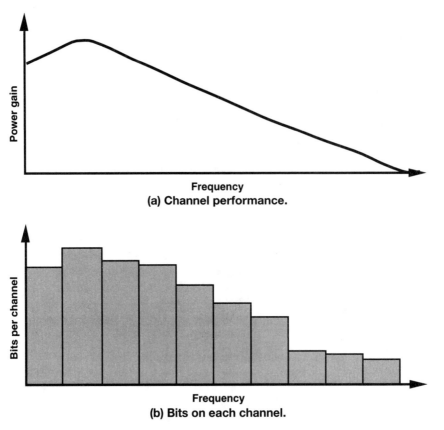

Frequency
(a) Channel performance.

Frequency
(b) Bits on each channel.

Figure 2–11   Discrete multitone (DMT) modulation.

DMT can be further refined to adjust to impulse noise and radio frequency interference (RFI), as shown in Figure 2–12. It is assumed that crosstalk is more pronounced in certain frequencies than others in the channel, as is RFI. So, DMT allows performance to be maximized not only for each circuit but also the frequencies in the circuit. This operation is particularly attractive in local loops that suffer crosstalk and local interference.

Some additional thoughts are appropriate to bring into our analysis at this time. ADSL systems require a higher transmit level (+20 dBm) than traditional distribution plant systems. However, this higher power is spread over a wider bandwidth. Thus, the overall power spectral density (PSD) operates within the levels acceptable to existing equipment.

Consequently, crosstalk between ADSL and ISDN is no different from self-crosstalk between two ISDN systems running in the same wire.

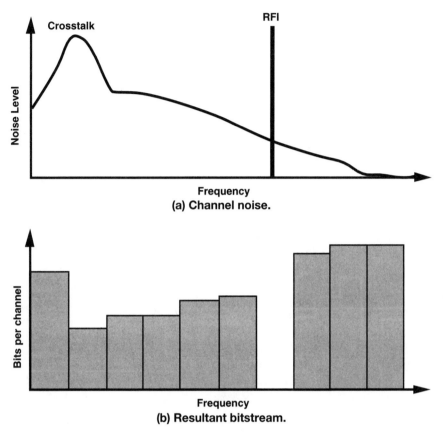

Figure 2–12   Discrete multi-tone (DMT) modulation.

Moreover, each subchannel can be allocated different power values, which allows the application of the power in a nonuniform manner.

CAP/QAM VERSUS DMT

Table 2–1 reflects the conclusions reached by British Telecom (BT) in its research on QAM, CAP, and DMT.[5] BT groups CAP and QAM together in this comparison because they are quite similar to each other. In

---

[5]For the reader who wishes to know more about BT's study, I refer you to an excellent paper published in *BT Journal,* 13 (4), October 1995. This paper was published by Gavin Young, Kevin T. Foster, and John Cook. My examples of DMT are also sourced from this paper.

Table 2–1   CAP/QAM versus DMT

Attribute/Issue	CAP/QAM	DMT
Optimum bandwidth (theoretical)	+ Adaptively shapes allocation of information	
Performance	+ Better at high transmission rates, more usable bandwidth	
Delay	– Processing delays may not conform to standards at ADSL speeds	+ Within international specifications
RF interference	+ More adept	– Experiences more errors
Clipping noise	– More susceptible, resulting in expensive analog to digital conversion	+ Not a serious issue
Echo cancellation	– Not a "trivial" matter	+ Not complex
Impulse noise	+ Greater immunity	– Less immunity
FEC		+ Able to use simpler methods
Upstream/downstream adaptability	+ More flexible in supporting a variety of data rates	
Activation time	– Complex startup procedure	+ Simple startup procedure

a nutshell, these techniques all work well. The end user will not be able to tell the difference between them. The issue is, which technology will an RBB provider choose? Since these technologies are placed in modems, the RBB customer may be tied to a specific RBB service provider. If the customer wishes to change service providers, it may require the replacement of the user's ADSL modems.

Presently, ANSI is working only on DMT as a standard, but CAP has been set forth by private groups as an alternative standard, and a proposal has been given to ANSI.

ASYMMETRICAL DIGITAL SUBSCRIBER LINE (ADSL)

Asymmetrical Digital Subscriber Line (ADSL) was introduced in Chapter 1, and the underlying technologies for ADSL (QAM, CAP, DMT) have just been described. Recall that it is based on the premise that the current traditional telephone services that are symmetrical (equal band-

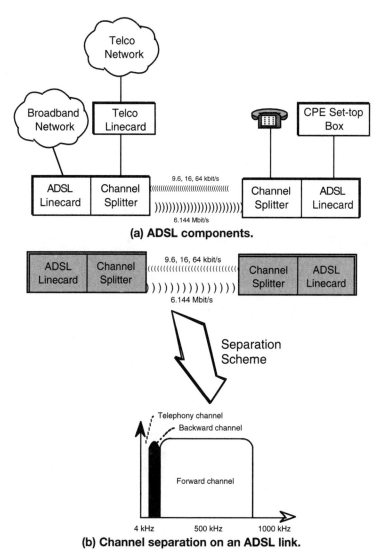

(a) ADSL components.

(b) Channel separation on an ADSL link.

Figure 2–13   ADSL architecture.

width in both directions) must evolve to an asymmetric system. ADSL is designed to provide asymmetric bandwidth and to take advantage of reduced bandwidth in one direction by using the extra bandwidth in the other direction.

The ADSL technology was originally defined as a downstream and upstream technology wherein the downstream signal (network to user) was a 1.5 Mbit/s channel and the upstream channel (user to network) operated at 16 kbit/s. Conventional telephone services were supported on same wire pair. In 1994, a 6 Mbit/s system was introduced that provides for four high-capacity channels over 12 kft of copper wire. The current ANSI T1E1 standard defines the downstream channel (toward the subscriber) to operate in the simplex mode between 1.5 and 6.1 Mbit/s. The other channels can operate downstream and upstream at rates between 16 and 576 kbit/s. The system also supports traditional voice service on the same twisted pair as ADSL. ADSL uses a frequency spectrum ranging between 0 and 1.1 MHz. The 0–4 Hz spectrum is reserved for POTS (see Figure 2–13).

ADSL uses adaptive signal-processing techniques to make up for distortions of the signal on the subscriber loop. It is designed to provide the high bit rates over two-wire cable.

ADSL ARCHITECTURE

As just mentioned, the installation of ADSL on the local loop does not disturb the existing cable in the distribution plant, nor does it necessitate taking the customer's phone service out for a long time. As shown in Figure 2–13, the customer's location is outfitted with a POTS splitter and an ADSL remote unit. These interfaces allow the existing copper wire to be split into multiple channels: Forward: central office to customer (upstream to downstream), and Return: customer to central office (downstream to upstream).

The return channel operates at much lower frequency than the forward channel(s) (an asymmetrical configuration). Consequently, crosstalk is not so great a problem in comparison to conventional symmetrical configurations. The POTS voice signals are isolated from the ADSL signals by the low-pass voiceband splitter filter. It can be packaged with the interface card at the central office or CPE, or it can be packaged separately.

RADSL and VDSL

Two variants of ADSL are rate adaptive DSL (RADSL) and very-high-speed DSL (VDSL). RADSL adjusts the bit rate of the transmission based on line quality. The DMT technology is seen as an effective tool for RADSL.

VDSL defines a short-distance link with a downstream 60 Mbit/s bandwidth and an upstream 6.4 Mbit/s bandwidth as one possibility. Another VDSL prototype modem operates at 13, 26, or 52 Mbit/s downstream options and 2 Mbit/s upstream. This modem is also designed to operate at 4500, 3000, or 1000 feet, respectively, for these downstream rates.

RADSL and VDSL technologies are far from settled and work continues on their refinement.

ITU-T V SERIES MODEMS

In the last few years, the ITU-T V Series recommendations have become the prevalent standards for modems designed for use on telephone-type circuits. X.25 also permits the use of these specifications at the physical layer. Table 2–1 provides a summary of the V Series interfaces, and the legend explains the entries in Table 2–1. The column labeled "modulation technique" describes the physical signaling between the modems.

CROSSTALK

The information-carrying capacity of the twisted pair is determined by a number of factors. One factor is collectively known as "impairments" and consists of (1) near-end crosstalk (NEXT), (2) far-end crosstalk (FEXT), (3) radio frequency interference (RDI), (4) impulse noise, and (5) white noise. Each of these factors, working in combination, will limit the capacity of a channel to carry information, as will the attenuation of the signal itself.

As depicted in Figure 2–14, NEXT occurs when transmitters in the same multi-pair cable affect other pairs in the cable. A transmitter on one pair interferes with the input of a transceiver at the same end of the cable pairs. Due to capacitive and inductive coupling, the transmitted signal leaks into the receiver. NEXT is usually the most common (significant) source of noise and affects the operations on high transfer rate systems.

FEXT occurs when transmitters in the same multipair cable leak into the receivers at the other end of the cable. For symmetrical digital transmission systems, FEXT is not a big problem, because the FEXT signal experiences more decay than the signal itself. For asymmetrical sys-

Table 2-2 ITU-T V Series Modems

Series Number	Line Speed	Channel Separation	Modulation Rate	FDX or HDX	Modulation Technique	Bits Encoded	Switch Lines	Leased Lines	Use of V.25
V.29	9600	4-Wire	2400	Either	QAM	4:1	No	PP 4W	ND
V.29	7200	4-Wire	2400	Either	PS	3:1	No	PP 4W	ND
V.29	4800	4-Wire	2400	Either	PS	2:1	No	PP 4W	ND
V.32	9600	EC	2400	FDX	QAM	4:1	Yes	PP 2W	Yes
V.32	9600	EC	2400	FDX	TCM	5:1	Yes	PP 2W	Yes
V.32	4800	EC	2400	FDX	QAM	2:1	Yes	PP 2W	Yes
V.33	14400	4-Wire	2400	FDX	TCM	7:1	FS	PP 4W	ND
V.34	28800	EC	Varies	FDX	TCM	Varies	Yes	PP 2W	Yes
V.34+	33600	EC	Varies	FDX	TCM	Varies	Yes	PP 2W	Yes
V.35	48000	4-Wire	NA	FDX	FM	NA	No	Yes	ND

A V series number may be entered into the table more than once. This means that the recommended standard permits more than one option. The initials "ND" means not defined in the specification. The initials "NA" mean not applicable, and "FS" means for further study.

Entries	**Explanation**
Line speed	Speed in bits per second (bit/s).
Channel separation	If the recommended standard permits multiple channels, the method of deriving the channels is noted as:
	FD: Frequency Division
	4-Wire: Each set of wires carries a channel
	EC: Echo Cancellation
Modulation rate	The rate of the signal change of the carrier on the channel, in baud.
Full duplex or	FDX: Full Duplex
Half duplex	HDX: Half Duplex
Modulation technique	The description of the modulation technique where:
	FS: Frequency Shift
	PS: Phase Shift

Entries	**Explanation**
	QAM: Quadrature Amplitude Modulation
	FM: Frequency Modulation
	TCM: Trellis Coded Modulation
Bits encoded	Describes the number of bits encoded per signal change (baud).
	For example, 2:1 means two bits encoded per baud.
	Describes the use of conventional dial-up circuits.
Switched lines	O: Optional 2W: Two-wire
	PP: Point-to-point 4W: Four-wire
	MP: Multipoint
Leased lines	
V.25	A ITU-T specification that describes the procedures for automatic dial- and-answer. May also offer features on call and answer beyond that of V.25.

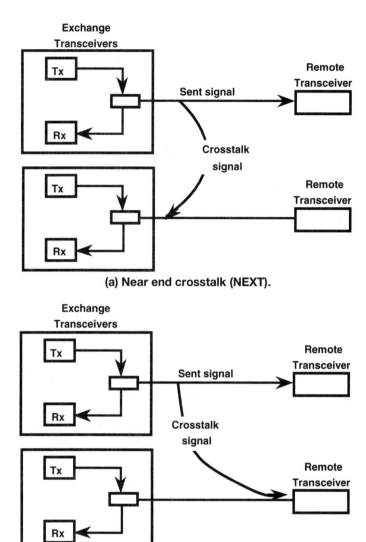

(a) Near end crosstalk (NEXT).

(b) Far end crosstalk (FEXT).

Figure 2–14   Crosstalk.

tems, it is significant. Also, FEXT is often more severe when the signals on the other pairs are the same kind as those that are experiencing interference. This problem is known as self-FEXT.

Figure 2–15 shows the effect of NEXT and propagation loss on category 5 VTP cable (3). This category of cable is explained in Appendix B.

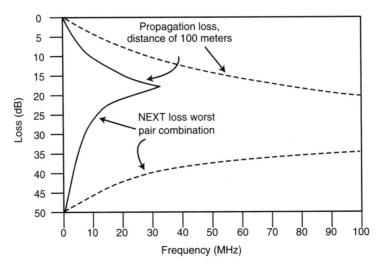

Figure 2–15 Propagation and delay loss (*Source:* See foot-note 5).

SUMMARY

Modern transmission systems use multilevel modulation, with QAM being the most common modulation technique. The V series modems form the basis for most modems today. Discrete multi-tone (DMT) modulation and carrierless amplitude modulation (CAP) are being implemented in many systems. QAM, CAP, and DMT are the coding/modulation schemes for ADSL.

3

GR-303:
Current RBB Architecture

This chapter provides an overview of Bellcore's GR-303, the specifications for the Integrated Digital Loop Carrier (IDLC) system. It also compares IDLC to its predecessor, the Universal DLC (UDLC). The GR-303 layers are examined with examples of how the layers are used in ground start and loop start systems. It will be helpful if the reader is familiar with the material in Appendix A while reading this chapter.

GR-303 ARCHITECTURE

GR-303 establishes specifications for the operations between the local digital switch (LDS) and the remote digital terminal (RDT). The intent of these specifications is to permit the interconnection of LDSs and RDTs from different manufacturers or suppliers. This set of systems is also known as a generic *integrated digital loop carrier* (IDLC) system. In addition to the goals just cited, GR-303 also aims to reduce the burden and expense of multiple proprietary interfaces.

Figure 3–1 depicts a functional view of the IDLC system in relation to a UDLC. The principal difference between and IDLC and UDLC is the absence of the central office terminal (COT). Figure 3–1 compares the IDLC (at the top of the figure) to the UDLC (at the bottom of the figure).

The basic assumption is that IDLC is more beneficial from the standpoint of performance, because fewer components are involved, which is evident from the bottom part of Figure 3–1. As mentioned earlier, the COT is eliminated as is the analog interface unit (AIU).

The connection through the devices is based on conventional DS1 and the extended superframe (ESF) formats. A separate DS0 data link, the embedded operations channel (EOC), is used to transmit operation messages between the RDT and LDS. The EOC is derived from the LAPD protocol, found in ISDN, as well as the ISO/ITU-T CMIP/ASN.1 messages. In addition, a separate 64 kbit/s data link is used to perform per call timeslot assignments and, as an option, to transmit the call processing messages between the RDT and LDS. Yet another option is the

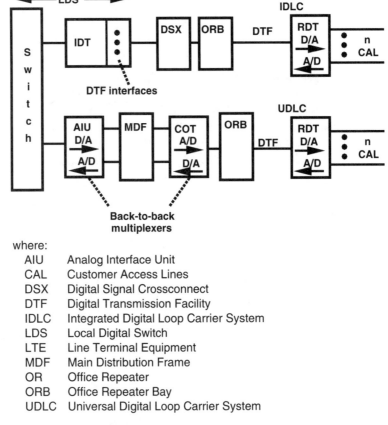

where:

AIU	Analog Interface Unit
CAL	Customer Access Lines
DSX	Digital Signal Crossconnect
DTF	Digital Transmission Facility
IDLC	Integrated Digital Loop Carrier System
LDS	Local Digital Switch
LTE	Line Terminal Equipment
MDF	Main Distribution Frame
OR	Office Repeater
ORB	Office Repeater Bay
UDLC	Universal Digital Loop Carrier System

Figure 3–1   GR-303 architecture.

conventional signaling employing the ABCD bits found in many DS1-based systems today.

IDLC systems support a wide range of special services and provide a flexible and inexpensive means to offer these services. Costs can be reduced substantially by providing services when the carrier serving area (CSA) concept is used. The system can also provide ISDN basic access to a large number of lines in the distribution plant.

IDLC ARCHITECTURE

Figure 3–2 shows a functional view of the IDLC architecture. In this particular installation, IDLC includes the DSX-1 frame over which the physical cross-connects occur for the DS1 signals. The remote digital terminal (RDT) provides the interface between the customer access lines (CALs)

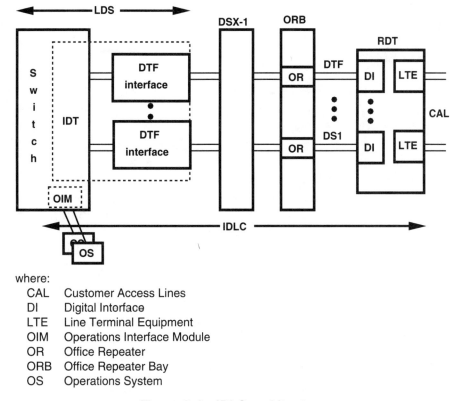

where:
   CAL   Customer Access Lines
   DI   Digital Interface
   LTE   Line Terminal Equipment
   OIM   Operations Interface Module
   OR   Office Repeater
   ORB   Office Repeater Bay
   OS   Operations System

Figure 3–2   IDLC architecture.

and the DS1 facility. The DTF interface terminates one DS1 facility and provides several digital terminal services, such as frame alignment, multiplexing/demultiplexing, signaling insertion, and signaling extraction.

The DTF facility also includes power feed, fault location with loopbacks, and signal regeneration. These functions operate in the line terminal equipment (LTE) card, which is installed into the RDT or LDS. These LTE functions can also be installed in other external equipment, such as office repeater bays (ORBs) located either at the central office or at the RDT.

While the ORB is part of the DTF, it is installed as a separate piece of equipment (located in the central office or the RDT). In addition, the office regenerators (ORs) provide the signal characteristics that are needed for the connection of the DTF to the DSX-1 frame. These functions must include DC powering for all line repeaters, equalization, signal regeneration, impedance matching, and metallic pair termination.

The integrated digital terminal (IDT) is a piece of equipment that replicates the functions of a UDLC systems COT, with the exception of D/A and A/D conversions.

TYPES OF SERVICES

The GR-303 interface provides for five major types of services. The first service is *DS1 facility operations,* used to support the signals across the interface with DS1 alarms, loopbacks, and protection switching. *Call processing* is the second major function it allows setup and clearance of calls, timeslot assignment, and use of autoband signaling (with some options). The third function, *information transport,* supports the transport of user traffic; voice, video, data, and so on. The fourth function is *IDLC System/Terminal Operations,* which encompasses provisioning, performance monitoring, and so on. The fifth function is part of DS1 facility operations and is called *loop testing.* Loop testing is controlled in a proprietary fashion between lines in the CO or in a remote maintenance center at an RTU at the RDT location.

REMOTE DIGITAL TERMINAL (RDT)

The components to the IDLC are examined in more detail in this section. To begin the analysis, the remote digital terminal (RDT) provides interfaces between the customer access lines and the DS1 lines. Typically, the RDT is divided into three major parts, shown in Figure 3–3.

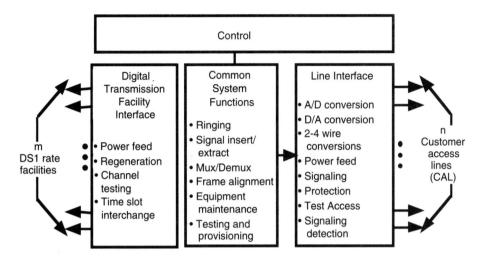

Figure 3–3 Remote digital terminal (RDT).

- Line interface functions: These functions are responsible for A/D and D/A conversions, 2-alarm to 4-alarm conversion, signaling (including ringing and detection as well as power feed)
- Common system functions: The principal functions in the common system include multiplexing/demultiplexing, timeslot interchange, channel testing, frame alignment, and signaling insertion/extraction. The line interface functions can be configured to meet specific customer access line needs.
- Digital transmission facility (DTF) interface functions: The DTF is part of the LDS and the RDT. The DTF interface provides digital terminal functions and terminates a DS1 facility. Its operations include multiplexing/demultiplexing, signaling insertion/extraction, as well as frame alignment, power feed, loopback testing, and regeneration and fault location. Some of these functions are delegated to be line terminal equipment (LTE) functions, but can be incorporated into either the RDT or the LDT. These functions can also be provided by external equipment such as an office repeater bay (ORB) located either at the CO or the RDT. While the ORB is considered to be part of the DTF, it is a separate equipment bay also located at the CO or RDT.

In general, the RDT supports operations for maintenance testing and conditioning. The operations can be provided by an operations channel through the switch, a supervisory system, or simply a local crafting interface.

INTEGRATED NETWORK ACCESS

The integrated digital terminal (IDT) is part of the LDS and duplicates the functions of the "old" UDL systems COT. It does not, however, perform the COT operations of D/A and A/D conversions. The idea of the IDT is to define a common operation for an RDT, including management and administration. A set of DTF interfaces and all LDS common equipment comprise the IDT. Also, there is a 1:1 correspondence between the IDT and RDT. In effect, the IDT is designed to mirror the functions of the RDT with the exception of interface operations such as the D/A and A/D conversions. Figure 3–4 provides a functional view of the IDT structure.

The IDT also requires operations interfaces for maintenance, testing, and provisioning. The maintenance functions include error reporting and performance monitoring. In the RDT, these interfaces are provided to the LDS and IDT or through a craft interface device (CID). The IDT

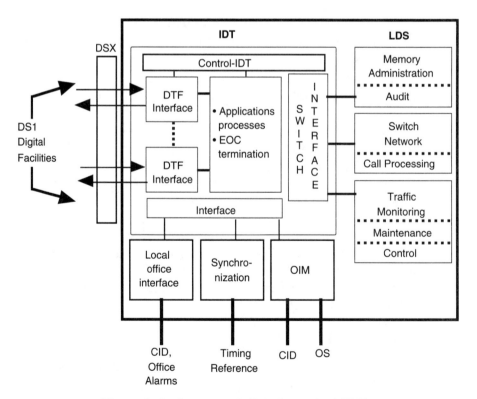

Figure 3–4   Integrated digital terminal (IDT).

only needs a synchronization network interface, whereas the RDT includes timing from its incoming DS1 signals.

The integrated network access (INA) architecture is shown in Figure 3–5. This system provides direct digital connectivity between the digital facilities and the distribution plant loop area and the digital interface facilities. The INA can perform field grooming at the RDT, the side door rout-

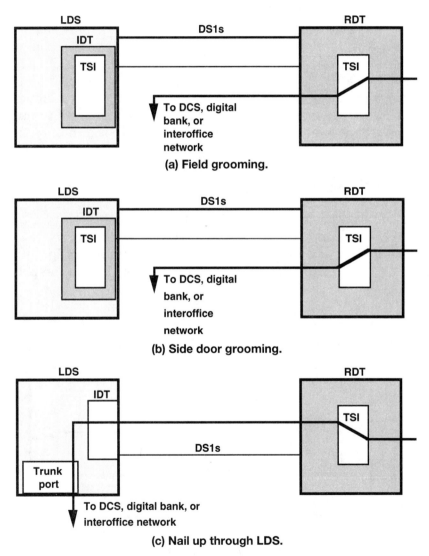

(a) Field grooming.

(b) Side door grooming.

(c) Nail up through LDS.

Figure 3–5 Integrated network access.

ing of the circuits at the IDT. It can also "nail up" the circuits of the LDS to the port trunk. All of these choices are shown in the figure. The actual implementation must be defined by the specific user requirements.

THE GR-303 LAYERED MODEL

The IDLC interface is organized around the OSI Model, as shown in Figure 3–6. Layer 1 is also known as the transmission interface; layer 2 refers to a conventional data link control mechanism and is based on the ISDN layer 3 protocol, link access for the D channel, LAPD; and applications refers to a protocol set derived from the ISDN layer 3, Q. 931.

The GR-303/IDLC system supports ISDN access as well. Two interfaces are available at the CO: the conventional ISDN line termination (LT), and termination at an IDT. All configurations are defined through the ISDN U reference point. The ISDN configurations are shown in Figure 3–7.

GR-303 FRAMING CONVENTIONS

The physical layer of the GR-303 interface is based on DS1 technology. The system can support 2 to 28 DS1s across the interface. A low-speed operation of two DS1s is designed to allow small configuration options as well as provide backup operations (but it does not support full

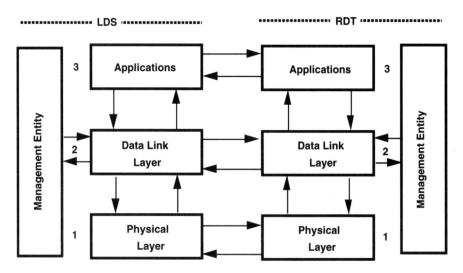

Figure 3–6   The layered model.

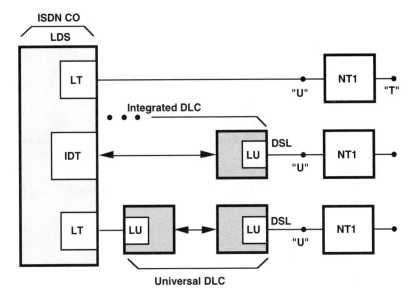

Figure 3–7   ISDN basic access capability.

protection switching). The maximum configuration of 28 DS1s allows the support of large systems. With the larger installations, automatic facility protection switching is provided.

All DS1 line formats must adhere to the extended superframe (ESF) format in accordance with TR-NWT-000499. Figure 3–8 shows a general

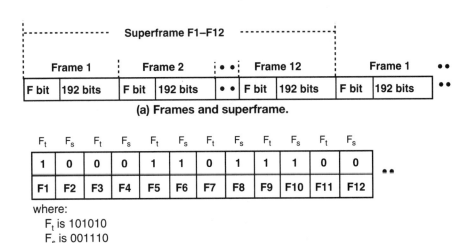

Figure 3–8   Framing conventions.

view of EFS. The original D1 channel bank used the 193rd bit to locate the beginning of the frame. Since the 1960s, the succeeding frame formats of D2, D3, D4, and the extended superframe (ESF) format have been used to improve the T1 systems, all using the 193rd bit.

The D4 frame format is illustrated in the bottom part of Figure 3–8. The terminal framing (F_t) bits are used to align the receiving channel bank onto the proper sequence of the 24 channels. The receiver searches for the F_t pattern to synchronize the incoming frames to the channel bank.

The signal framing bits or multiframe alignment bits (F_s) indicate which frames are used for signaling bits (the robbed bits). They are also

Frame Number	F_t	F_s}	→	SF		ESF
1	1			1		DL
2		0		0		CRC
3	0			0		DL
4		0		0		F = 0
5	1			1		DL
6		1		1		CRC
7	0			0		DL
8		1		1		F = 0
9	1			1		DL
10		1		1		CRC
11	0			0		DL
12		0		0		F = 1
13						DL
14						CRC
15						DL
16						F = 0
17	Repeat	Repeat		Repeat		DL
18	every 12	every 12		every 12		CRC
19	frames	frames		frames		DL
20						F = 1
21						DL
22						CRC
23						DL
24						F = 1

Figure 3–9   Extended superframe format (193rd bit).

used to synchronize the timing between the channel bank multiplexer and the carrier's central office equipment.

The F_t and F_s framing bits are consolidated into the entire framing pattern that is used with a D4 channel bank. This composite framing convention, now known as the superframe (SF) format, is the D4 framing convention. This framing bit sequence repeats every 12 frames and constitutes the superframe. To find the 193rd bit, the receiving channel bank looks for a repeating bit pattern of 100011011100.

The extended superframe (ESF) format is illustrated in Figure 3–9. As just stated, the terminal framing (F_t) bits are used to align the receiving channel bank onto the proper sequence of the 24 channels. The channel bank searches for the F_t pattern to synchronize the incoming frames to the channel bank.

CALL PROCESSING OPTIONS

Two different call processing techniques are supported across the GR-303 interface (summarized in Table 3–1). The first technique is called *hybrid switching* and entails the use of ABCD codes for call supervision. With this technique, a timeslot is assigned to a line unit. The call timeslot is managed over a 64 kbit/s timeslot management channel (TMC). This channel carries the messages between the RDT and LDS. As we shall see later, the purpose of these messages is to make and break the timeslot assignments between the line units and the DS0s on a per-call basis.

Table 3–1 Call Processing Options

Hybrid Signaling
ABCD codes used for call supervision.
Per-call timeslot assignment performed with a 64 Kbit/s timeslot management channel (TMC).

Out of Band Signaling
Consists of a 64 kbit/s common signaling channel (CSC).
CSC carries messages for making timeslot assignments and for call supervision.
TMC and CSC are based on LAPD and Q.931.
A separate DS0 data link (Embedded Operations Channel [EOC]) used for operations messages between RDT and LDS (ESF 4 kbit/s frame is used).

The second call processing technique is *out-of-band signaling,* which consists solely of a 64 kbit/s common signaling channel. The common signaling channel (CSC) also carries messages for making timeslot assignments and for overall call management.

Both signaling techniques use a variation of the LAPD layer 2 protocol that was initially designed for the ISDN channels. For layer 3, the Q.931 specification (also designed for ISDN signaling) is employed.

A separate DS0 signal is used to transmit operational traffic between the RDT and RDS and between the RDT and OSs. This channel is called the embedded operations channel (EOC). It also uses a variation of the LAPD protocol and the 4 kbit ESF data link is used for transmission protection switching and for loopback messages.

The interface also supports ISDN basic access capabilities and provides guidance for the mapping of the B and D channels into the DS1 facilities at the RDT. The specification allows the LDS to locate and process all the B and D channels.

GR-303 AND THE SIGNALING BITS

Signaling is a procedure for indicating to the receiving end equipment: (1) the digits dialed by the calling customer at the transmitting end, and (2) special signaling for that customer's circuit. Signaling is accomplished during every sixth frame, where one bit of each channel's eight bits is used as a signaling bit. In other words, five frames convey eight bits for voice, while the sixth frame conveys seven bits for voice plus one bit for signaling. The one bit for signaling is the "robbed bit."

The earlier T1 channel banks use the eighth bit in every slot for control signaling. Examples of control signaling are off-hook, on-hook, ringing, busy signals, and battery reversal. When the 256-step quantizers were initially conceived, it was thought the eighth bit would be used to represent all possible 256-step values (2^8=256). However, during the development of the D channel bank, the designers recognized that every eighth bit was not needed for signaling and chose to minimize the number of bits required. The D2 channel banks (and later channel banks) use the eighth bit of every sixth and twelfth frame to provide signaling information. The least significant bit in these frames is overwritten with a signaling bit. This concept is called *bit robbing* and the respective sixth and twelfth robbed frame bits are called the A and B bits (see Figure 3–10).

The A and B bits are used in conjunction with each other. For example, an on-hook condition is indicated if the A and B bits equal 1 in both

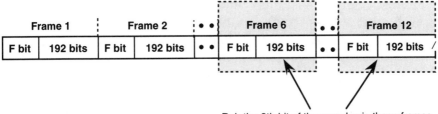

Rob the 8th bit of the samples in these frames

Note: For new systems, the ABCD bits are placed in the robbed bit slots of frames 6, 12, 18, and 24, respectively.

Figure 3–10   Bit robbing.

directions. When a caller goes off-hook the A/B bits are then set to 0. Generally, the called end of the link responds by sending the 0s in both positions for a brief period of time. The scenarios are numerous, but this brief summary gives the reader an idea of the use of the A and B bits.

This eighth bit is often a source of confusion, because it is also used to transmit status information. The office channel unit (OCU) inserts a 1 into bit position 8 when the customer is sending data. When the customer's device is idle, the OCU places a 0 in bit position 8 and 1s into bit positions 2 through 7. This technique provides the assurance that the signal has no more than seven consecutive 1s. Consequently, this convention effectively uses 8 kbit/s of the transmission.

If the user phone is a dual tone multifrequency tone device, signaling is sent over the voice path. In this case, the signaling bit is used only to convey on-hook or off-hook states.

The AB bits have been "upgraded" to support ABCD bits. The ABCD bits are placed in the robbed bit slots of frames 6, 12, 18, and 24, respectively. They reside in the DS1 ESF format, and are discussed in relation to GR-303 later in this chapter.

LAPD IN GR-303 OPERATIONS

I stated earlier that LAPD has been modified for layer 2 operations on the GR-303 interface. It is beyond the scope of this book to provide a full treatise on LAPD. Rather, our approach will be to summarize the major functions and architecture of LAPD in the next section and in the following section concentrate on how LAPD is used in the IDLC operation.

The ISDN provides a data link protocol for devices to communicate with each other across the D channel. This protocol is LAPD, which is a subset of the high level data link control (HDLC), the widely used international standard. The protocol is independent of a transmission bit rate and it requires a full duplex, bit transparent, synchronous channel. Figure 3–11 depicts the LAPD frame and its relationship to the ISDN layer 3, Q.931 specification. The Q.931 message is carried within the LAPD frame in the I (information) field. LAPD ensures that the Q.931 messages are transmitted across the link, after which the frame fields are stripped and the message is presented to the network layer. The principal function of the link layer is to deliver the Q.931 message error-free despite the error-prone nature of the communications link. In this regard, it is quite similar to LAPB in X.25.

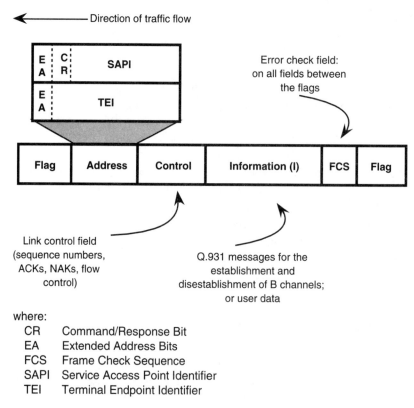

where:
CR   Command/Response Bit
EA   Extended Address Bits
FCS   Frame Check Sequence
SAPI Service Access Point Identifier
TEI   Terminal Endpoint Identifier

Figure 3–11   The LAPD frame.

LAPD has a frame format similar to HDLC, but LAPD defines specific octets for the address field. As we learned earlier, these octets identify the TEI and SAPI. Two other fields are coded in the address field. The command/response (C/R) bit is set to 1 to indicate if the frame is to be interpreted as a command; otherwise it is interpreted as a response. The receipt of a command frame dictates certain actions at the receiver, such as responding immediately by sending back a certain type of frame. In this particular example, the C/R bit acts as a poll command.

The extended address (EA) bits can be used to stipulate a larger address field if the data link connection identifier (TEI/SAPI) needs to be expanded.

Figure 3–12 summarizes the HDLC commands and responses that are used with LAPD. A connection is set up through the sending of a set asynchronous balanced mode extended frame (SABME) and the receipt of an unnumbered acknowledgment frame (UA). After this connection is established, ongoing traffic is exchanged with information frames (I), and unnumbered information frames (UI). The information frame mode uses sequence numbers, ACKs, NAKs, and retransmissions of errored frames. The UI frame mode does not employ these services.

The flow control capabilities are implemented with the receive ready (RR) and receive not ready (RNR) frames. Negative acknowledgments are signaled with the reject (REJ) frames. Upon the receipt of a REJ frame, the terminal must initiate retransmission procedures.

The disconnect frame (DISC) logically disconnects the LAPD session. It means that the terminal will no longer acknowledge frames. The disconnect mode frame (DM) informs the recipient of the frame that the station does not acknowledge frames.

Example of LAPD Operations

Figure 3–13 provides several examples of LAPD operations and the exchange of frames between two machines, a TE and an NT. The full contents of the frames are not shown for purposes of simplicity. The LAPD retransmission timer (T200) is also introduced in Figure 3–13.

The process begins by the TE sending a set asynchronous balanced extended frame (SABME) to the NT; the NT responds with an unnumbered acknowledgment frame (UA). The effect of this initial "handshake" is to set up a connection by reserving buffer space for the receipt of frames and initializing several counters, variables, and sequence numbers that are used to keep track of the frames sent across the channel.

Control Field Bit

Format	Encoding							Commands	Responses
	1	*2 through 8*		*9*	*10 through 16*				
Information	0	- N(S)		-	•	-	N(R)	-	I	

	1 through		*4*	*9*	*10 through 16*				
	(5–8 are all 0s)								
Supervisory	1	0	0	0	•	—	N(R)	—	RR	RR
	1	0	0	1	•	—	N(R)	—	REJ	REJ
	1	0	1	0	•	—	N(R)	—	RNR	RNR
	1	*2*	*3*	*4*	*5*	*6*	*7*	*8*		
Unnumbered	1	1	0	0	•	0	0	0	UI	
	1	1	0	0	•	0	1	0	DISC	
	1	1	0	0	•	1	1	0		UA
	1	1	1	0	•	0	0	1		FRMR
	1	1	1	1	•	0	0	0		DM
	1	1	1	1	•	1	1	0	SABME	
	1	1	1	1	•	1	0	1	XID	XID

where:

I	Information
RR	Receive Ready
REJ	Reject
RNR	Receive Not Ready
UI	Unnumbered Information
FRMR	Frame Reject
DISC	Disconnect
XID	Exchange Identification
DM	Disconnect Mode
SABME	Set ABM Extended Mode
•	The P/F Bit

Figure 3–12   Commands and responses in the LAPD control field.

This handshake also creates a process in each machine to govern the upcoming dialogue; this process is managed with a state diagram.

GR-303 Requirements for LAPD

This section provides a description of how LAPD is used across the GR-303 interface. First, the 16-bit FCS field is employed between the RDT

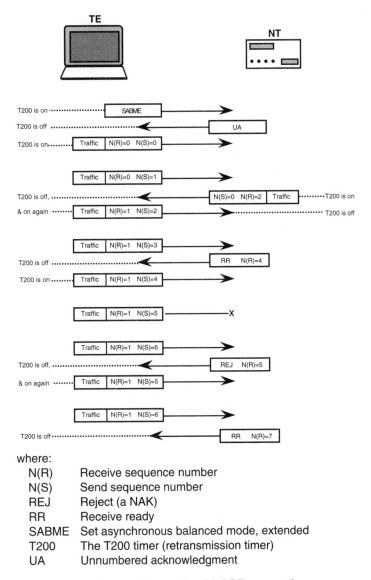

Figure 3–13   Example of LAPD operations.

and IDT. Furthermore, several of the command and response messages in the LAPD specification are used and were summarized in Figure 3–12. Other LAPD operations are not supported for the IDLC. These include frame reject (FRMR), unnumbered information (UI), exchange identification (XID), disconnect (DISC).

Because there are scores of off-the-shelf LAPD implementations that are available from a variety of vendors, it is possible that LAPD products might not interwork. With this in mind, GR-303 stipulates rules on the use of "unsupported" commands and responses. The idea is to set boundaries on the options and yet preserve the IDT-RDT interoperability.

For example, if either device does not understand the LAPD frame, it will send a diagnostic coded as "GR-303 unsupported." The reception of this frame must not take the system down. In addition, if any new frames come in that are not understood by the node, the frames shall be ignored.

It was anticipated that the FMR response and the DISC command would be desirable features for the interface. Currently, they are under study and will likely be incorporated into this specification at a later date.

The specific GR-303 requirements for LAPD are summarized here:

- The I field (in a command mode) is used to transmit Q.931 messages across the link
- Set asynchronous balance mode extended (SABME) (also in a command mode) is used to initialize the link
- The receive ready (RR) and receive not ready (RNR) (issued as command R responses) are used for flow control operations on I frames
- Reject (REJ) (issued as a command R response) is used as a NAK to request the retransmission of I frames
- Unnumbered acknowledgment (UA) (issued only as response) is used to acknowledge the receipt of SABME; it may also be used to clear a busy condition reported with the RNR frame
- Disconnect mode (DM) (issued only as a response) is used to report that the data link layer cannot support operations at this time

The Basic Rate Interface (BRI) Topologies

GR-303 establishes requirements for the use of the terminal endpoint identifier (TEI) and service access point identifier (SAPI) fields in the LAPD frame. Before discussing those requirements, we will review the purpose of the TEI and SAPI (see Figures 3–14 and 3–15).

The ISDN interface is configured as a point-to-point or multipoint topology at the S/T reference point. The U reference point does not support multipoint connections (nor do the PRI or B-ISDN interfaces). The

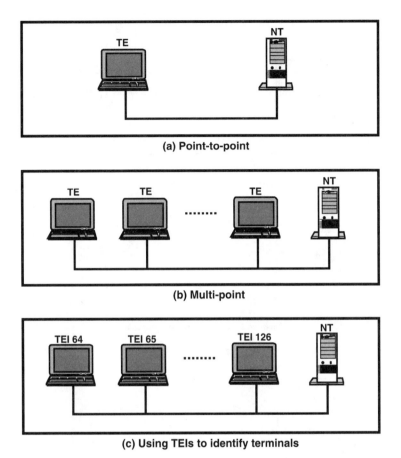

(a) Point-to-point

(b) Multi-point

(c) Using TEIs to identify terminals

Figure 3–14   Basic rate interface (BRI) topologies.

point-to-point arrangement is a common implementation for dial-up services, for example, from a home to an Internet service provider. The multipoint arrangement is useful in situations where multiple terminals must share one physical channel—for example, in a business office.

The traffic on the BRI is placed into a LAPD frame. The address field in the frame contains a terminal endpoint identifier (TEI) and a service access point identifier (SAPI). The TEI and SAPI fields are known collectively as the data link connection identifier (DLCI). These entities are discussed in the following paragraphs.

The TEI identifies either a single terminal (TE) or multiple terminals that are operating on the BRI link. The TEI is assigned automatically by a separate assignment procedure. A TEI value of all 1s identifies a broadcast connection. TEI values ranging from 0 through 63 make up

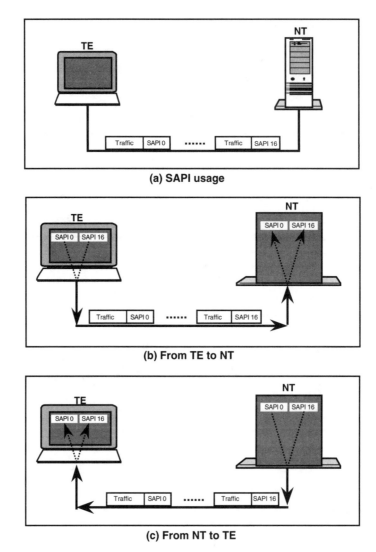

(a) SAPI usage

(b) From TE to NT

(c) From NT to TE

Figure 3–15   Identifying processes with SAPIs.

the fixed TEIs and are assigned prior to a terminal logging on and accessing the ISDN channel. TEI values ranging from 64 through 126 make up the values that are assigned automatically by the network during the logon procedure. TEI 127 is used during this assignment procedure.

As a general practice, fixed TEIs are used with point-to-point configurations, and multipoint configurations use the automatic assignment procedure.

The Service Access Point Identifiers (SAPI)

The service access point identifier (SAPI) identifies the entity where the data link layer services are provided to the layer above (that is, layer 3). The SAPI is based on the OSI service access point concept.

The services invoked at a layer are dictated by the upper layer (e.g., ISDN's layer 3) passing primitives (transactions) to the lower layer (e.g., ISDN's layer 2).

Services are provided from the lower layer to the upper layer through a service access point (SAP). The SAP is nothing more than an identifier. It identifies the entity in the lower layer that is performing the service(s) for the upper layer.

It is the responsibility of the receiving lower layer (in concert, of course, with the operating system in the receiving machine) to pass the traffic to the proper destination SAP in the upper layer. If multiple entities (e.g., processes) exist in the machine, the SAP serves to properly identify the process.

One way to view the SAP is to consider it to be a software "port." It is akin to the socket concept found in the UNIX operating system environment.

At the present time, these SAPIs are defined in ISDN:

SAPI Value	Frame Carries
0	Signaling (call control) information
1–15	Reserved
16	User traffic
17–31	Reserved
63	Management information
Others	Not available for layer 2 operations

Other LAPD Operations

LAPD operates with states. The states control the behavior of the protocol across the link. For GR-303, only four states are supported:

1. TEI assigned
2. Awaiting multiple frame operation
3. Multiple frame operation
4. Timer recovery

Multiple frame operation simply means that more than one information frame can be transmitted (perhaps one behind the other) and the receiver is allowed to acknowledge the several frames simultaneously with the inclusive acknowledgment feature, discussed earlier.

Some other specific rules follow with regard to use of LAPD with GR-303:

- Maximum window size (the value k) is 7
- The maximum number of retransmission timer (n200) can range from 1 to 10 inclusive, with the default range of 3
- For SAPI=1 at the EOC and TMC/CFC, the maximum number of bytes in the I field cannot exceed 256 (SAPI=1 is used for operation messages)
- For SAPI=0 of the TMC/CFC, the maximum number of bytes in the I field cannot exceed 32 (SAPI=0 is used for call processing messages)

Timers T200, T201, T202, and T203 also have rules established regarding their maximum and default values.

SAPI/TEI Addressing Conventions

As discussed earlier in the introduction to LAPD, service access point identifiers (SAPIs) and terminal endpoint identifiers (TEIs) are used in the address field of the LAPD frame to identify stations and SAPs operating at the stations. The rules for coding the SAPI/TEI and TMCs/CSCs are shown in Table 3–2.

GR-303 establishes rules for the use of the SAPI/TEI. I will summarize some of the rules here and refer you to Section 12.4 of the specification if more detail is needed.

During initialization for the interface, all SAPIs/TEIs must be put into the TEI assign state. The IDT or RDT must establish multiple frame operations on both TMC/CMC paths for the TNSC/CSC SAPI = 1 TEI = 0 when the IDT or RTD is initialized or reinitialized.

Finally, to complete this summary of the GL-303 requirements for LAPD, errors are handled at both the IDT and RDT in the following manner. When an error occurs (which cannot be solved by the data link layer), local diagnostics may be initiated and corrective action can take place in accordance with the specific machine. If this corrective action does not clear the problem, then the data link management cannot enter

Table 3–2   Rules for the Use of SAP1 and TE1

SAPI	TEI	Data-Link Function
1	0	EOC Path Switching Operations
1	1	RDT—Provisioning/Memory Administration OS
1	2	RDT—Maintenance/Surveillance OS
1	3	RDT—Testing OS
1	4	RDT—IDT
1	5	RDT—Test System Controller 1
1	6	RDT—Test System Controller 2 (if required)
1	7	RDT—Test System Controller 3 (if required)
1	8	User assignable
1	9	User assignable
1	10	User assignable
1	11	User assignable
SAPI	**TEI**	**Data-Link Function**
0	0	Call Processing
1	0	TMC/CSC Path Switching Operations

the automatic data link path protection switching. If the later operation fails to clear up the problem, then alarm messages must be sent to the maintenance OS. Two types of alarms are defined in this scenario. A major alarm is reported by those IDLC systems that terminate up to 28 lines; a critical alarm is reported on systems terminating more than 128 lines.

Earlier discussions established that the IDLC interface has one option that uses the ABCD codes for hybrid signaling. These codes are based on their use in other telephone-based systems. But for this specification, their use is controlled by the rules established in Tables 3–3 and 3–4.

Remember that ABCD bits are placed in the robbed bit slots of frames 6, 12, 18, and 24, respectively. Remember also that they reside in the DS1 ESF format.

These tables pertain to loop start, ground start, and loop reverse battery. GR-303 also defines the ABCD codes for coin and multiparty lines, which are not shown in these tables.

Table 3–3   ABCD Codes for Locally Switched Circuits for IDT to RDT

ABCD Code	Loop Start	Ground Start	Loop Reverse Battery
0000	-R ringing	-R ringing	
0001			
0010	DS0 AIS	DS0 AIS	DS0 AIS
0011			
0100	RLCF	RLCF	
0101	LCF	LCF	LO
0110			
0111	DS0 Yellow	DS0 Yellow	DS0 Yellow
1000	*Reserved*	*Reserved*	*Reserved*
1001	*Reserved*	*Reserved*	*Reserved*
1010			
1011			
1100			
1101	*Reserved*	*Reserved*	*Reserved*
1110			
1111	LCFO	LCFO	LC

Table 3–4   ABCD Codes for Locally Switched Circuits for RDT to IDT

ABCD Code	Loop Start	Ground Start	Loop Reverse Battery
0000		Ring Ground	
0001			
0010	DS0 AIS	DS0 AIS	DS0 AIS
0011			
0100			RLCF
0101	LO	LO	LCF
0110			
0111	DS0 Yellow	DS0 Yellow	DS0 Yellow
1000	Reserved	Reserved	Reserved
1001	Reserved	Reserved	Reserved
1010			
1011			
1100			
1101	Reserved	Reserved	Reserved
1110			
1111	LC	LC	

GR-303 LAYER 3 OPERATION

This section describes the layer 3 messages that are exchanged between the IDT and RDT. They are categorized as either TMC or CSC messages, and their use is summarized in Table 3–5. If the reader has studied any ISDN protocols, this table should be quite familiar. The messages are derived from the ITU-T Recommendation Q.931. Because requirements differ between an ISDN and an IDLC system, the messages in this table are considered to be extensions of the Q.931 messages.

Assignment Initiations

This section will examine timeslot management procedures used for hybrid signaling. Once a timeslot has been assigned for the connection, ongoing supervision is performed through ABCD codes. For the reader who has read earlier versions of GR-303, the operations described herein were originally called on-hook transmission. These operations are now known as TMC operations.

Table 3–5   TCM and CSC Messages

Message	Function	TMC	CSC
SETUP	Begins the timeslot assignment	Yes	Yes
SETUP ACK	On CSC tells RDT which timeslot to use	No	Yes
ALERTING	Informs that it has successfully alerted customer on terminating call	No	Yes
CALL PROCEEDING	RDT sends after seizing a loop reverse battery circuit	No	Yes
NOTIFY	Informs the IDT has received a DISCONNECT, or RDT has started a start dial	No	Yes
INFORMATION	Informs that customer has returned to on-hook	Yes	Yes
CONNECT	Informs that IDT and RDT have connected the line to the time slot being used for the call	Yes	Yes
CONNECT ACK	Acknowledges the CONNECT	Yes	No
DISCONNECT	Used to clear a call	Yes	Yes
RELEASE	Releases the connection	Yes	Yes
RELEASE COMPLETE	Sent in response to RELEASE	Yes	Yes
STATUS	Part of error-handling procedures	Yes	Yes
STATUS ENQUIRY	Handles possible call state mismatches	Yes	Yes

Figure 3–16 shows the timeslot management operations that are initiated by the IDT, which sends a SETUP message to the RDT. The SETUP message identifies the called line termination and identifies the DS0 assigned to the call. Before sending the SETUP message, the IDT inserts ABCD signals into the DS0. Upon receiving the SETUP message, the RDT determines if it can complete the connection. If so, it connects the line unit to the allocated DS0 and returns a CONNECT message to the IDT. Before returning the CONNECT message, the RDT reports on the status of the called line by inserting ABCD codes into the DS0 slot.

The customer may also initiate a timeslot assignment, as shown in Figure 3–16. The service request shown in Figure 13–5 corresponds to a loop closures on loop start circuits and a ring ground on ground start circuits.

Upon the RDT receiving the service request, it sends a SETUP message to the IDT. If the IDT accepts the call, it returns the CONNECT

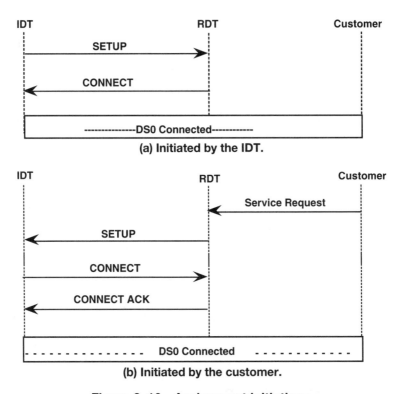

Figure 3–16   Assignment initiations.

message which informs the RDT which DS0 is to be used for the connection. Before sending the CONNECT message, the IDT inserts ABCD codes into the DS0. When the CONNECT message is received by the RDT and the DS0 channel is available, the RDT begins reporting on the status of the calling line with ABCD codes inserted into the assigned DS0. It also must react to the received ABCD codes. If all goes well, the RDT sends a CONNECT ACKNOWLEDGMENT message to the IDT. After these operations, the DS0 is disconnected.

Timeslot Clearing

Figure 3–17 shows a timeslot clearing operation. The IDT determines that the timeslot is no longer needed. It learns this situation usually by receiving ABCD coding information that indicates the customer has gone on-hook. Upon learning of the on-hook condition, it sends a disconnect message to the RDT. Before it sends this disconnect message, the IDT stops reacting to the ABCD signals in the DS0.

When the RDT receives the disconnect message, it stops reacting to the received ABCD signals and disconnects line unit from the DS0. It then sends a RELEASE message to the IDT. In turn, the IDT, upon receiving the RELEASE message, disconnects the DS0 and sends a release COMPLETE MESSAGE to the RDT. After this operation, the DS0 bandwidth is available for other users.

The DISCONNECT message sent by the IDT must contain a clause value. Ordinarily, this is set to "normal clearing," although other reasons for the clear can be identified.

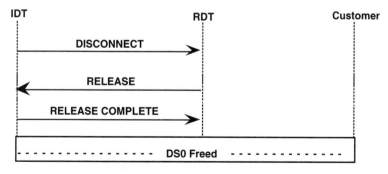

Figure 3–17   Timeslot clearing.

LOOP START CIRCUITS

The information that follows deals with common signaling channel operations and was called timeslot assignment in the earlier releases of GR-303. Figure 3–18 shows the operations on loop start circuits where the IDT initiates the call by sending a SETUP message to the RDT. This message identifies the called line, allocates a DS0, and instructs the RDT what ALERTING signal is to be applied to the line. Upon receiving this message, the RDT initiates the ring pretrip test.The RDT then seizes the line to the customer in accordance with the alerting signal specified by the IDT. (On loop start circuits, the seizure consists of applying an alerting signal to the line. On ground start circuits, the seizure consists of applying tip ground and an alerting signal to the line.) It then sends an ALERTING message that informs the IDT that the customer has indeed been alerted. Next, at the beginning of the first silent interval, the RDT sends a NOTIFY message to the IDT. Next, the IDT forwards the calling number to the RDT and the RDT signals the customer. When the customer goes off-hook and the RDT detects loop closure, it sends a CONNECT message to the IDT.

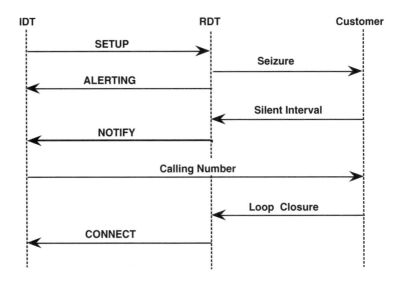

Figure 3–18   Loop start circuits.

Establishment by Customer (Loop Start Circuits)

Figure 3–19 shows an example of a call that is initiated by the customer. The seizure signal is detected by the RDT (a loop closure on an idle loop start circuit). It sends a SETUP message to the IDT which informs the IDT that the customer wants to make a call. After the IDT determines that the call can be accepted, it sends a SETUP ACKNOWLEDGE to the RDT. This message tells the RDT which DS0 to use. Upon receiving this message, the RDT connects the line unit to the allocated DS0 and gets ready to receive addressing information from the customer. Notice that a dial tone is sent from the IDT to the customer.

As the Figure 3–19 also indicates, the RDT and customer can use the tip-ring voltage/loop closure operation for ground start circuits. The figure also indicates that the customer can provide addressing information to the network with either dial pulses or dual-tone multifrequency

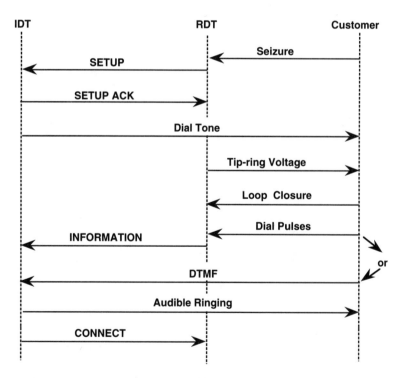

Figure 3–19   Establishment by customer (loop start circuits).

(DTMF) signals. Dial pulses are interpreted by the RDT, and DTMF passes through the RDT to be interpreted by LDS. The dial pulses are interpreted by the RDT and the digits are placed in the INFORMATION message and sent to the IDT. When the IDT determines that the address is complete, it returns a CONNECT message to the RDT.

Clearing (Loop Start Circuits)

Figure 3–20a provides an example of the IDT initiating the clearing of a connection. It starts this operation by sending a DISCONNECT message to the IDT. The RDT then applies the forward disconnect to the customer. Upon detecting loop open from the customer, it disconnects the

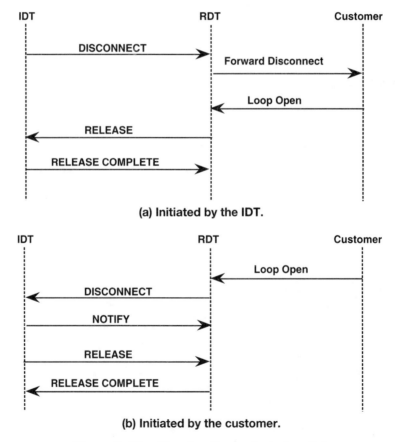

(a) Initiated by the IDT.

(b) Initiated by the customer.

Figure 3–20   Clearing (loop start circuits).

line unit from the DS0 and sends a RELEASE message to the IDT. Upon receiving the RELEASE message, the IDT disconnects the DS0 and returns a RELEASE COMPLETE message to the RDT. Under ordinary conditions, the DISCONNECT message contains a "normal clearing" cause code.

Figure 3–20b shows the operations when the clearing is initiated by the customer. The RDT detects a loop open from the customer and then sends the DISCONNECT message to the IDT. In this situation, the IDT must send a NOTIFY message to the RDT while the LDS determines if the call can be cleared through the network. If the call can be cleared, the IDT disconnects the DS0 slot that was allocated for the call and sends a RELEASE message to the RDT. In turn, the RDT disconnects its line unit from the DS0 and returns a RELEASE message to the RDT.

Ground Start Circuits

The previous operations have dealt with loop start circuits. The next scenarios deal with ground start circuits. The operations are quite similar to the loop start circuit discussions earlier in this chapter.

The operations begin with the IDT sending a SETUP message to the RDT. See Figure 3–21. This message identifies the call line and allocates a DS0. It also informs the RDT what alerting signal it is to apply to the line. Upon receiving this message, the RDT performs the ring pretip test.

The RDT then seizes the line to the customer by applying both tip ground and the alerting signal that was specified by the IDT. Next, it sends an ALERTING message back to the IDT to inform the IDT that the customer alerting has started. The RDT sends a NOTIFY message to the IDT at the beginning of the first silent interval, in accordance with ongoing specifications.

The calling number is then forwarded from the IDT through the RDT to the customer. Then, upon the RDT detecting loop closure, it removes the alerting signal and sends a CONNECT message to the IDT.

Establishment by Customer (Ground Start Circuits)

Figure 3–22 shows the ground start circuit operation when the call emanates from the customer. Upon detecting a ring ground by the RDT on an idle ground start circuit, a SETUP message is sent to the IDT. If the IDT accepts the call, it sends a SETUP ACK message back to the RDT. This message informs the RDT which DS0 slot is to be used for the connection. Dial tone is applied from the IDT through the RDT to the

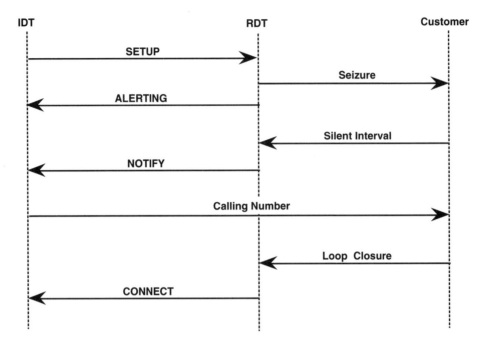

Figure 3–21   Look ground start circuits.

customer. Also, in response to the SETUP ACK message, the RDT applies tip-ring voltage (with the tip conductor grounded) and connects the line unit to the proper DS0. The RDT is now ready to receive addressing information from the customer.

As Figure 3–22 shows, the customer may use dial pulses or DTMF signals for its addresses. The DTMF tones are passed through the RDT to be processed by the LDS.

We assume the called party is available and is alerted. Therefore, audible ringing is passed back to the customer from the IDT. In accordance with these specifications, the IDT must return a CONNECT message to the RDT when the IDT has received a complete called address. (Be aware that this approach is different from conventional ISDN operations in how the CONNECT message is used.)

Figure 3–23c provides an example of the IDT initiating the clearing of a connection. Figure 3–23b provides an example of the customer initialing the clear. These operations are identical to those described earlier pertaining to loop start circuits, so I shall not repeat the descriptions here.

ANSI T1.405-1989 stipulates the use of three pulsing control signals for loop reverse battery circuits. These are wink-start, immediate-dial,

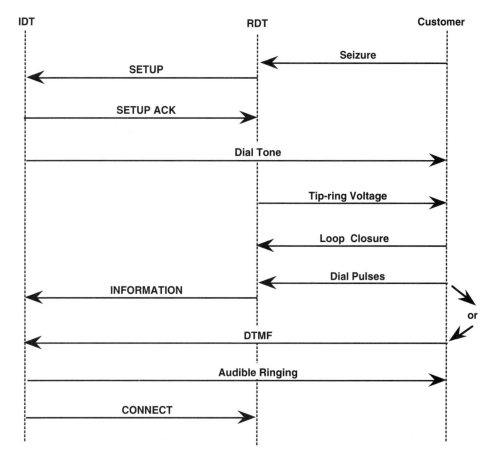

Figure 3–22 Establishment by customer (ground start circuits).

and delay-dial (these signals are described in Appendix A of this book). The RDT must be capable of supporting all three of these out-pulsing protocols.

With these thoughts in mind, let us turn our attention to Figure 3–24, which shows a call establishment setup by the IDT on a loop reverse battery circuit.[1] The operations proceed in the same manner as some of our earlier examples. The one notable point to this figure is the operation labeled Start Dial. This signal can be a wink signal for a wink-start interface. For the delay-dial operation, the signal is a transition

---

[1]This operation requires that call establishment is initiated only by the IDT. The customer is not allowed to initiate a call with this arrangement.

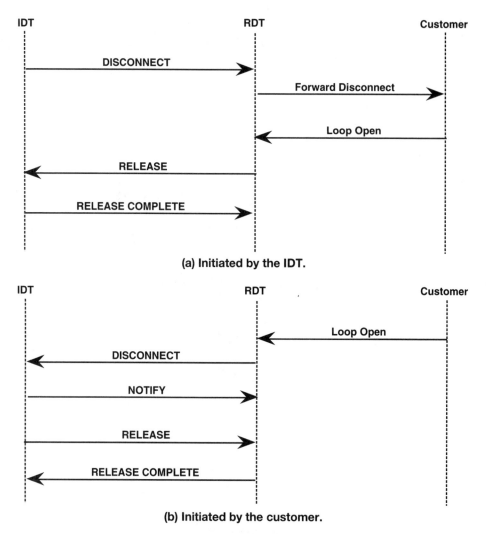

(a) Initiated by the IDT.

(b) Initiated by the customer.

Figure 3–23   Clearing (ground start circuits).

from reverse to normal battery. For the immediate-dial operation, there is no explicit start dial signal stipulated.

Call Clearing (Loop Reverse Battery Circuits)

Figure 3–25 shows a call clearing for loop reverse battery circuits. Figure 3–25a shows the clear initiated by the IDT; Figure 3–25b shows

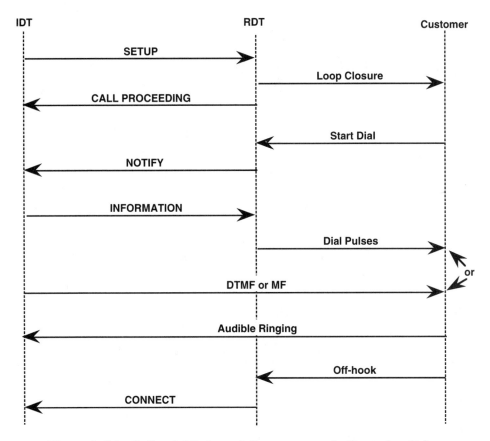

Figure 3–24   Call establishment (loop reverse battery circuits).

the clear initiated by the customer. The only difference between these clear operations and those discussed earlier is that the RDT detects an on-hook signal from the customer (CPE) in both parts of Figure 3–25. The on-hook signal is used in a loop reverse battery circuit in contrast to the loop open signal that we explained in loop start circuits and ground start circuits.

911 Calls (Loop Reverse Battery Circuits

GR-303 defines the rules for call clearing during a 911 call. Figure 3–26a shows the clear initiated by the customer, and Figure 3–26b shows the clear initiated by the IDT. Both operations proceed in the identical manner to previous discussions dealing with clears. But Figure 3–26

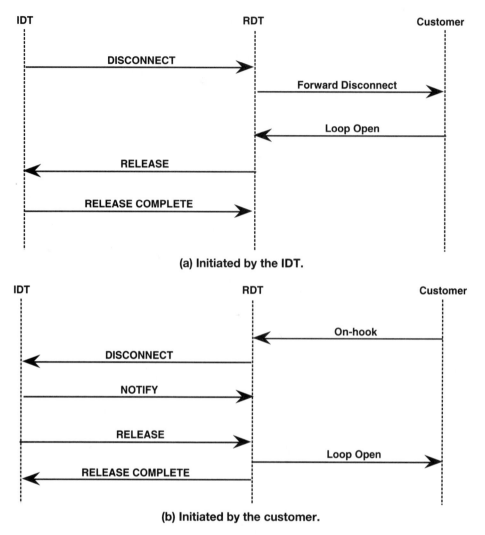

(a) Initiated by the IDT.

(b) Initiated by the customer.

Figure 3–25   Call clearing (loop reverse battery circuits).

warrants some additional discussion. The customer sends the on-hook signal to the RDT, which precipitates the exchange of the DISCONNECT and NOTIFY messages. During this time, the LDS is determining if the call can be cleared.

If the LDS recognizes the call as an emergency 911 and the call should not be cleared, the IDT sends an INFORMATION message to the RDT. In turn, the RDT applies ring back to the customer and sends back an ALERTING message to IDT to so indicate that the operation has oc-

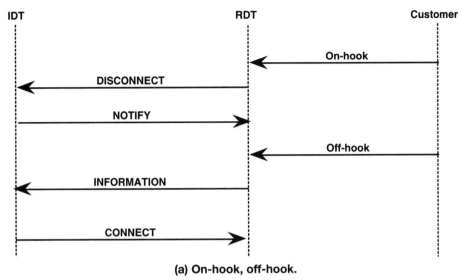

(a) On-hook, off-hook.

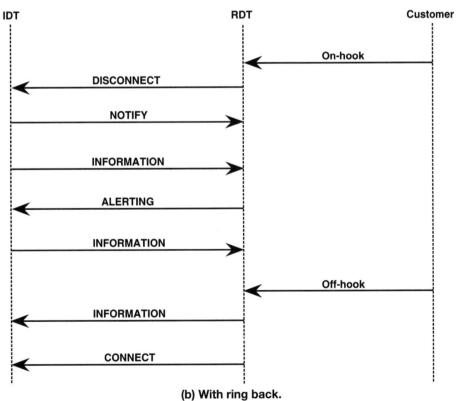

(b) With ring back.

Figure 3–26   911 Calls (loop reverse battery circuits).

curred. Next, the IDT may send another INFORMATION message back to the RDT. This message could direct the RDT to stop ring back or to resend ring back to the customer. In either case, the RDT returns an IN-FORMATION message back to the IDT that acts as an acknowledgment.

Finally, when the customer goes off-hook, the RDT sends a CONNECT message to the IDT. If all goes well, this latter operation re-establishes the call.

Reverting Call Establishment (Multiparty Option)

Figure 3–27 shows an example of multiparty operations and is based on loop-start signaling. GR-303 defines the specifications for two-to-four party service. This example shows the reverting call operation—this term refers to a call in which the calling and called parties are on the same multiparty circuit. To start the operation, the RDT detects loop closure on an idle multiparty circuit. The result of this operation precipitates the exchange of the SETUP and SETUP ACK messages between the RDT and IDT.

As in previous examples, the customer may use either dial pulses or DTMF signals.

ISDN Basic Access Circuits

This section examines the procedures for ISDN. The IDT begins the operations by sending a SETUP message to the RDT. This is quite similar to other examples in this chapter, except that the SETUP message identifies the B channel that is to be used for the connection. Nonetheless, the effect of this operation is still to allocate a DS0. The RDT connects the B channel on the line unit to the proper DS0 and returns a CONNECT message to the IDT.

One notable rule for this operation is that the ABCD signals cannot be used on this interface. An ISDN B channel requires the full 64 kbit/s slot.

Figure 3–28b shows the clearing operation on an ISDN basic access interface. The result of this operation is to release the DS0 and the associated B channel.

GR-303 MESSAGES

The messages use a format depicted in Figure 3–29. The message contains several parameters to define the connection and the attributes

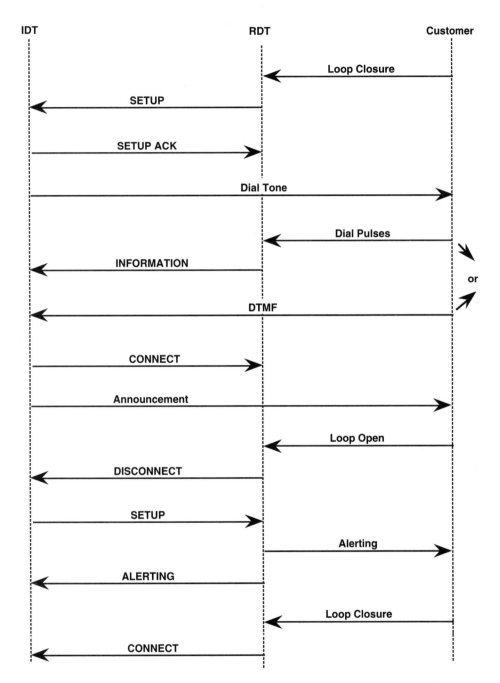

Figure 3–27   Reverting call establishment (multiparty option).

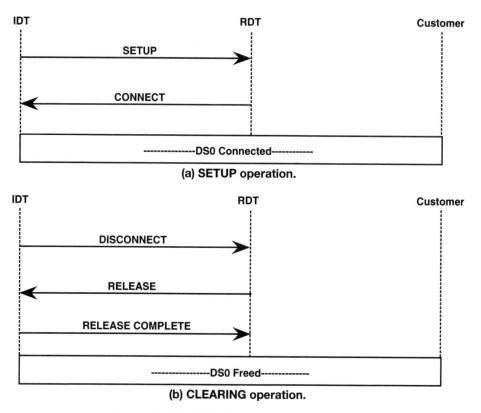

Figure 3–28   ISDN basic access circuits.

of the connection. The parameters are examined by the called party (and, if applicable, the intervening network nodes) to determine the exact nature of the call.

As an example, the parameters in the message can request services from the network and/or called party, such as a transfer rate (in bit/s) or the type of voice encoding (PCM, adaptive PCM).

Every message exchanged between the user and the network must contain these three parameters:

- *Protocol Discriminator:* This parameter distinguishes between ISDN user-network call control messages and other messages, such as in other technologies that use Q.931 (such as ATM and Frame Relay). The field is coded as 00001000 for Q.931 messages.

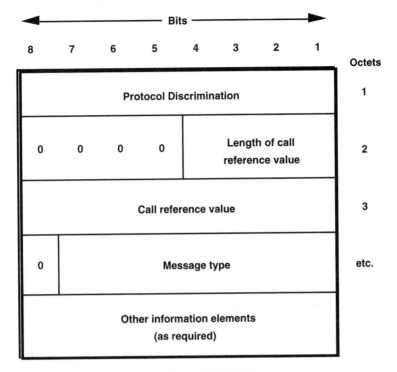

Figure 3–29   The TMC/CSC message.

- *Call Reference:* This parameter identifies a specific call at the local UNI. It is a unique identifier of each call on a UNI and, with its use, a call can be distinguished from other calls.
- *Message Type:* This parameter identifies the message function, such as a SETUP or a DISCONNECT, etc.

Figure 3–29 shows the information elements (IEs) field(s) residing behind the three mandatory parameters in the Q.931 message. The information element may consist of many entries (fields), and its contents depend on the message type. Later, we explain each TR-303 message type and its associated information element(s).

Functions of the Messages

This section provides a description of the functions of the TCM and CSC messages. Table 3–6 provides a useful reference tool during this discussion.

Table 3–6   TMC and CSC Messages

Message Name	TMC	CSC
SETUP	Yes	Yes
SETUP ACKNOWLEDGE	No	Yes
ALERTING	No	Yes
CALL PROCEEDING	No	Yes
NOTIFY	No	Yes
INFORMATION	Yes	Yes
CONNECT	Yes	Yes
CONNECT ACKNOWLEDGE	Yes	No
DISCONNECT	Yes	Yes
RELEASE	Yes	Yes
RELEASE COMPLETE	Yes	Yes
STATUS	Yes	Yes
STATUS ENQUIRY	Yes	Yes

- *ALERTING:* This message is sent on the CSC by the RDT to indicate that the called user party has been alerted and the call is being processed. This message is sent after the RDT has placed ringing signals on the line to the called party. The channel identification element identifies the timeslot used for the call. This message is not used on the TMC.

- *CALL PROCEEDING:* This message is sent on the CSC to the RDT after the RDT successfully seizes a loop reverse battery circuit. The channel identification information element identifies the timeslot used for the call. This message is not used on the TMC.

- *CONNECT:* Both the IDT and the RDT use this message. On the TMC, the IDT uses this message to inform the RDT which DS0 slot to use for the originating call. The RDT uses this message on the TMC to enable the IDT to verify that the RDT has used the correct slot for a terminating call. On the CSC, the message is used by the IDT to signal to the RDT to stop scanning for dial pulses from the calling party. The RDT sends this message to the IDT after detecting that the called party has answered the call.

- *CONNECT ACKNOWLEDGE:* This message is sent on the TMC by the RDT to indicate that it has connected the unit to the timeslot and is now inserting and processing ABCD codes. This message is not used on the CSC.

- *DISCONNECT*: This message is used on both the TMC and CSC. On the TMC, the IDT uses it to begin the clearing of a timeslot, and on the CSC, the IDT sends upon determining that a call is to be cleared. On the CSC, the RDT sends it to report that a party has gone on-hook.

- *INFORMATION*: This message is used on the TMC and CSC. The RDT uses it to notify the IDT that a party in a permanent signal state has returned to on-hook. The RDT must place the switch-hook information element in this message. In turn, the IDT uses this message to acknowledge the receipt of the INFORMATION message from the IDT. On the CSC alone, the IDT uses the message to forward the RDT digits that are to be outpulsed to the customer.

- *NOTIFY:* This message is not often used, but is available for the user or the network to provide information regarding a connection. The NOTIFY message contains a field called the notification indicator, which is used as follows:

IDT

- To report receiving a DISCONNECT from the RDT
- For special testing procedures

RDT

- During call establishment to report the detection of a start dial signal from the customer on a loop reverse battery circuit.
- Altering induce being applied to a loop/ground start circuit is entering its first long silent interval.

- *RELEASE:* This message is invoked in response to the reception of a DISCONNECT message. It is sent by the network or the user to notify its recipient that the equipment has disconnected the circuit that had been reserved for the connection. In essence, it tells the receiver that it should also release the circuit. The RELEASE message is designed also to free and make available the call reference numbers (and the associated resources) associated with the call.

- *RELEASE COMPLETE:* As the name implies, this message is sent in response to the RELEASE message, and it indicates by its invocation that the sender has released the circuit, the call reference and, of course, the resources associated with the connection. The combination of the RELEASE and RELEASE COMPLETE messages means that the circuit has been completely cleared and made available for other calls, and that the call reference is no longer valid.

- *SETUP:* The setup message contains more information elements than any of the other Q.931 messages. It is used to begin the call setup procedure. The SETUP message is always issued by the calling user to the network at the originating end and by the network to the called user at the terminating end. Both the IDT and RDT use this message to begin timeslot assignment, and the IDT is responsible for specifying the DS0 for the call.

- *SETUP ACKNOWLEDGE:* This message is sent in response to the SETUP message to indicate that the SETUP message has been received correctly. It is used to indicate that call establishment has been initiated. It may also indicate that additional information may be required to complete the call. For the latter case, the recipient of the SETUP ACKNOWLEDGE is required to send the additional information, which is coded in an INFORMATION message. On the CSC, the IDT uses this message to inform the RDT of the timeslot to use for the originating call.

- *STATUS:* This message is sent in response to a STATUS ENQUIRY message. It may also be sent in the event of certain error conditions that occur at a network node.

- *STATUS ENQUIRY:* This message is sent by either the IDT or RDT to inquire about the status of a call, specifically if a mismatch occurs in a call stage operation.

Information Elements (Parameters) in the Message

Most GR-303 messages contain only a few parameters (information elements). Table 3–7 lists these information elements and their use/nonuse on TMC and CSC.

To conclude this chapter, the following material explains how the message information elements are used between the IDT and RDT.

1. The protocol discriminator is coded as 01001111 to distinguish IDLC call processing from other Q.931 messages, such as ISDN or Frame Relay.

2. The call reference correlates the message with a specific call. Its use differs from that of an ISDN, in that it can be used also to identify the line termination to which the message pertains, as well as the specific call on that line.

3. The message type identifies the type of message, such as SETUP or CONNECT.

Table 3–7   Information Elements

NAME	TMC	CSC
Protocol Discriminator	Yes	Yes
Call Reference	Yes	Yes
Message Type	Yes	Yes
Bearer Capability	Yes	Yes
Cause	Yes	Yes
Call State	Yes	Yes
Channel Identification	Yes	Yes
Notification Indicator	No	Yes
Keypad Facility	No	Yes
Signal	No	Yes
Switchhook	Yes	Yes

4. The bearer capability is included in GR-303 to be compatible with the Q.931 ISDN signaling protocol. Here are some examples of information that can reside in this information element:

   • Request for an information transfer capability, such as speech, 3.1 kHz audio, or 7 kHz audio.

   • Request for circuit or packet transfer mode.

   • Request for a specific transfer rate, such as 64 kbit/s or 384 kbit/s.

   • Identification of user's encoding and compression algorithm (A-law, μ-law).

   • Request for data transfer rate, if data are to be transmitted during the connection.

   • Request for rate adaptation in a data connection.

5. The cause is used primarily to report a problem, but it is used also to provide status information about a call. For the first use, it can be coded to indicate that the called user went on-hook, a DS0 is not available to several others.

6. A call goes through various states (idle, call proceeding, wait). The call state is used in a STATUS message to report the current state of a call.

7. The channel identification is used to identify (1) the DS1 and (2) the DS0 on the DSM to which the call is associated. The DS1

range is 1 to 28 (to support DS3, if necessary), and the DS0 range is 1 to 24 (to support the 24 DS0s on the DS1).

8. The notification indicator is used on the CSC to support coin, multiparty, and custom calling services.

9. The keypad is used by the IDT to forward to the RDT the digits that are to be outpulsed on the loop reverse battery circuits. Conversely, the RDT uses it to send to the IDT the pulse digits received from the customer. It is also used by the RDT to inform the IDT that a customer has finished the switchhook.

10. The signal is used on the CSC by the IDT to specify the alerting pattern the RDT is to apply to a loop/ground start circuit.

11. The switchhook is used by the RDT or IDT to indicate or acknowledge that a customer is on-hook or off-hook.

SUMMARY

GR-303 defines the components in the distribution plant and the major types of service that are offered. GR-303 is based on the use of T1. LAPD and variations are employed at layer 2, while Q.931 and variations are employed at layer 3. ABCD codes are used for signaling. Additionally, operations on loop start and ground start circuits are supported. GR-303 represents the present generation for digital signaling techniques and protocols for the local loop. Chapter 8 provides examples of a new generation.

4

Fiber in the Loop
and the Synchronous Optical
Network (SONET)

This chapter describes the deployment of fiber in the loop (FITL). Several approaches to FITL have been proposed; this chapter examines the Bellcore proposal. I cite the Bellcore concepts because they include the deployment of both coax and copper to the customer's dwelling from the fiber facility. The second part of the chapter explains the major features of SONET and how it is being deployed in RBB.

Additional discussions on fiber in the loop are contained in Chapter 5. I placed this information in Chapter 5 for purposes of continuity with the ATM Forum's specification on fiber for an ATM Home Network.

ACTIVE NETWORK INTERFACE DEVICE (ANID)

A key issue in RBB is how the optical fiber is deployed in the local loop. The "how" entails the engineering of the fiber plant, including the optical fiber signal requirements for quality, testing, and protection. Equally important is the definition of the interfaces to coaxial cable and twisted pair. Bellcore has been the coordinating body to address these issues with (1) GR-2890-CORE, Fiber in the Loop Active Network Interface Device (ANID); (2) TA-NWT-000909, Generic Requirements for Fiber in the Loop (FITL) systems; and (3) GR-49-CORE, Generic Requirements for Network Interface Devices.

These specifications focus on the ANID that supports voice and video services. As shown in Figure 4–1, it consists of the ANID network interface unit (NIU), the ANID subscriber interface unit (SIU), and the optical network unit (ONU). The functions of these three units are:

Network Interface Unit (NIU)

- Physically terminates the FITL (for example, at the customer's dwelling)
- Acts as the network termination point for voice and video services
- Receives power for voice services from the ONU
- Receives power for the video services from the customer

Subscriber Interface Unit (NIU)

- Resides between the NIU and the customer's appliance (e.g., video)
- The subscriber interacts with the SIU with a remote, a telephone keypad, or other device.
- Employed only for video services
- Connection to NIU is by a coaxial cable
- Power is provided by the customer

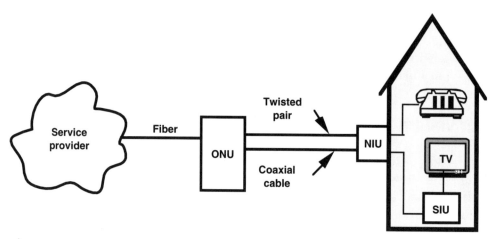

where:
NIU   Network interface unit
ONU   Optical network unit
SIU   Subscriber interface unit

Figure 4–1   FITL configuration.

Optical Network Unit (ONU)

- Terminates optical fiber distribution
- Provides optical/electrical conversion
- Provides A/D and D/A conversions, if necessary
- Multiplexes traffic into and out of the optical facility
- Provides ongoing testing and maintenance
- Serves 128 to 500 dwellings

COAXIAL SPECTRUM ALLOCATION

The Bellcore plan for the coaxial frequency spectrum allocation is shown in Figure 4–2. The upstream channel occupies the 5 to 54 MHz spectrum. Analog video channels occupy the next bands from 54 to 550 MHz, but more bandwidth can be allocated, if necessary.[1] Digital video occupies the spectrum at 650 to 750 MHz. The spectrum above 750 MHz is reserved for future services.

THE ANID INTERFACES AND LAYERS

The ANID is modeled around the OSI layers and operates with three of the seven layers, as illustrated in Figure 4–3. The layers in the figure are noted as PL (physical layer), DLL (data link layer), and SL (session layer), and the numbers in parentheses [(1), (2), etc.] are used as shorthand notation to indicate the layers' functions, described next.

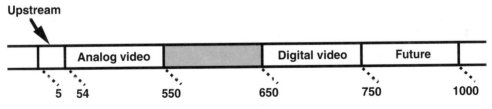

Figure 4–2 Spectrum allocation.

---

[1]The 550 to 650 MHz band is utilized with proposed RBB protocols (see Chapter 7).

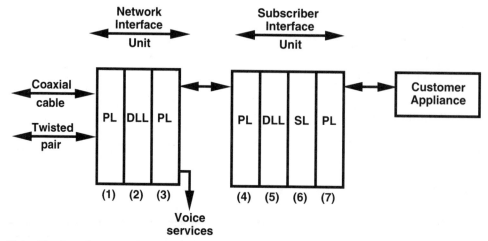

Note: Numbers in parentheses indicate layer services (see text).

where:

   PL   Physical layer
   DLL   Data link layer
   SL   Session layer

Figure 4–3   Interfaces and layers.

Physical Layer to Coaxial and Twisted Pair Plant at NIU (1)

The physical layer at the NIU for the cable connections is concerned with the physical connectors as well as the electrical specifications. For the physical connections, the modular jacks and plugs are established in Bellcore's GR-49-CORE and the specifications for surge protectors are defined in GR-974-CORE or GR-1361-CORE.

No power level to the customer premises is stipulated for coaxial cable. Notwithstanding, the coaxial cable must institute surge protection, once again in accordance with GR-2098-CORE, and a bonding block for the coaxial cable sheet must be implemented in accordance with GR-2910-CORE. The coaxial cable interface power fault tests and lightning surge tests, as well as the AC power fault tests, must meets the standards listed in Table 4–1.

Data Link Layer at the NIU (2)

The data link layer is stipulated for the coaxial cable services; no data link layer is stipulated for twisted pair cables. For coaxial service, the data link layer defines signaling and modulation as well as error cor-

Table 4–1   Coaxial Cable Specification

First-Level Lightning Surge Test

Surge Test	Minimum Open-Circuit Peak Voltage	Minimum Short-Circuit Peak Current	Maximum Rise/ Duration Time for Voltage and Current	Repetitions, Each Polarity
1	1000 V	100 A	10/1000 μs	25
2	2000 V	1000 A	10/250 μs	5

First-Level AC Power Fault Test

Surge Test	Voltage	Current	Duration	Repetitions
1	600 Vrms	40 Arms	1 second	1

Second-Level Lightning Surge Test

Surge Test	Minimum Open-Circuit Peak Voltage	Minimum Short-Circuit Peak Current	Maximum Rise/ Duration Time for Voltage and Current	Repetitions, Each Polarity
1	2000 V	1000 A	10/250 μs	1

Second-Level AC Power Fault Test

Surge Test	Voltage	Current	Duration	Repetitions
1	600 Vrms	40 Arms	15 minutes	1
2	600 Vrms	60 Arms	1 minutes	1
3	600 Vrms	120 Arms	10 seconds	1

rection, encryption, and decryption. This layer also defines MPEG-2 transport stream services as an NTSC pass-through option (if necessary). Several additional sublayers exist within the data link layer, including video, audio, and data layers as well as a signaling information entity.

Physical Layer on the Customer Side NIU (3)

This interface defines the connection, including connectors and cables to the voice services (the telephone set) and the video services (known as the plant). The requirements for the voice services are no different than ongoing telco specifications. The video interface is not defined at this time by Bellcore.

Physical Layer on the Customer Side (SIU) (4)

This layer interfaces with (and complements) the NIU physical layer operation at the NIU.

Data Link Layer at the SIU (5)

This layer provides the MPEG-2 transport stream entity, the NTSC pass-through entity, signaling information, demultiplexing/decompression, video D/A, audio D/A, as well as an NTSC video/audio stream combiner.

Session Layer at the SIU (6)

The session layer is responsible for data formatting and storage of applications. It also contains a signaling formatter and is responsible for the overall dialogue between the customer appliance interface and the overall components in the ANID.

Physical Layer Interface between SIU and Customer Plant (7)

This layer provides the interface into the customer appliance (for example, the TV set). It is designed to provide a transparent interface to user premises equipment. The intent is for any conversions or interface changes to be made at the SIU without any alterations required for the customer equipment.

OTHER FITL SERVICES

Several other services are stipulated in the FITL services. First, as I mentioned in the previous section, is the use of MPEG-2. This service must be provided with ongoing specifications, principally, the ISO/IEC 1318 entitled, *Information Technology-Generic Coding for Moving Pictures and Associated Audio Information.*

In addition, several security features are stipulated by Bellcore in the Bellcore FITL specification, but the specific security measurements are not cited. Once again, companion specifications provide guidance on security services. The reader can refer to Bellcore TA-NWT-000909 for more detailed information.

Briefly, the FITL video security requirements are divided into (1) network security, (2) per-channel security, and (3) pay-per-view security. Network security prevents unsubscribed users from accessing any of the video services. This feature can be embedded in either the ONU or the NIU section of the NAID. It is intended that a network security module, if located in NIU, can be removed. If problems occur, it can be replaced. The security module must be programmable through both the local user and the remote service provider.

The pay-channel security describes a service that may be purchased periodically. The intent is to allow this service to be dynamic and safe from month-to-month. Like network security, pay-per-view security can be installed in NIU and it should be (1) programmable, (2) removable, and (3) replaceable.

Finally, the pay-per-view security feature is a shorter range service, in contrast to pay-channel security. It is intended that pay-per-view would be configurable on a day-to-day or even hour-to-hour basis. Pay-per-view security is located in the NIU and is, once again, removable, replaceable, and programmable. However, the pay-per-view security module is independent of the network security module and the pay-channel module. That is to say, the removal, reprogramming, or replacement of the pay-per-view security module should not affect the network security module and the pay-channel module.

The Bellcore specifications also stipulate that the NIU security access panel can be locked, and proprietary tools must be employed to remove the NIU housing. In addition, the NIU security module shall be designed to indicate if the NIU has been tampered with.

SONET IN RESIDENTIAL BROADBAND

The Synchronous Optical Network (SONET) was deployed initially as part of the service provider's backbone network. In the past few years it has reached into the local access network as well. A logical implementation for SONET in RBB is to deploy it in the access network from the service provider node to a SONET service adapter where the optical network unit resides (refer to Figure 4–1). With this configuration in mind, the remainder of this chapter describes the SONET features that are germane to RBB.

Figure 4–4 shows a typical topology for a SONET network. End-user devices operating on LANs (FDDI, 802.3, 802.5, etc.) and digital transport systems, such as DS1 and E1, are attached through a SONET service adapter to the network. This service adapter is also called an access node, a terminal, or a terminal multiplexer. This machine is responsible for supporting the end-user interface by sending and receiving traffic from LANs, DS1, DS3, E1, and others. It is really a concentrator, and at

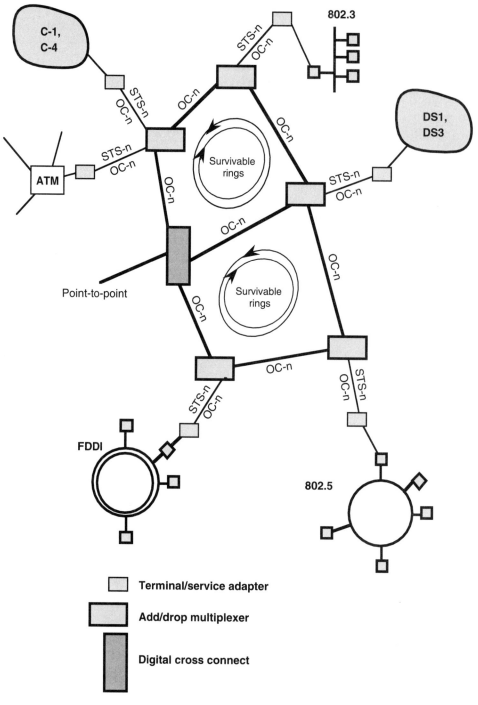

Figure 4–4   SONET topology.

a sending site, it consolidates multiple user traffic into a payload envelope for transport onto the SONET network. It performs a complementary but opposite service at the receiving site.

The user signals are converted (mapped) into a standard format called the synchronous transport signal (STS), which is the basic building block of the SONET multiplexing hierarchy. The STS signal is an electrical signal, and the notation of "STS-n" means that the service adapter can multiplex the STS signal into higher integer multiples of the base rate.

Strictly speaking, the access node (service adapter) is implemented as the end-user interface machine, or as an add-drop multiplexer. The latter implementation multiplexes various STS-n input streams onto optical fiber channels, which are now called an optical carrier (OC) signal and designated with the notation OC-n, where n represents the multiplexing integer. OC-n streams can also be multiplexed and demultiplexed with this machine. The term "add-drop" means that this machine can add or drop payload onto one of two channels.

The digital cross-connect (DCS) machine usually acts as a hub in the SONET network. It not only adds and drops payload, but it also can operate with different carrier rates, such as DS1, OC-n, or CEPT1, and can make two-way cross-connections between them. It consolidates and separates different types of traffic.

The topology can be set up as a ring or as point-to-point. In most networks, the ring is a dual ring, operating with two optical fibers (working and protection). The structure of the dual-ring topology permits the network to recover automatically from failures on the channels and in the channel/machine interfaces. This is known as a self-healing ring and is explained later in this chapter.

STRUCTURAL DIVERSITY IN THE ACCESS NETWORK

Ideally, one would like to have the working and protection fiber in different paths (different feeders) between the network elements. This option is not always possible, but as seen in Figure 4–5a, it may be possible to place two fiber cable sheaths in the same conduit structure, and separate them physically within the conduit.

Since many systems and their conduits are laid out in a grid structure, it may be possible, as in Figure 4–5b, to place the working and protection fibers in separate conduits for at least part of the feeder connection.

Yet another possible alternative (Figure 4–5c) is to use different feeders for the working and protection fibers. Finally, Figure 4–5d shows

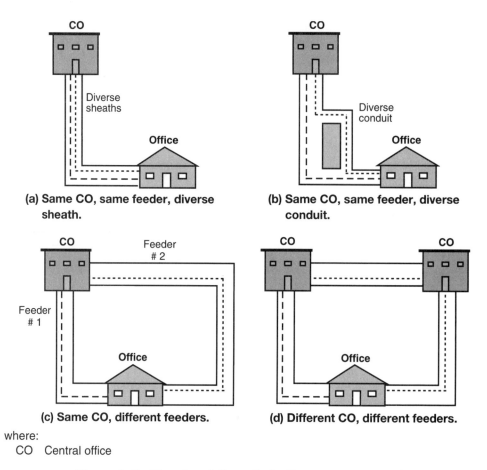

(a) Same CO, same feeder, diverse sheath.

(b) Same CO, same feeder, diverse conduit.

(c) Same CO, different feeders.

(d) Different CO, different feeders.

where:
CO   Central office

Figure 4–5   Structural diversity in the access network.

another possible way to separate the cables. Since some feeder routes in densely populated areas may intersect or be situated close together, it may be feasible to use two dual paths to two separate central offices and have the ring connected through these offices.

LINE PROTECTION AND PATH PROTECTION

Since optical fiber has such a large information carry capacity and supports many simultaneous connections, the loss of the fiber can be quite serious and disruptive. Several approaches are used to reduce the chances of this disruption.

One approach is called *line protection switching,* or *1:1 switching,* and is shown in Figure 4–6a. This configuration consists of two point-to-point fiber pairs between two network elements. If the working fiber is lost or the signal degraded, the protection pair assumes the job of carrying the traffic between the network elements. In a fully protected system, this configuration requires four fibers.

Another approach is called *1+1 protection switching* (or *path protection switching*). The switching takes place at the low speed or STS-1 input into the network element. As shown in Figure 4–6b, the traffic in this arrangement is sent on both the working and protection fibers. The two copies of the traffic are received at the receiving network element. Here, they are compared, and only the better copy is used.

For example, a fiber might carry 48 STS-1s: 1 to 24 are used to carry traffic, and 25 to 48 are used for protection. In the event one of the working channels is faulty, the receiving network element will replace it with the other copy on the protection fiber. This approach is quite fast and does not result in any loss of traffic. Problem restoration is quite efficient and the other 23 STS-1s are not affected.

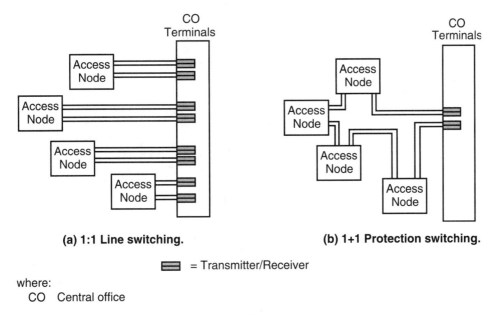

(a) 1:1 Line switching.   (b) 1+1 Protection switching.

▭ = Transmitter/Receiver

where:
  CO   Central office

Figure 4–6   Line protection and path protection.

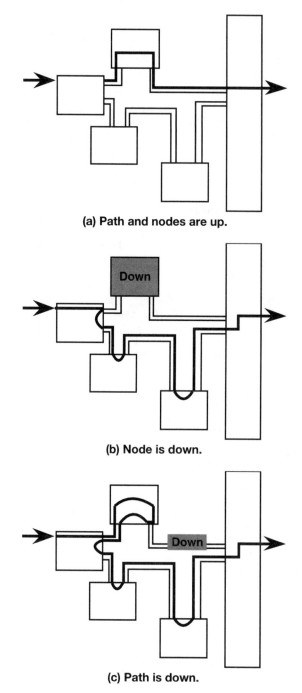

(a) Path and nodes are up.

(b) Node is down.

(c) Path is down.

Figure 4–7   Restoration alternatives.

Restoration Alternatives

Using Figure 4–6b as a reference point, Figure 4–7 shows how a shared protection ring (for example, the SONET nodes and their associated channels) can reconfigure and recover from a node or fiber failure.

SUMMARY OF OPTIONS FOR PROTECTING THE DISTRIBUTION NETWORK

The RBB service provider has a number of options for how SONET is configured to protect the distribution network. Some were mentioned earlier; this section provides a summary of these options (4).

1+1 and 1:1 Linear Configurations

In these configurations, two signals are monitored and compared to select the better one. In 1+1, the head-end signal is permanently bridged onto the protection fiber and cannot be used to support extra traffic. In 1:1, the signal is not bridged onto the protection fiber until a failure that affects the working fiber is detected. In this case, the protection fiber can be used to support extra traffic. These schemes can use route diversity for survivability against link failures.

1:N Linear Configuration

With this scheme, one standby facility provides protection for A number of working channels. In this configuration, when a failure is detected on a working fiber, the traffic is bridged onto the protection loop and sent to the other end using the protection channel facilities. When not in use, the protection fiber can support extra traffic.

Regenerator

In this configuration, the system receives, reshapes, retimes, and retransmits the optical signals to compensate for losses and distortior that build up as the signals travel over the fiber.

Two- or Four-Fiber Ring/Add-Drop Multiplexer

In this configuration, traffic is either passed through or selectively added to or dropped from the payload at the STS-1 level. This topology offers enhanced survivability by rerouting traffic around equipment failures, cable cuts, and nodal failures.

SONET PAYLOADS

SONET is designed to support a wide variety of payloads. Table 4–2 summarizes typical payloads of existing technologies.

The SONET multiplexer accepts these payloads as sub-STS-1 signals (or VTs). The VT of these subrates is designated as a VT-type in the following manner:

- DS1 = VT1.5
- CEPT1 = VT2
- DS1C = VT3
- DS2 = VT6

SONET is designed to be backward compatible with technologies in Europe, North America, and Japan. Therefore, the DS payloads and the CEPT payloads are supported and carried in the SONET "envelope." These payloads range from the basic DS 0/CEPT 0 of 64 kbit/s up to the higher speed rates of DS 4 and CEPT 5.

In addition, cells are also carried in the SONET envelope. Therefore, the technology is both backward compatible, supporting current technology, and forward compatible, supporting cell technology.

SONET is designed to support a concept called virtual tributaries (VT). Through the use of pointers and offset values, VTs such as DS1, DS3, or CEPT1 can be carried in the SONET envelope. The standard provides strict and concise rules on how various VTs are mapped into the SONET envelope.

Figure 4–8 shows two examples of payload mapping. In Figure 4–8a 23 DS0 channels are multiplexed into a conventional DS1 payload

Table 4–2   Typical Payloads

Digital Bit		Voice		
Type	Rate	Circuits	T-1	DS3
DS1	1.544 Mbit/s	24	1	—
CEPT1	2.048 Mbit/s	30	—	—
DS1C	3.154 Mbit/s	48	2	—
DS2	6.312 Mbit/s	96	4	—
DS3	44.736 Mbit/s	672	28	1

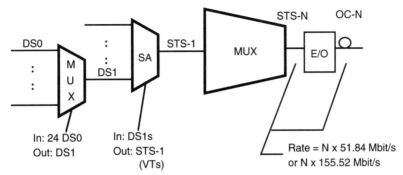

(a) Mapping into virtual tributaries.

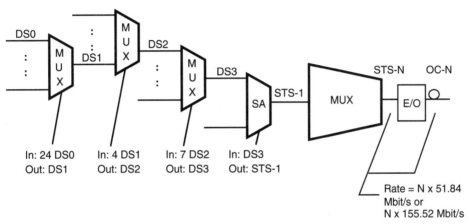

(b) Mapping into STS-1.

where:

OC   Optical carrier
SA   Service adapter
STS   Synchronous transport signal
VT   Virtual tributary

Figure 4–8   Examples of payload mapping.

through a DS1 multiplexer. The next stage of multiplexing and mapping occurs when 1 to n DS1 streams are multiplexed together through a SONET service adapter. This output is an STS-1 stream. Next, 1 to n STS-1 streams can be further multiplexed into a STS-N stream. This signal is then converted into an optical carrier (OC) signal.

Figure 4–8b is similar to 4–8a, except that it shows the asynchronous multiplexing hierarchy operations that lead to the DS3 payload. The intermediate rates are DS2 and DS3.

SONET CONFIGURATION

Figure 4–9 shows a simplified diagram of a SONET configuration. Three types of equipment are employed in a SONET system: (1) path terminating equipment, (2) line terminating equipment, and (3) section terminating equipment. The path terminating equipment consists of a SONET terminal or switch. The line terminating equipment is a SONET hub. The section terminating equipment is a SONET regenerator.

Each of these components utilizes substantial OAM&P information (overhead). Path level overhead is inserted at the SONET terminal and carried end-to-end. The overhead is added to DS1 signals when they are mapped into virtual tributaries (VT, explained shortly) and for end-to-end STS-1 payloads.

Line overhead is used for STS-N signals. This information is created by line terminating equipment such as STS-N multiplexers. The section overhead is used between adjacent network elements such as SONET regenerators.

Figure 4–10 shows one scenario of the SDH/SONET and ATM layer interactions. The dashed lines indicate the flow of traffic. This stack may vary in different implementations. For example, at an ATM switch, the SONET path layer might not be accessed because it is intended as an

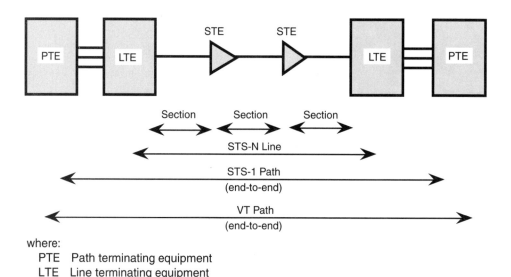

where:
  PTE   Path terminating equipment
  LTE   Line terminating equipment
  STE   Section terminating equipment

Figure 4–9   SONET configuration.

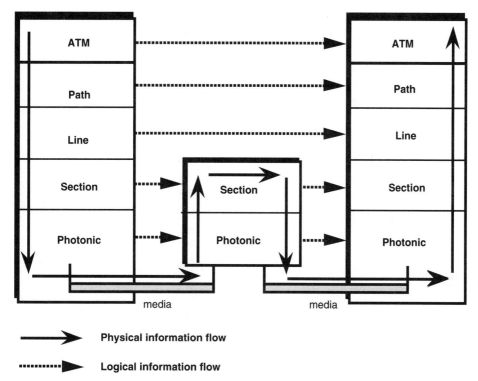

Physical information flow

Logical information flow

Note: Layer stacks may vary at multiplexers, switches and other line terminating equipment.

Figure 4–10   Interactions between and among the layers.

end-to-end operation. The manner in which the layers are executed depends on the actual design of the equipment.

SONET SIGNAL HIERARCHY

The synchronous transport signal-level 1 forms a basis for the optical carrier-level 1 signal. OC-1 is the foundation for the complete synchronous optical signal hierarchy. The higher level signals are derived by the multiplexing of the lower level signals. The high level signals are designated as STS-N and OC-N, where N is an integer number. As illustrated in Table 4–3, OC transmission systems are multiplexed by the N values of 1, 3, 9, 12, 18, 24, 36, 48, and so on. Presently, signal levels OC-3, OC-12, and OC-48 are the most widely supported multiples of OC-1

Table 4–3   SONET Signal Hierarchy

OC Level	STS Level	Line Rate (Mbit/s)
OC-1*	STS-1	51.840
OC-3*	STS-3	155.520
OC-9	STS-9	466.560
OC-12*	STS-12	622.080
OC-18	STS-18	933.120
OC-24	STS-24	1244.160
0C-36	STS-36	1866.230
OC-48*	STS-48	2488.320
OC-96	STS-96	4876.640
OC-192*	STS-192	9953.280

*Currently, the more popular implementations
(Note: Certain levels are not used in Europe, North America, and Japan.)

SONET Transmission and Relationship to Asynchronous Payloads

As we have learned, in the SONET hierarchy the basic building block is the optical carrier-1 (OC-1), which is 51.84 Mbit/s made up of one DS3 and SONET overhead.

Just as the asynchronous DS3 signal was used in integer multiples for higher level multiplexing in the asynchronous digital hierarchy, they

Table 4–4   SONET Transmission and Relationship to Asynchronous Payloads

Electrical	Optical Hierarchy	Transmission Line Rate (Mbit/s)	DS-3 Equiv.	DS-1 Equiv.	DS-0 Equiv.
STS-1	OC-1	51.840	1	28	672
STS-3	OC-3	155.520	3	84	2,016
	OC-9	466.560	9	252	6,048
	OC-12	622.080	12	336	8,064
	OC-18	933.120	18	504	12,096
	OC-24	1244.160	24	672	16,128
	OC-36	1866.240	36	1008	24,192
	OC-48	2488.320	48	1344	32,256
	OC-192	9953.280	192	5376	129,024

are also used as integer multiples in the OC hierarchy. The STS-1 is scrambled and converted from electrical pulses to optical pulses to form the OC-1 signal. Three STS-1 signals can be multiplexed together to create the STS-3 signal. The STS-3 (155.52 Mbit/s) signal is the electrical component of the OC-3 signal and likewise will be scrambled and converted from electrical-to-optical format to form the OC-3 signal. The OC-9 is comprised of 9 DS3s, the OC-12 is comprised of 12 DS3s, and so on. Table 4–4 shows the DS-1 and DS-3 equivalents; that is, the number of these payloads that are "carried" in the various SONET envelopes.

THE ENVELOPE (FRAME)

The basic transmission unit for SONET is the envelope (frame) (see Figure 4–11). It is comprised of 8-bit bytes (octets) that are transmitted serially on the optical fiber. For ease of documentation, the payload is depicted as a two-dimensional map. The map is comprised of n rows and m columns. Each entry in this map represents the individual octets of a synchronous payload *envelope* (the "F" stands for flag, and is explained later).

The octets are transmitted in sequential order, beginning in the top left-hand corner through the first row, and then through the second row, until the last octet is transmitted—the last row and last column.

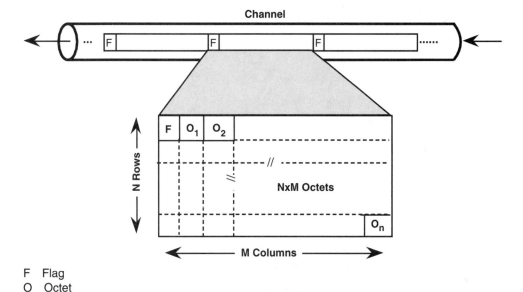

F   Flag
O   Octet

Figure 4–11   The envelope (frame).

The envelopes are sent contiguously and without interruption, and the payload is inserted into the envelope under stringent timing rules. Notwithstanding, a user payload may be inserted into more than one envelope, which means the payload need not be inserted at the exact beginning of the part of the envelope that is reserved for this traffic. It can be placed in any part of this area, and a pointer is created to indicate where it begins. This approach allows the network to operate synchronously, yet accept asynchronous traffic.

The basic transmission unit for SONET is the STS-1 frame (see Figure 4–12). The frame consists of 90 columns and 9 rows of 8-bit bytes (octets). Therefore, the frame carries 810 bytes or 6480 bits. SONET transmits at 8000 frames/second, making the frame length 125 microseconds. This approach translates into a transfer rate of 51.840 Mbit/s ($6480 \times 8000 = 51,840,000$). The first three columns of the frame contain transport overhead, which is divided into 27 bytes with 9 bytes allocated for section overhead and 18 bytes allocated for line overhead. The other 87 columns comprise the STS-1 envelope capacity (although the first column of the envelope capacity is reserved for STS path overhead).

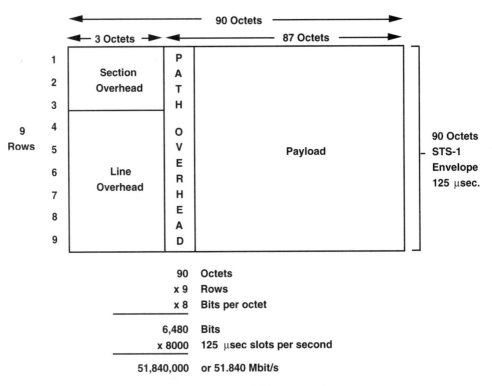

Figure 4–12   STS-1 signal.

The 87 columns are also called the synchronous payload envelope (SPE). The reader should be aware that the actual user payload consists of 86 columns or 774 bytes. Therefore, user payload operates at 49.536 Mbit/s ($774 \times 8000 = 49,536,000$). Obviously, the user payload can support VTs up to the DS3 rate (44.736 Mbit/s).

The STS-1 frame is transmitted row-by-row from left to right. Each byte is transmitted with the most significant bit first.

POINTER OPERATIONS

SONET uses a new concept, called *pointers,* to deal with timing variations in a network. The purpose of pointers is to allow the payload to "float" within the VT payload. The SPE can occupy more than one frame. The pointer is an offset value that shows the relative position of the first byte of the payload. During the transmission across the network, if any variations occur in the timing, the pointer need only be increased or decreased to compensate for the situation. Several options are available in how the payload is mapped into the frame. The option just discussed is called the *floating mode,* for obvious reasons.

Another option is called the *locked mode.* With this approach, the pointers are not used and the payload is fixed within the frame. It cannot float. This approach is much simpler, but it requires that timing be maintained throughout the network. Since all signals have a common orientation, the processing of the traffic is efficiently performed.

The location of the payload in the SONET frame is identified by a pointer in the transport overhead. These pointers are labeled H1, H2, and H3 and are used for identifying the position of the payload in the envelope (perhaps for adjusting the payload in the envelope) (see Figure 4–13). The dynamic alignment allows the payload to "float" within the frame. The pointers can adjust to both phase (time) changes and frequency (bit/frame rate) differences.

The pointer values can range from 0 to 782. This pointer indicates the relative position of the SPE within the payload. If the pointer is 0, the SPE begins in the byte adjacent to the H3 byte. Thereafter, the pointer value is adjusted to signify the relative position away from H3 byte.

The pointer value is a binary number in bits 7 through 16 of H1 and H2. The first four bits of the payload pointer are used to indicate a change of the payload. These are called the n bits (for the new data flag bits) and are used to indicate that a payload is new within the envelope.

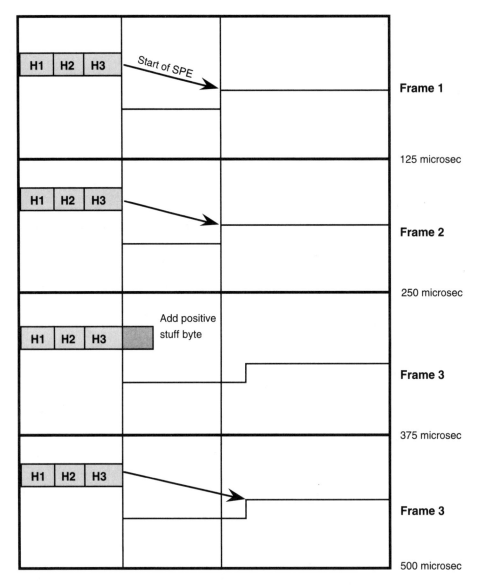

Figure 4–13   Pointer operations.

If SONET encounters a timing difference in the payload or flags, it can adjust a pointer value to reflect this difference, as shown in Figure 4–14. For example, if the SPE that is being placed in the STS-1 envelope is "too slow" in relation to the STS-1 rate, the H1 and H2 bits are manipulated as the signal is sent through the SONET nodes. These operations

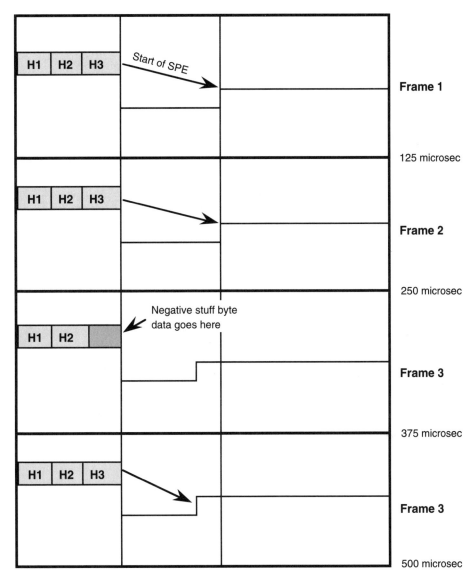

Figure 4–14   Pointer adjustments.

will eventually reveal that the SPE is about 1 byte slower than the STS-1 and *positive byte stuffing* will occur, shown in Figure 4–14, where a byte is stuffed into the envelope, allowing the payload to "slip back."

The stuff byte contains no useful information. It follows the H3 byte. Figure 4–14 also shows that the pointer is incremented by 1 byte to indicate the beginning of the SPE in the next relative position of the frame. The pointer is actually incremented by 1 in the next frame and in the subsequent pointers containing the new value.

Negative byte stuffing is the opposite of positive byte stuffing. In this situation, the SPE is too fast for the rate of the STS-1 frame. This situation requires that the SPE move forward into the envelope. To do so, the data is written in the H3 byte. Additionally, the pointer is decremented by 1 byte value in the next frame, with all subsequent pointers containing the new value. In essence, the SPE has been speeded up to match the alignment with the STS-1 frame.

While the use of pointers provides an effective means of adjusting to frequency and phase problems in the network, it does provide a problem known as *payload output jitter*. This timing impairment manifests itself on a received signal after recovery from a payload pointer change. This jitter, if excessive, can influence the timing in the network equipment that is processing the signal immediately downstream from where the change was made. Therefore, it is wise to design synchronous networks that use floating payload in a careful manner such that payload adjustments are rarely needed. Otherwise, jitter will accumulate through the network as payload adjustments are made.

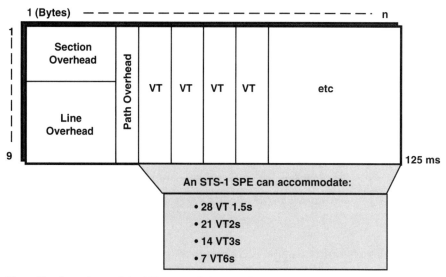

Note: The four sizes of the VT are as follows: VT 1.5 = 1.728 Mbit/s, VT 2 = 2.304 Mbit/s, VT 3 = 3.456 Mbit/s, VT 6 = 6.912 Mbit/s

Figure 4–15   VT/VC groups.

VT/VC GROUPS

Virtual tributaries are used to support sub-STS-1 levels, which are simply synchronous signals used to support low-speed signals (as shown in Figure 4–15). To support different mixes of VTs, the STS-1 SPE can be divided into seven groups. Each group occupies 12 columns and 9 rows of the SPE and may actually contain 4, 3, 2, or 1 VTs. For example, a VT group may contain one VT 6, two VT 3s, three VT 2s, or four VT 1.5s. Each VT group must contain one size of VTs, but different VT groups can be mixed in one STS-1 SPE.

WAVE DIVISION MULTIPLEXING (WDM)

A relatively new technology in the fiber arena is called wave division multiplexing (also called wavelength division multiplexing in some circles, both are known as WDM). This is illustrated in Figure 4–16. The technology uses an external coupling device that mixes different optical signals. Two forms of WDM are employed: unidirectional WDM sends multiple wavelengths in one direction on the fiber, while bidirectional WDM allows these signals to pass in opposite directions.

In addition, WDM systems are classified as broadband (which is also called crossband), narrowband, or dense. Wideband WDM doubles a capacity of a fiber span by combining a 1310 nm wavelength with a second wavelength that ranges between 1528 and 1560 nm. The figure shows an example of a broadband configuration using 1310 and 1550 nm wavelengths. Broadband WDM can support OC-12 rates.

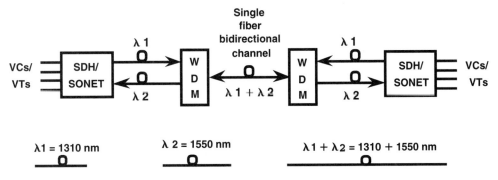

Figure 4–16 Wave division multiplexing.

A narrowband configuration can also provide a twofold increase in the capacity of the span. However, this approach uses two low-loss wavelengths operating at 1533 and 1557 nms. This operation can support OC-48 and OC-92 rates.

If system distance is an important consideration for long-haul networks, narrowband WDM is considered a better choice than broadband WDM, because the signal loss is less in these technologies.

The third WDM technology, dense WDM, employs as many as eight wavelengths, yields an eight-fold increase in capacity over conventional fiber span. The wavelengths fall between two bands. The first band is called the blue band and ranges between 1529 and 1541 nm. The second band is called the red band and falls between 1549 and 1557 nm. Each band is used for a particular transmission direction.

BANDWIDTH MANAGEMENT

Most of the SONET nodes in RBB have the ability to groom and reconfigure payload on demand. These operations are summarized here (4).

Timeslot assignment.   Enables traffic to be added to any SONET line from an optical tributary or be dropped from any line to any tributary. Routing traffic at low levels of STS-1 granularity allows operators to fill their SONET/SDH pipes more efficiently. When traffic does not have to be added or dropped, it simply passes through the bandwidth management unit.

Timeslot interchange.   Enables pass-through traffic to be switched from an STS-1 timeslot on an incoming link to a different STS-1 timeslot on the outgoing link when the corresponding timeslot on the outgoing link is already filled.

Hairpinning.   Allows STS-1 signals coming in on one tributary to be looped back directly to another tributary within a SONET network element, without having to go out on the backbone network.

Drop and continue/broadcast.   Enables an incoming signal from an OC line to be dropped to any tributary and simultaneously pass through to an outgoing line. This capability is commonly used for video distribution, where a cable head end distributes a feed to many sites. While drop and continue allows the signal to be dropped to many different nodes, broadcast allows the signal to be sent out on multiple tributaries on the same node.

SUMMARY

Optical fiber and SONET are viewed as key components in the residential broadband technology. A number of standards groups have been defining the specification for running fiber in the loop (FITL), and SONET is gaining in use as an RBB technology. Wave division multiplexing is a relative newcomer to fiber technology but is now deployed as part of the SONET network.

5

ATM Networks in Two-Way Access Systems

T his chapter is divided into two parts. The first part provides a short tutorial on ATM, and the second part explains how ATM is deployed in RBB and describes the specifications from both the ATM Forum and the ADSL Forum.

FEATURES OF ATM

The asynchronous transfer mode (ATM) forms the basis for some broadband networks. This technology provides for demand access to a network by multiplexing user information into fixed length slots called *cells*. The traffic is identified and managed through virtual connection identifiers.

ATM provides convergence functions for connection-oriented and connectionless variable bit rate (VBR) applications. In addition, provision is made for synchronous services, such as voice, video, and music, with functions to provide support for constant bit rate (CBR) services. Figure 5–1 shows the ATM layers. Segmentation and reassembly operations are provided for data services that may use PDUs different from those of an ATM cell. These convergence services provide standardized interfaces to the ATM layer. This layer is then responsible for relaying, routing, and

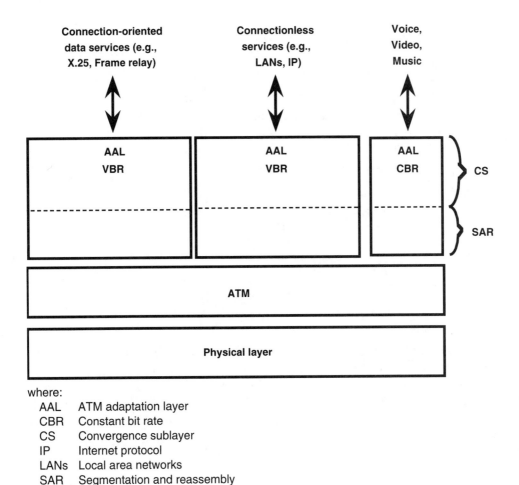

Figure 5–1   ATM layers.

multiplexing the traffic through the ATM network. The physical layer is made up of a variety of technologies such as twisted pair and HFC.

THE ATM Cell

Most of the values in the 5-octet cell header consist of the virtual circuit fields of VPI and VCI, and 24 bits are available with 8 bits assigned to VPI and 16 bits assigned to VCI. The cell header is depicted in Figure 5–2.

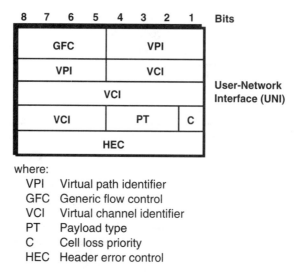

Figure 5–2   The ATM cells.

A payload type identifier type field identifies the type of traffic residing in the cell. If this field is not used, it is set to 0. The cell loss priority (CLP) field, if set to 1, means that the cell is subject to being discarded. Whether the cell is discarded depends on network conditions. The header error control (HEC) field is an error check field. The genetic flow control field (GFC) provides a variety of functions, but is not used in some implementations.

Switching

Switching is performed in an ATM-based network through the use of the VPI/VCI that is contained in the header of the ATM cell. The VPI/VCI is not an explicit address, such as a 32-bit IP address, or a fourteen-digit X.121 address. Rather, it is a label. The label is used at the ATM switch to determine how to relay traffic to the next node.

Explicit addresses are not feasible in cell technology due to the very short size of the header. Five bytes of header precludes using lengthy explicit addresses.

The ATM switch receives an incoming cell on a port and reads the VPI/VCI value (see Figure 5–3). This value has been reserved to identify a specific user for a virtual circuit. It also identifies the next node that is to receive the traffic. The ATM switch then examines a table for the match of the incoming number and the incoming port to that of an outgo-

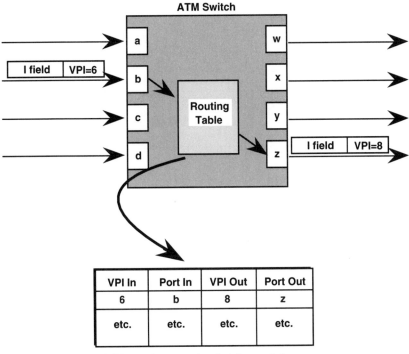

Note: Both VPI and VCI may be examined at the switch.

Figure 5–3   ATM routing table operations.

ing number and an outgoing port. In this manner, relaying can be performed quite quickly at the switch.

The header in the outgoing cell is changed with the new VPI/VCI value placed in the field of the cell header. The new value is used by the next ATM switch to perform subsequent routing operations.

Examples of Protocol Placement in the Broadband-IDSN (B-ISDN) Layers

The three B-ISDN planes are shown in Figure 5–4 with the placements of likely protocols residing in the layers. Strictly speaking, the B-ISDN model defines SONET for the physical layer, although Figure 5–4 shows other choices.

The ATM Adaptation Layer (AAL) is designed to support different types of applications, and different types of traffic, such as voice, video, and data. The AAL plays a key role in the ability of an ATM network to support multiapplication operations. It isolates the ATM layer from the

Control Plane	User Plane	Managment Plane
Q.2931	TCP/IP, FTP, etc.	LMI, SNMP, CMIP
AAL	AAL	AAL
ATM		
SDH, SONET, DS1, E1, etc.		

Notes:

SNMP and CMIP are actually user applications and operate in the user plane, but they can be invoked in the management plane.

AAL is "tailored" to support each plane (and application within a plane), but certain AAL features are common to each plane.

where:

AAL	ATM adaptation layer
CMIP	Common management information protocol
FTP	File transfer protocol
LMI	Local management interface
SNMP	Simple network management protocol
TCP/IP	Transmission control protocol/Internet protocol

Figure 5–4   Examples of protocol placement in the B-ISDN layers.

myriad operations necessary to support diverse types of traffic. AAL is divided into a convergence sublayer (CS) and a segmentation and re-assembly sublayer (SAR). CS operations are tailored, depending on the type of application being supported. SAR operations entail the segmentation of payload into 48-octet SDUs at the originating SAR and reassembling the SDUs into the original payload at the receiver.

The ATM layer's primary responsibility is the sending and receiving of cells between the user node and the network node. It adds and processes the 5-octet cell header.

On the left side of the Figure 5–4 is the control plane. It contains the Q.2931 signaling protocol that is used to set up connections in the ATM network (Q.2931 is a variation of Q.931). The layer below Q.2931 is the signaling ATM adaptation layer (SAAL), which is an AAL tailored for Q.2931.

In the middle of Figure 5–4 is the user plane, which contains user and applications-specific protocols, such as Transmission Control Protocol/ Internet Protocol (TCP/IP), File Transfer Protocol (FTP), and so on. These protocols are chosen arbitrarily, as examples of typical user protocols.

The management plane provides the required management services and is implemented with the ATM Local Management Interface. The Internet Simple Network Management Protocol (SNMP), and/or the OSI Common Management Information Protocol (CMIP) can also reside in the management plane.

The ATM ADAPTATION Layer (AAL)

The AAL is organized to support different types of service classes. The classes are defined with regard to:

- Timing needed between source and destination
- Bit rate (variable or constant)
- Connectionless or connection-oriented operation

Classes A and B require timing relationships between the source and destination; classes C and D do not require timing relationships. A constant bit rate is required for class A; variable bit rates are permitted for classes B, C, and D. Classes A, B, and C are connection-oriented; class D is connectionless.

These classes are used to support different types of user applications. For example, class A is designed to support a constant bit rate requirement for voice or video coding. On the other hand, class B, while connection-oriented, supports a variable bit rate. Class B supports applications such as variable bit rate video. For example, variable bit rate coding could be supported by information retrieval services in which large amounts of video traffic are sent to the user and then long delays occur as the user examines the information. As a result of this type of exchange, a variable bit rate is needed. Class C services are the connection-oriented data transfer services such as X.25-type connections. Conventional connectionless services such as datagram networks are supported with class D services.

Relationships of ATM Class and AAL Types. Since the original publication of the ATM specifications and standards, the relationships between the ATM service classes and the AAL types that support these services have changed. Table 5–1 shows these changes. Originally, a one-to-one relationship existed, with class A supported by AAL type 1, class B support by AAL type 2, and so on. As designers became more familiar with ATM, it was decided that the definition of separate types 3 and 4 were unnecessary. Therefore, these types were combined and are now called AAL type 3/4.

Due to the overhead (headers and trailers) in AAL type 3/4, another type was created, called AAL type 5. While this can be used with any ATM service class, its initial, principal use has been to run "under" other layers (protocol families), such as TCP/IP and SNMP. However, due to its small protocol control information (PCI) field, it is being used now in some video applications. One vendor has run MPEG compressed video over AAL5.

Also, type x was defined to describe a private, user-defined service class.

The AAL PDUs.   Different formats are shown for the AAL PDU types in Figure 5–5. Their functions are explained below.

The ATM adaptation layer (AAL) uses type 1 protocol data units (PDUs) to support applications requiring a constant bit rate transfer to and from the layer above AAL1. It is also responsible for the following tasks: (1) segmentation and reassembly of user information, (2) handling the variable cell delay, (3) detecting lost and missequenced cells, (4) providing source clock frequency recovery at the receiver, (5) correcting all 1-bit errors in the PDU and detecting of all 2-bit errors.

The AAL type 1 PDU consists of 48 octets, with 47 octets available for the user's payload. The first header field is a sequence number (SN) used for detection of mistakenly inserted cells or lost cells. The other

Table 5–1   Relationships of ATM Class and AAL Types

Class	Original Type of Service/PDU	Class	Revised Type of Service/PDU
A	1	A	1
B	2	B	2
C	3	C	3/4 or 5
D	4	D	3/4 or 5
X	not defined	not defined	not defined

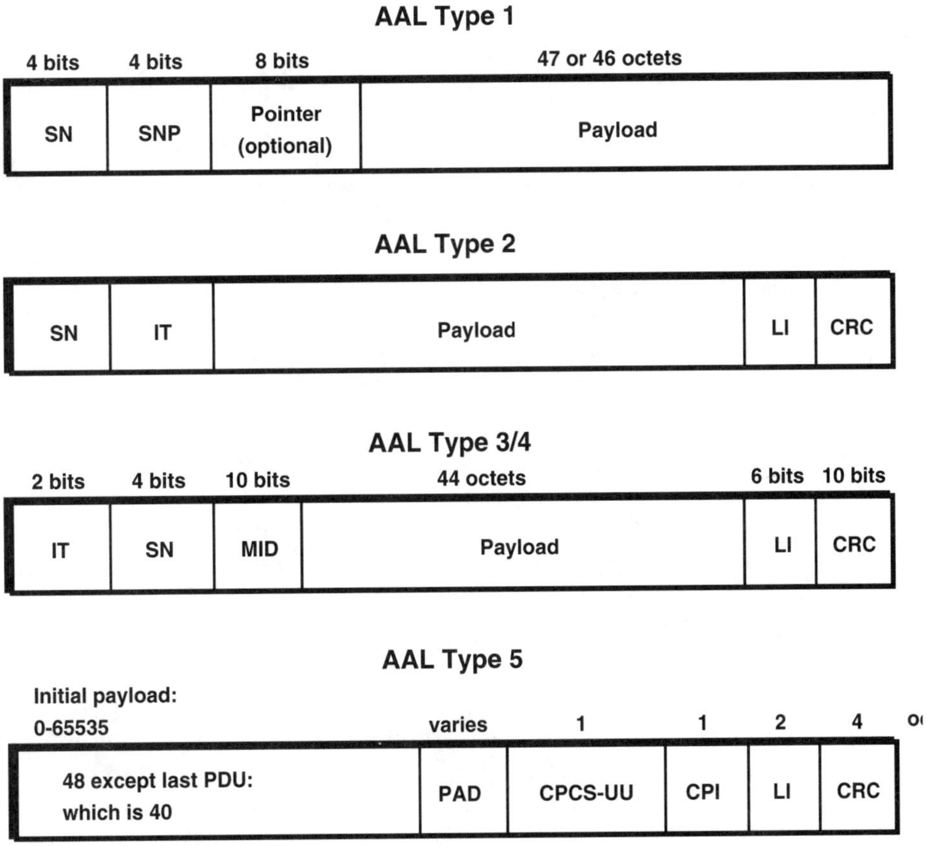

AAL Type 1

4 bits	4 bits	8 bits	47 or 46 octets
SN	SNP	Pointer (optional)	Payload

AAL Type 2

SN	IT	Payload	LI	CRC

AAL Type 3/4

2 bits	4 bits	10 bits	44 octets		6 bits	10 bits
IT	SN	MID	Payload		LI	CRC

AAL Type 5

Initial payload:

0-65535		varies	1	1	2	4	o(
48 except last PDU: which is 40		PAD	CPCS-UU	CPI	LI	CRC	

where:

CPCS-UU	Common part convergence sublayer-user to user indication
CPI	Common part ID
CRC	Cyclic redundancy check
IT	Information type
LI	Length Indicator
MID	Message ID (or multiplexor ID)
PAD	Padding to fill 48 bytes (if necessary)
SN	Sequence number
SNP	Sequence number protection

Figure 5–5   The AAL PDUs.

header field is the sequence number protection (SNP), and it is used to provide for error detection and correction on the SN. The AAL type 1 conversion sublayer is responsible for clock recovery for both audio and video services.

The AAL type 2 is employed for variable bit rate (VBR) services where a timing relationship is required between the source and destination sites. For example, class B traffic, such as variable bit rate audio or video, would fall into this category. This category of service is responsible for handling variable cell delay as well as the detection and handling of lost or missequenced cells.

The PDU for AAL type 2 consists of both a header and a trailer. The header consists of a sequence number (SN) as well as an information type (IT) field. The length of these fields and their exact functions have not been determined as of this writing. Obviously, the SN will be used for detection of lost and mistakenly inserted cells. The IT field can contain the indication of beginning of message (BOM), continuation of message (COM), or end of message (EOM). It may also contain timing information for audio or video signals.

The AAL type 2 trailer consists of a length indicator (LI) that is used to determine the number of octets residing in the payload field. And finally, the cyclic redundancy check (CRC) will be used for error detection.

The original ATM standards established AAL3 for VBR connection-oriented operations and AAL4 for VBR connectionless operations. These two types have been combined and are treated as one type. As the AAL standard has matured, it became evident that the original types were inappropriate. Therefore, AAL3 and AAL4 were combined due to their similarities.

The AAL 3/4 PDU carries 44 octets in the payload and 5 fields in the header and trailer. The 2-bit segment type (ST) is used to indicate the beginning of message (BOM), continuation of message (COM), end of message (EOM), or single segment message (SSM). The sequence number is used for sequencing the traffic. It is incremented by one for each PDU sent, and a state variable at the receiver indicates the next expected PDU. If the received SN is different from the state variable, the PDU is discarded. The message identification (MID) subfield is used to reassemble traffic on a given connection. The length indicator (LI) defines the size of the payload. Finally, the cyclic redundancy check (CRC) field is a 10-bit field used to determine if an error has occurred in any part of the cell.

AAL 5 was conceived because AAL 3/4 was considered to contain unnecessary overhead, and it was judged that multiplexing could be pushed up to an upper layer and that the BAsize operations to preallocate buffers at the receiver were not needed.

Figure 5–5 shows the format of the type 5 PDU. It consists of an 8-octet trailer. The PAD field acts as a filler to fill out the PDU to 48 octets. The CPCS-UU field is used to identify the user payload. The common part indicator (CPI) has not been fully defined in ITU-T I.363. The length field (L) defines the payload length, and the CRC field is used to detect errors in the SSCS PDU (user data).

Service Classes

The initial ATM specifications and standards focused on constant bit rate (CBR) and variable bit rate (VBR) applications. As more experience was gained with the ATM technology, it became evident that other classes should be defined, as well as methods and techniques to handle these other classes. Figure 5–6 shows the bit rates for the service classes.

Two more service classes are now defined by the ATM Forum: (a) unspecified bit rate (UBR), and (b) available bit rate (ABR). UBR is the lowest quality of service that an ATM network offers. A UBR user takes

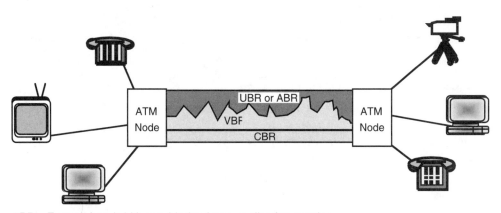

ABR   Enough bandwidth provided to keep application running
CBR   Fixed service for assured steady supply of bandwidth
UBR   Bandwidth as available with no assurance
VBR   Bursty service with assured supply of bandwidth

where:
  ABR   Available bit rate
  CBR   Constant bit rate
  UBR   Unspecified bit rate
  VBR   Variable bit rate

Figure 5–6   Service classes.

what is left on the channel (or logical connections) after CBR and VBR have had their go. As two writers have phrased it, UBR is like flying standby (D. Hughes and K. Hooshmand of Stratacom). UBR provides no way for a user to negotiate with the network, and the network provides no guarantee that the user's traffic will be delivered.

ABR is similar to UBR in that the user is not given as much preferential treatment as the users of the CBR and VBR services. However, the network provides enough bandwidth to keep the user application up and running. Additionally, flow control mechanisms are available to throttle the user's traffic in the event of problems.

ATM FORUM RBB

Because ATM is being accepted in the marketplace and its features are becoming known, some vendors, network managers, and potential customers view ATM as a viable technology for deployment in residential broadband. As discussed in other parts of this book, one of ATM's principal attributes is well-documented standards on (1) quality of service provision, (2) traffic management, and (3) overall network management.

The ATM Forum is now defining the role of ATM technology for residential broadband, and this committee has issued a baseline document draft titled, "Residential Broadband Baseline Text," which is published as document #BTD-RBB-001-02, April 1997. This document provides various levels of detail on the role of ATM. Some of the specifications in this document are complete and some are not. Therefore, as the title name suggests, this is a baseline specification that will undergo specification changes over time. However, there is enough substance to the document to warrant a discussion here.

ATM RBB Reference Architecture

As depicted in Figure 5–7, the ATM RBB Reference Architecture defines five functions including networks, terminations, and equipment. They are:

1. Core ATM network
2. ATM access network
3. Access network termination
4. Home ATM network
5. Terminal network

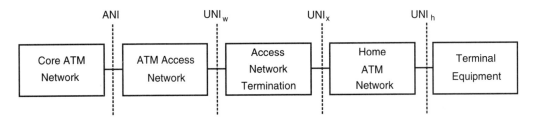

Figure 5–7   The ATM residential broadband architecture.

Each of these functional entities is described in the next sections. Note from Figure 5–7 that each entity is defined by an interface to one of the associated entities. The interfaces are the access network interface (ANI) and the user network interface (UNI) in which three UNIs are defined (UNI_w, UNI_x, and UNI_h)

Core ATM Network.   The core ATM network consists of one-or-more ATM switches (see Figure 5–8). ATM network management includes ITU-T OAM and the ATM Forum network management. It also includes servers that might act as level one or level two gateways into and out of

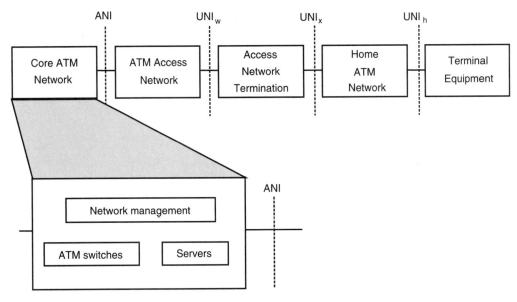

Figure 5–8   The core ATM network.

the ATM core network. The ATM Forum has not defined the functions of the core ATM network beyond this general description. However, in most instances it need not go into further detail, since the ATM switch design is left to the discretion of the vendor and the network management entities are well defined. The servers will be more application-specific and also tailored to the specific RBB environment.

ATM Access Network.   The ATM access network is the first network located in the local loop (see Figure 5–9). It is comprised of an ATM digital terminal (ADT) and the access distribution network. The ATM Forum does not intend to define all the functions of the ATM access network, because many variations will be required to meet the different services. Notwithstanding, the ATM Forum specification does provide considerable detailed information about the operations with the ATM access network at the ANI, UNI_w, and UNI_x. I will provide a summary of these operations' interfaces here.

As stated earlier, the ATM access network consists of an ATM digital terminal (ADT) that provides the ANI to the core ATM network. This interface must be in compliance with existing ATM standards with no variations to the ATM physical and ATM layers specified. The other side

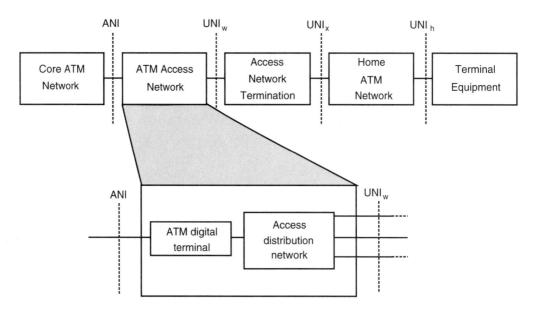

Figure 5–9   The ATM access network.

of the ADT consists of HFC, which implements the third major function shown in Figure 5–7, the access termination network.

This HFC access network transports RF signals between the ADT and the ATM interface unit (AIU), located in the terminal equipment at the customer premises. The specifications for this interface is defined in various ATM specifications as well as the IEEE 802.14 standard (which is still undergoing development).

Access Network Termination (NT).   The access network termination (NT) connects the ATM access network with the home ATM network (see Figure 5–10). The NT may be passive or active. If passive, it is restricted to operating with passive components such as electrical protectors. If active, it may house OSI bearer services.

OSI bearer services operating in the lower three layers of the OSI Model and the NT may consist of ATM and AAL operations operating on top of a media access control (MAC) layer. The IEEE 802.14 draft specification defines several operations of ATM operating over a MAC defined especially for RBB. See Chapter 7 for more information.

The Home ATM Network.   The ATM home network is placed between the ATM access network and the terminal equipment (see Figure 5–11).

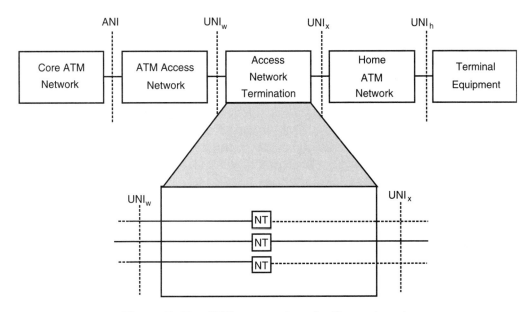

Figure 5–10   ATM access termination network.

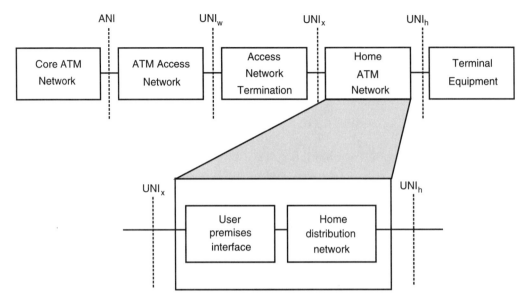

Figure 5–11   ATM home network.

Its functions vary and may consist of a simple pass-through passive network to a full network with switching and traffic management capabilities. I say may, because work is underway to define further the specific operations of this part of the RBB ATM system. Thus far, the ATM home network has been divided into the user premises interface (UPI) and the home distribution network (HDN). The UPI is responsible for translating ATM access termination network to/from home ATM network traffic. Its contents and functions vary and may support L_1, L_2 operations as well as ATM Q.2931 signaling capabilities. The HDN is responsible for transporting ATM cells across the UNI_h to and from the terminal equipment. Again, the operations of the HDN are under study, but information is available from the draft specification TIA-TR41.5 *Draft Proposal, Multimedia Premises Reference Architecture.*

Terminal Equipment.   The components described thus far are the "means to the end"—that is, transporting traffic to and from the end user terminal, such as a computer or a television set. The "end" is the user terminal (see Figure 5–12). The adapter may or may not be part of this configuration. The function of the adapter is to act as a gateway between the non-ATM-based user terminal and the ATM-based RBB operations. It is reasonable to expect this gateway to be an essential component of

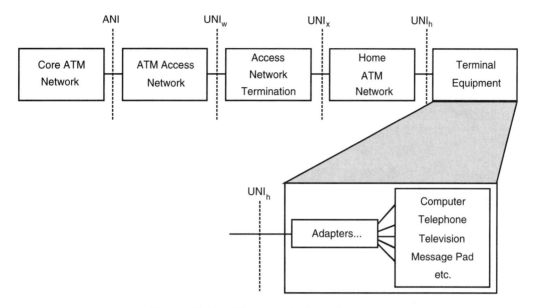

Figure 5–12   The terminal equipment.

the terminal equipment, because it allows current user machines (such as a TV) to operate without any modification to the user equipment.

ATM Digital Terminal (ADT)

The principal function of the ADT is to interface with the HFC at a splitter/combiner and the other side with the ATM core network with an HFC specific ANI. As depicted in Figure 5–13, the ADT consists of four major entities:

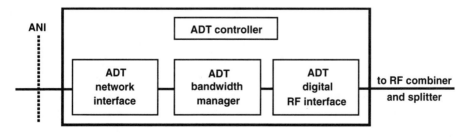

Figure 5–13   The ATM digital terminal (ADT).

- The *ADT RF interface (ADTRFI)* connects with the HFC and modulates the downstream digital signal onto the HFC. These signals must contain the ATM cells received from the ADT bandwidth manager (ADTBM). On the receive side, the entity demodulates the signals received across the HFC and extracts the cells as necessary for delivery to the ADT bandwidth manager. Undecided at this time is the role of this entity in performing forward error correction (FEC).
- The *ADT bandwidth manager (ADTBM)* implements an access control protocol to manage the upstream ATM bandwidth. The BM must react to AIU requests for ATM upstream bandwidth and this service request must be met within the ongoing ATM QOS parameters.
- The *ADT network interface (ADTNI)* terminates the physical and ATM layers at the UNI. Its functions include ongoing ATM operations such as traffic management and multiplexing. It is responsible for the interleaving of the upstream virtual connections for the AIUs into one single ATM interface.
- The *ADT controller* is the overall managing entity for the other three entities. The specific functions of the controller are not defined as of this writing.

ATM Interface Unit (AIU)

The AIU acts as the ADT peer on the customer side of this interface. It also consists of four major entities as depicted in Figure 5–14. It is responsible for terminating all HFC operations and provides the interface into the dwelling. The functions of the four entities in the ADT are as fol-

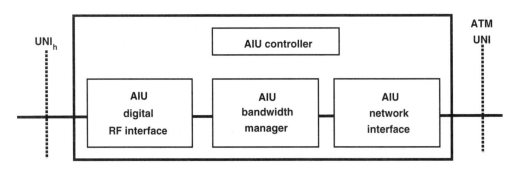

Figure 5–14   The ATM interface unit (AIU).

lows. On the UNI HFC side, the *AIU digital RF interface (AIURI)* terminates the modulate RF signals and decouples the ATM cells from the RFC interface. Also under study for the ADURI is the possibility of performing FEC. The *AIU bandwidth manager (AIUBM)* is the peer of the ADTBM and, like its peer, it terminates the access control protocol and presents ATM cells to the AIU network interface (AIUNI). The bandwidth manager also controls the delivery of cells upstream for delivery across the HFC. The *AIU network interface (IUNI)* implements the standard ATM UNI as defined in the ATM Forum specifications (for example, UNI version 4.0). It is not anticipated that this interface will differ from the ongoing UNI specifications just cited.

In addition to these operations, the AIU will also contain the IEEE 802.14 MAC and physical layer functions (with ATM running on top of MAC) and a security feature (which will use likely existing security specifications), although this part of the ATM RBB is still under study.

Finally, the three entities just described are managed by the AIU controller. Although like its counterpart in the ADT, the full functions in this controller have not been defined.

ATM over HFC

Figure 5–15 depicts the RBB ATM model running on HFC. The UNI_w is retitled UNI_{hfc} to denote the use of a hybrid fiber and coax distribution plant. The NTs may be passive or active and the UNI_{hfc} can include taps, amplifiers, and fiber nodes.

The technology independent interface (TII) connects the AIU to the user terminal (also refer to Figure 5–12). Its function is to act as a gateway between the user terminal and the ATM access network or the home ATM network and isolate the user from these technologies.

Physical Interface for the Home ATM Network

The physical interface for the home ATM network is plastic optical fiber (POF), operating at 50 Mbit/s with light emitting diodes (LEDs) and fiber length of up to 50 meters. This aspect of the physical layer is actually in the physical media dependent (PMD) sublayer of the physical layer. At the transmission convergence (TC) sublayer, several proposals are being considered: (1) 25.6 Mbit/s, (2) 51.2 Mbit/s, and (3) 64.8 Mbit/s.

The requirement for the optical fiber must be in conformance with the IEC 793-1 (1992) specifications. It is beyond the scope of this book to delve into the details of IEC 793-2, so a summary of these standards is provided in Table 5–2. The optical line coding for the cable is binary non-

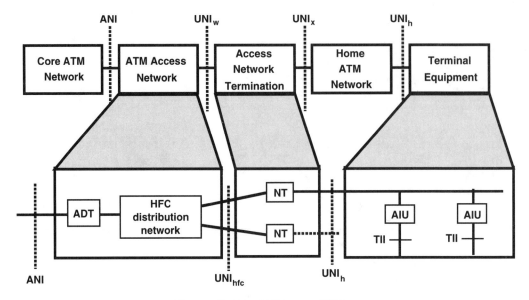

Figure 5–15   ATM over HFC.

return to zero (NRZ), with a binary 1 represented as a high light condition. The POF receiver must operate with a bit error rate (BER) no worse than 10^{-10}.

Transmitter Characteristics.   The values prescribed below are for worst case operation conditions and end of life. The following parameters are specified for the transmitter.

- The enter wavelength is from 640 to 600 nm.
- The maximum full width half-maximum (FWHM) spectral width is 40 nm.
- The mean launched power into POF is from −9 to −2 dBm.
- The source NA is from 0.2 to 0.3.
- The minimum extinction ratio is 10 dB.
- The transmitter exit rise (fall) time is less than 5.5 ns.
- The maximum transmitter overshoot is 25%.
- The systematic interface jitter at the transmitter output is less than 4.8 ns.
- The random interface jitter at the transmitter output is less than 1.8 ns.

Table 5–2   50 m Plastic Optical Fiber (POF) Worst Case Loss Increments

Parameters	Unit	Min	Max	Loss Increment	Test Method Reference
Source center wavelength	nm	640	660	3.4 dB	IEC 793-1-C1A
Source spectral length (FWHM)	nm		40	3.4 dB	IEC 793-1-C1A
Cable bends—radius	mm	25.4		0.5 dB	(TBD)
Cable bends—number of 90° bends			15	0.5 dB	(TB)

Receiver Characteristics.   The following characteristics are specified for the receiver.

- The minimum receiver sensitivity is –26 dBm.
- The minimum receiver overload is –2 dBm.
- The receiver optical input rise (fall) time is less than 6.0 ns.
- The systematic interface jitter at the receiver input is less than 6.0 ns.
- The random interface jitter at the receiver input is less than 1.8 ns.
- The minimum receiver eye opening at a 10E-10BER is 3.69 ns.

POF Transmitter and Receiver Characteristics.   The POF transmitter and receiver characteristics listed previously are all required (no options). In addition, the optical parameters for the POF interface are provided in Table 5–3.

ATM over ADSL

ATM Forum's View.   Other discussions in this text focus on the use of ATM in residential broadband and discuss several of the ATM Forum's specifications for these operations. The ATM Forum is in the process of formulating its specifications for the use of ATM over ADSL. Although the specifications are not complete, they are complete enough to warrant discussion here. Figure 5–16 shows the ATM Forum approach in defining the relationship of the residential broadband architecture with the ADSL functional module.

The V interface can consist of interfaces to one or more switches, and its implementation is optional. The T interface is also optional if the

Table 5–3   Optical Parameters for POF Interface

	POF	Unit
Transmitter Interface Characteristics		
Center wavelength	640 to 660	nm
Maximum spectral width (FWHM)	40	nm
Mean launched power	–9v to –2v	dBm
Source NA	0.2 to 0.3	
Minimum extinction ratio	10	dB
Maximum rise (fall) time (10–90%)	5.5	ns
Maximum overshoot	25	%
Maximum systematic interface jitter	4.80	ns
Maximum random interface jitter	1.80	ns
Receiver Interface Characteristics		
Minimum receiver input power	–26	dBm
Minimum overload	–2	dBm
Maximum rise (fall) time (10–90%)	6.0	ns
Maximum systematic interface jitter	6.0	ns
Maximum random interface jitter	1.80	ns
Minimum receiver eye opening	3.69	ns

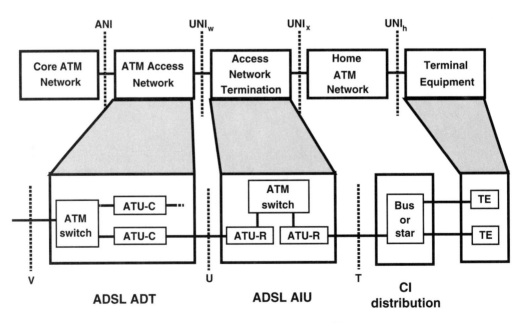

Figure 5–16   ATM over ADSL.

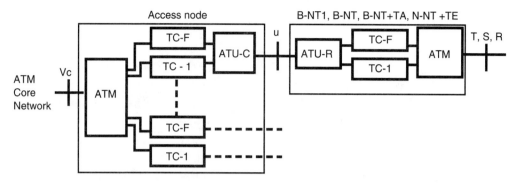

Figure 5–17   ADSL Forum's View of ATM over ADSL.

elements connected by this interface are within a common processing element. One example of the V interface is the implementation of a SONET carrier that could be connected at this interface with ADSL transceiver unit central office (ATU-C). The U reference point requires that the transmitting signals must be physically separated at this interface.

The ADSL ADT (the ADSL digital terminal) at this stage of the evolution of the ATM Forum's specifications could contain: (1) a concentrator/switch, (2) a multiplexer/demultiplexer, (3) the ADSL transceiver unit central office (ATU-C), (4) the ongoing ATM layer operations, (5) the interface into the core ATM network, and (6) a POTS splitter to delineate between the POTS and ADSL channels.

Under study as of this writing are the specific functions of the ATU-C in relation to ATM. It is anticipated that this unit will provide the physical layer functions such as modulation/demodulation, FEC, and cell interleaving. It will likely also provide the POTS splitter function, although this function may be separate.

The ADLS transceiver unit/remote terminal end (ATU-R) resides at the access network termination entity. In effect, the ATU-R operates in the inverse of the ATU-C; therefore, it also houses downstream demodulation, upstream modulation, FEC, scrambling operations, and cell interleaving.

The ADSL Forum's View.   Like most efforts in the telecommunications industry, more than one specification for a technology emerges. The ADSL Forum is also involved in defining the operations of ATM over ADSL.[1] Many of the concepts espoused by the ATM Forum have already been covered (see Figure 5–17).

---

[1]See ADSL Forum TR-002, ATM over ADSL Recommendations, March 1997.

The operations of the components in the ATM/ADSL systems are as follows:

- *Access Node:* The access node performs the adaptation between the ATM core network and the access network. In the downstream direction it performs routing/demultiplexing. In the upstream direction it performs multiplexing/concentration.
- *B-NT1, B-NT, B-NT+TA or N-NT+TE:* This terminates the ADSL signal entering the user's premises via the twisted pair cable and provides either the T, S, or R interface towards the terminal equipment. Its functions are: terminating/originating the transmission line and handling the transmission interfacing and OAM functions.

ATM Connection-Oriented Options on Residential Broadband

The ATM Forum has defined several options for establishing virtual channel connections (VCCs) on the RBB network. In the original ATM work, simple point-to-point connections were established; but for RBB with services such as video-on-demand, web browsing, e-mail downloading, and other client-server operations, a simple point-to-point relationship is not sufficient. Consequently, using the ITU-T connection types, the ATM Forum has expanded these types for the RBB services. The types discussed here are:[2]

- Type 1: *Bidirectional point-to-point.* The type 1 connection is a bidirectional point-to-point connection between two parties. Bandwidth is independently specified in each direction. Asymmetric bandwidth can be supported, and unidirectional connection is the special case with zero bandwidth in one direction. Type 1 also specifies that the physical route taken by the connection in each direction must be identical.
- Type 2: *Unidirectional point-to-multipoint.* The type 2 connection is a point-to-multipoint connection that involves three or more parties, one of which is the root. This is a unidirectional connection for which the root is the only source and multicasts its information over the type 2 connection to all the other parties of the connection (called leaves). The root is responsible for adding and dropping parties. The leaf parties can also drop from such a connection independently. It is up to the root to specify during the

---

[2]ATM Forum, BTD-RBB-001.02, April 1997, pp. 15–16.

connection setup time whether the root should be notified of such actions. The type 2 connection is required to support multicast services, such as broadcast TV.

- Type 3: *Unidirectional multipoint-to-point.* The type 3 connection is a unidirectional connection between three or more parties with multiple sources and a single destination. This has the same logical configuration as type 2 connection, except the information flow is reversed, from the leaves back to the root.

    Since the cells from different sources (leaves) arrive at the destination (root) carrying the same VPI/VCI, the root cannot reassemble the AAL PDU because the root will receive interleaved cells from different leaves. This cell interleaving problem is the main challenge for designing the signaling protocols to support the type 3 connection. There are two special cases, however, for which interleaving is not a problem. The first exception is when AAL 3/4 is used (which as MID field for demultiplexing), and the second is if only single cell messages are sent.

- Type 4: *Bidirectional multipoint-to-multipoint.* Type 4 is a bidirectional multipoint-to-multipoint connection that allows three or more parties to communicate with each other. The information sent by any party will be received by all other parties to the connection. This connection type faces the same challenge of cell interleaving as the type 3 connection, and hence can be solved similarly. The type 4 connection is important for supporting group communication, such as multiuser games and multiparty video calls.

Relationship of the ATM Forum and IEEE 802.14 Specifications

The relationship of the ATM Forum and IEEE 802.14 specifications is shown in Figure 5–18. The IEEE 802.14 MAC operations take place

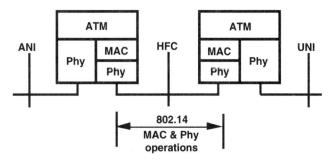

Figure 5–18   ATM and IEEE 802.14.

across the HFC UNI, between the AT and the AIU. The ATM layers rest on top of the MAC layer. Chapter 7 provides more information on ATM and the IEEE 802.14 RBB MAC layer.

SUMMARY

ATM is viewed as the switching component of residential broadband. The ATM adaptation layer is used to support different types of user applications (service classes). Several vendors are establishing plans for its use with HFC and ADSL. It is also a component in the IEEE 802.14 specifications.

6

Internet and
LAN Considerations

As the chapter title suggests, this chapter examines the operations and issues surrounding Internet and LAN access across the local loop. Most of the issues pertain to the capacity of the telephone and Internet service providers' facilities to support frequent high bandwidth transfers.

One of the problems in this area deals with the connecting of very high-speed LANs through traditional telephone lines that are inherently limited in bandwidth. Traditional LAN users expect to receive high-bandwidth utilization for their applications. Once these applications start passing through low-speed access networks to reach another LAN, inevitable delays are encountered.

Ideally, a customer would like to have a "transparent LAN" service, meaning that the long distance carriers provide the same type of communications capability between the LANs, including the local loop as well as the wide area backbone.

Systems are being developed today that address this problem. The goals of these systems are as follows:

For network providers:

- To support high-speed LAN/WAN applications
- To support the addition of new services in a rapid manner
- To be able to serve multiple customers with resources partitioned among these customers

For end users:

- To be able to out-source all their needs to one public provider
- To enjoy the advantages of private networking without the expense of owning that network
- To treat the customers' LANs transparently, that is to say, maintain separate bridge/routing tables for each customer for each network
- To provide security for each customer even though some of the resources may be shared due to economies of scale
- To support the customer's choice of levels and qualities of service

PROBLEMS WITH THE INTERNET SERVICE PROVIDERS (ISPs)

The bottom line for Internet access deals with the ability to access the telephone company's switch at the local central office and to then access the ISP's switch. The scenario for a typical Internet access entails the Internet subscriber's dialing a prescribed number to the ISP. However, the subscriber first connects to the local central office, which, upon examining the called number, dials to a multiplexer/router that acts as a gateway to the ISP network. As a general practice, the connection from the ISP to the central office is an ISDN or T1 (DS1) link or multiples thereof (multiple DS1s, perhaps a DS3).

The problem occurs when the bandwidth to the ISP is exhausted. Only 24 DS0 slots are available on each DS1 channel.[1] When these slots are not available, the user receives a busy signal.

To get a sense of the problem, consider American On Line (AOL). According to *Business Communications Review* ("What AOL's Troubles Say About the 'Net'," John Puttre, March 1997, p. 24), AOL had (in February 1997) eight million customers and 200,000 modems installed. A ratio of one modem to 40 customers. This ratio appears to be attractive to the customer. After all, not everyone logs onto the Internet at the same time. However, data calls are much longer than voice calls, and tie up re-

---

[1]Systems can divide the DS0 slots into 32 kbit/s slots and increase the capacity. One approach yields 44 channels (not 48, since 4 channels are used for control). Another approach is to use "unchannelized T1," which effectively treats the T1 1.544 Mbit/s bandwidth as a conveyor belt and allows more effective use of the link.

sources longer. In fact, only 2.5% of the customers could get service at any time. For example, if 5% of the customer base tried to connect (400,000) at the same time, only 50% would be able to get a connection.

Puttre reports that an acceptable ratio for modems (DS0 slots) to customers is 10 modems to 100 customers. It is evident that problems exist for network providers that offer a lesser ratio. And, as we have learned, Internet subscribers have been extending the length of their connections—further exacerbating the problem.

PROBLEMS WITH THE TELEPHONE SERVICE PROVIDERS

A principal problem is dealing with the ISP's flat rate pricing in contrast to usage pricing. At the risk of oversimplifying the situation, the flat-rate usage has led to extraordinarily long hold times. Several studies have shown that subscribers who are given flat-rate charges tend to use the services 40% more than customers who are charged usage-based rates.

The basic problem deals with the difference between voice-oriented circuit switched calls and data-oriented packet switched calls. The telephone network is designed for the former and Internet is designed for the latter, and therein lies the problem.

Bottlenecks occur due to the inability to support long-running connections in a system that was designed for short-running connections. The bottlenecks usually occur at the terminating central office (CO) that served the ISPs. They can also occur at the originating COs where there is a high concentration of Internet users.

The problem revolves around (1) the capacity of the CO switch, (2) the number of users requesting Internet access through the switch, and (3) the hold-time of these users (that is, the length of time they utilize the capacity of the switch).

SOME SOLUTIONS

One approach to solving some of the problems of congestion and service denial for Internet users is Nortel's Internet Thruway. A typical architecture is shown in Figure 6–1. The customer's dialed number is monitored by an "access vehicle," which is a Nortel AccessNode. This node contains a database of up to 1000 Internet Service Providers' (ISPs) phone numbers (or any other provider, such as a private corporate network).

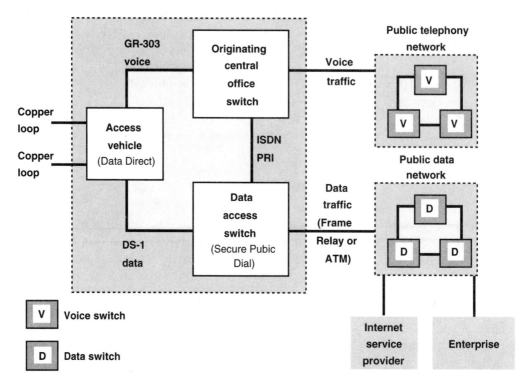

Figure 6–1   Internet Thruway functional architecture.

When a number matches a number in this database, the AccessNode disconnects the call from the switch (which is also collecting the DTMF digits), and routes the call via a DS0 clear channel within a PRI DS1 to a data access switch (in Nortel's configuration, a Rapport dialup switch).

The data access switch terminates the call and routes the user traffic via Frame Relay or ATM to the appropriate ISP or corporate user, based on the called party number. This switch maintains a list of ISP phone numbers and their associated IP addresses. It uses this list to correlate the dialed number to the IP address of the ISP.

When the subscriber goes on-hook, the switch removes the connection to the AccessNode and the Rapport switch and prepares the line for the next call.

The same procedure occurs on a customer ISDN link. The difference is that the digits of the called party are collected via the D channel.

The Internet Thruway approach is attractive to the customer, the local exchange carrier (LEC), and the ISP/corporation for several reasons.

The customer has a better chance of a call not being blocked (assuming the ISP has sufficient ports to support the call). In addition, for analog lines, the AccessNode's adaptive loop equalization provides for high-quality transmissions, such that 28.8/33.6 kbit/s data rates are feasible. The service requires no changes to user hardware or software.

The LEC does not have to tie up its circuit-switched resources for the data connection. This fact is a big attraction and should at least delay the need to upgrade/re-engineer the switch trunks and the voice switch. It also better aligns the LEC's costs versus revenues for data traffic. As a bonus, the statistics gathered allow the LEC to identify users who likely need high-speed asymmetrical services like xDSL.

The ISP should be able to better manage its lines, since these resources are operating with Frame Relay or ATM, which support data traffic more efficiently than voice lines. Additionally, the ISP still retains control of billing and authentication.

Modem Termination Options

Figure 6–2 provides three scenarios showing how the analog modem termination can be handled.[2] The goal is provide this termination as close to the subscriber as possible, which allows more efficient techniques to be used on the remainder of the link to the Internet or corporate node. The shadowed boxes in the figure numbered 1, 2, or 3 symbolize the demarcation point at which the modem signal (modem connection) is terminated. Thereafter, digital signaling is employed at the physical layer, with Frame Relay or ATM operating over the physical layer.

In scenario 1, the modem termination occurs at the trunk side of the terminating central office that is servicing the ISP. A data access switch is installed as a trunk-side peripheral at this CO. This configuration bypasses the line side of the remote CO.

In scenario 2, the modem termination occurs at the trunk side of the originating CO. The benefit of this approach is that it reduces or eliminates the need to upgrade the network's trunks to handle data traffic. The traffic is diverted to data networks before it hits the voice network. The data networks are designed to handle asynchronous data traffic.

Scenario 3 is the best approach. It terminates the connection before it enters the local switch. In this example, which was the scenario in the previous figure, most of the POTS facilities are not taxed with the data traffic.

---

[2]Additional information on these operations is available from *Telesis,* Issue 102, published by Nortel, telesis@barcam.com.

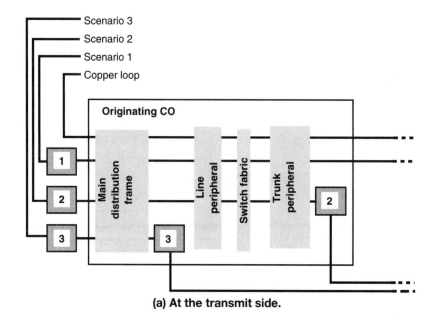

(a) At the transmit side.

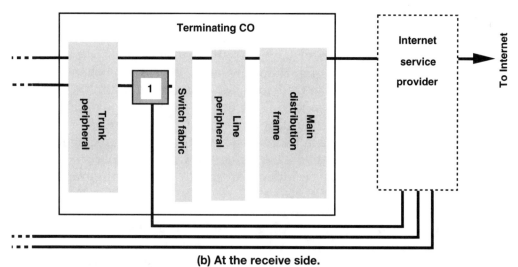

(b) At the receive side.

Figure 6–2   Modem termination options.

THE 56 KBIT/S MODEM

Recently, the 56 kbit/s modems have appeared on the scene. They are used on links where one end of the connection is digital. They are designed for the user at the CPE (customer premises equipment) to send at the conventional V Series modem speeds (say, 28.8, 33.6 kbit/s) and receive at the 56 kbit/s rate. If both ends of the connection are analog, then the 56 kbit/s rate is not employed.

The current technology is not yet standardized, and the two competing specifications are incompatible. So, if a user decides to purchase the modem, it must be determined that the modem is compatible with your ISP interface. Also, most of the current high-speed modems are capable of supporting this technology with a software upgrade. The two specifications are X2, developed by U.S. Robotics, and k56flex, developed by Lucent and Rockwell Semiconductor Systems, Inc.

In a typical setup, shown in Figure 6–3, digital/analog (D/A) or analog/digital (A/D) conversion occurs four times in each direction: (1) D/A at the sending modem, (2) A/D at the CO switch for transfer across the digital backbone, (3) D/A at the terminating CO, and (4) A/D at the receiving modem. Since many connections to ISPs are digital, the use of the 56 kbit/s modem entails only two conversions: (1) D/A at the sending modem, and (2) A/D at the CO switch.

Not all telephone lines will support this technology. Lines with high noise levels will present problems. In addition, the FCC places limits on phone lines that restrict their speeds to 53.3 kbit/s, but that restriction is supposed to be removed by the end of 1997.

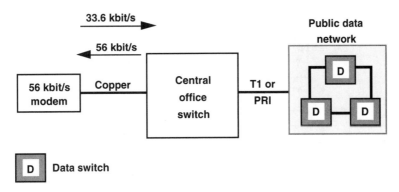

Figure 6–3   The 56 kbit/s modem.

The effect of all these operations on an analog signal is that information is lost in the analog-to-digital operation. This quantizing noise limits the transmission speeds on the local loop to about 35 kbit/s. Since quantizing noise only affects the A/D conversion and not the D/A, if the modem server in this figure uses digital transmission to the PTSN, no information is lost.

For this approach to work satisfactorily, one end of the connection (the server modem) must be able to operate on channelized T1, ISDN PRI, or ISDN BRI. The 56 kbit/s modem function must be in operation in both modems, and only one analog-to-digital conversion in the phone network can take place.

The 56 kbit/s limitation is due to the fact that not all the 256 discrete levels (codes) can be used, due to the nonlinear conversation process. The encoder users various subsets of the 256 codes that are the least susceptible to noise. U.S. Robotics uses 128 levels for 56 kbit/s, 92 levels for 52 kbit/s, and so on.

USING THE LOCAL LOOP FOR LAN ACCESS

A LAN user has expected to receive and send data at a very high rate—for example, at the 10 mbit/s exhaust speed. And applying the well-

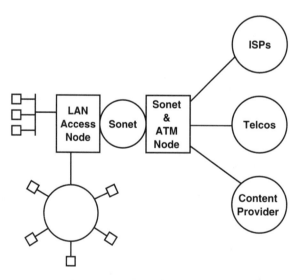

Figure 6–4   Interworking LANs and SONET.

testing 80/20 rule, 80% of the traffic stayed in the local LAN; 20% of the traffic went elsewhere.

The 80/20 rule no longer holds. With the increased use of enterprise WAN networks, companies are increasing their use of LAN-WAN-LAN data transfers. Moreover, the increased use of the Internet translates into significantly more traffic that goes beyond the local LAN boundaries.

To meet this requirement, equipment vendors and service providers are developing and deploying products to provide "transparent" LAN service though the RBB access network to the end-user.

Table 6–1   LAN/RBB Interworking Support

LANs Supported

Ethernet IOBASET
Token ring 4 Mbit/s
Token ring 16 Mbit/s
FDDI

Serial Ports

9.6 Kbit/s—1.544 Mbit/s

WAN Interfaces

ATM
Frame Relay
OC-3
DS1, DS3

Protocols Supported

L.2

LANs (cited above)
Spanning tree, transport bridging, source routing
Point-to-point protocol (PPP)

L.3

IP
IPX
Appletalk
OSPF and RIP
RTMP

Figure 6–4 shows an example of an RBB topology to suggest user LANs through a SONET distribution network.

The LAN access node supports both LAN and SONET interfaces, as well as serial ports. Table 6–1 provides a summary of the interfaces and protocols supported by this system.

SUMMARY

Growth of data use on the local loop has created congestion and bottleneck problems. Much of the growth has been due to the Internet. Bottlenecks at the local office and Internet Service Provider (ISP) occur. Bypassing the voice switch is one effective way to handle the problem. Modem termination options provide a range of choices for the service provider. Internet Thruway from Nortel is one example of this approach. In addition, systems are now being deployed to interwork the user LANs with the RBB access network.

7

New Generation Protocols for RBB HFC

This chapter explains the Adaptive Digital Access Protocol (ADAPt+), one of the Proposed MAC layer protocols for the IEEE 802.14 RBB standard.[1] As stated earlier in this book, the 802.14 is not finished, so the final ADAPt+ specification may reflect some differences from the material in this chapter. However, the differences should be minor, since IEEE 802.14 is nearing completion.

THE IEEE 802.14 SPECIFICATION

The IEEE 802.14 Working Group was formed in November 1994 to standardize the physical (PHY) and media access control (MAC) layers for HFC systems. The 802.14 specifications are not complete thus not available to the general public.[2] I will describe the major features of 802.14 in this section, but be aware that they may be changed as the specifications wind their way through the final approval process.

Figure 7–1 shows the layered structure of IEEE 802.14 and the major entities that reside in the layers.

---

[1]Another protocol, Extended Distributed Queuing Random Access Protocol (XDQRAP) is under consideration, but ADAPt+ appears to be the favorite candidate.

[2]Some twenty different proposals have been studied by the 802.14 Working Group.

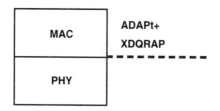

where:
ADAPt+   Adaptive Digital Access Protocol
XDQRAP   Extended Distributed Queuing Random Access Protocol

Figure 7–1   Layered architecture for IEEE 802.14.

THE ADAPTIVE DIGITAL ACCESS PROTOCOL (ADAPt+)

ADAPt+ defines the operations at the PHY and MAC layers of bidirectional HFC networks. It is designed to provide the support of multiservice traffic and QOS operations. It also permits the use of a variety of other protocols that can operate over the MAC layer—such as ATM, IP, IPX, and 802.3—and conventional synchronous transfer mode (STM) traffic, such as DS0, DS1, and so on.

ADAPt+ is located at the dwelling in a cable modem (CM) and at the network provider in the headend (HE). It manages and coordinates the broadcast downstream channels and the unicast, multiple access upstream channels. Since ADAPt+ must permit other protocols to operate over MAC (a self-evident statement, since these other protocols carry user traffic), it acts as the overall traffic manager for the HFC network. Figure 7–2 provides an illustration of the ADAP+ configuration.

ADAPt+ is an enhanced version of ADAPt. One of the major enhancements is ADAPt+'s support of variable length (VL) traffic. This version also stipulates the frame structures, which are not present in ADAPt.

ADAPt+ Functional Groups

ADAPt+ consists of three major functional groups. Their relationships to the upstream and downstream HFC channels are shown in Figure 7–3. Their functions are as follows:

- *Multiservice gateway (MSG).* This functional group acts as the interface to the upper layer protocols. It performs service and protocol mapping into and out of the ADAPt+ MAC layer.

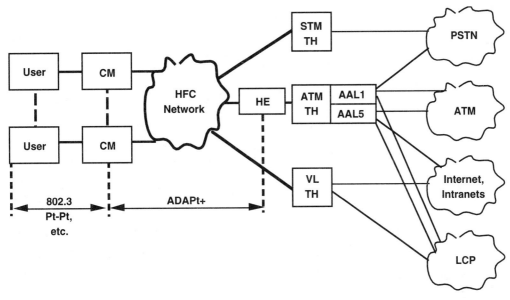

where:

AAL	ATM Adaptation layer
ATM	Asynchronous transfer mode
CM	Cable modem
HE	Headend
LCP	Local content provider (e.g., video on demand)
PSTN	Public switched telephone network
Pt-Pt	Point-to-point
HFC	Hybrid fiber coax
TH	Traffic handler
STM	Synchronous transfer mode
VL	Variable length

Figure 7–2   The ADAPt+ configuration.

- *Headend / bandwidth management (HE / BM).* This functional group operates as follows:
- For the downstream direction: Multiplexes traffic and performs QOS management from the HE to the CM, where the CM demultiplexes the traffic and address filters it to pass the traffic to the proper end-user appliance interface unit.
- For the upstream direction: Multiplexes traffic and allocates bandwidth from the CM to the HE, where the HE demultiplexes the traffic, analyzes status information, address filters it to pass the traffic to the appropriate traffic handler (TH).

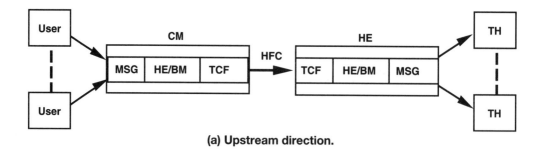

(a) Upstream direction.

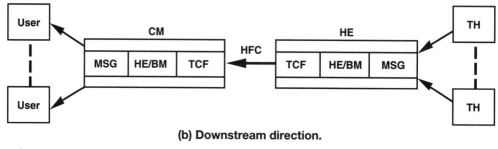

(b) Downstream direction.

where:
  BM   Bandwidth manager
  HE   Headend
  HFC   Hybrid fiber coax
  MSG   Multiservice gateway functions
  TCF   Transmission convergence function

Figure 7–3   ADAPt+ functional groups.

- *Transmission convergence function (TCF).* This functional group operates as follows:
  - For the downstream direction: Inserts forward error correction (FEC) bits, scrambles the bits, frames traffic, and modulates the traffic from the HE to the CM, where the CM performs complementary operations.
  - For the upstream direction: Performs the reverse operations of the downstream direction.

THE PHY LAYER

An RBB protocol should be able to operate over physical layers that employ a variety of modulation techniques on the HFC network. While ADAPt+ has not gone through its final approval, the techniques explained in this section are under consideration, with the first three slated to be included and the fourth added at a later time. The downstream direction will be able to use all these techniques. The upstream direction will use the first technique.

The first three techniques are based on using the conventional 6 MHz TV channel in the downstream direction and 1.8 MHz bands in the upstream (in the 5–42 MHz spectrum) direction.

- Quaternary phase shift keying (QPSK), with 2 bits per symbol
- 16 quadrature amplitude modulation (QAM), with 4 bits per symbol
- 64 QAM, with 6 bits per symbol
- 256 QAM, with 6 bits per symbol

Symbol Rates, Bit Rates, and Byte Rates for ADAPt+

These four modulation techniques use 5.12 Msymbols/s for the downstream direction and 1.28 Msymbols/s for the upstream direction. The bit rate for the five techniques (four downstream and one upstream) are:

Downstream

- QPSK: 2 bits per symbol × 5.12 Msymbols/second = 10.24 Mbit/s
- 16 QAM: 4 bits per symbol × 5.12 Msymbols/second = 20.48 Mbit/s
- 64 QAM: 6 bits per symbol × 5.12 Msymbols/second = 30.72 Mbit/s
- 256 QAM: 8 bits per symbol × 5.12 Msymbols/second = 40.96 Mbit/s

Upstream

- QPSK: 2 bits per symbol × 1.28 Msymbols/second = 2.56 Mbit/s

These bit rates are the complete throughput rate of these five techniques, which do not account for the ADAPt+ protocol control information (PCI); that is, the headers/trailers that must accompany the user payload. This PCI will be factored in later.

BANDWIDTH CAPACITY

For the present discussion, a key question to answer is, "How much capacity do these techniques provide on the HFC network?" To answer the question, we assume the upstream spectrum is 5 to 42 MHz, and the downstream spectrum is 550 to 750 MHz (the existing CATV spectrum is not disturbed).

These spectras yield the following capacity (results of calculations are rounded down). First, the 550 to 750 MHz spectrum yields about 33 6-MHz channels and the 5 to 42 MHz spectrum yields about 20 1.8-MHz channels. Given these yields, the total capacity for these techniques are:

Downstream

- QPSK: 33 FDM channels × 10.24 Mbit/s per channel = 337 Mbit/s
- 16 QAM: 33 FDM channels × 20.48 Mbit/s per channel = 675 Mbit/s
- 64 QAM: 33 FDM channels × 30.72 Mbit/s per channel = 1,013 Mbit/s
- 256 QAM: 33 FDM channels × 40.96 Mbit/s per channel = 1,351 Mbit/s

Upstream

- QPSK: 20 FDM channels × 2.56 Mbit/s per channel = 51 Mbit/s

These calculations answer the question of how much capacity these techniques yield on the HFC network. The next question is, "Is this enough capacity?" The answer depends upon how many users this capacity must support and, equally important, how often and when the users use the network. Once these two variables are known, then the third variable must be quantified: Given that the users require capacity, what is the nature of that requirement? For example, is the capacity requirement for a constant bit rate (CBR) or a variable bit rate (VBR)? For the former, the system must support synchronous operations; for the latter, the system must support the variable burst sizes (how many bits) and burst durations (for how long).

We could go further. What are the permissible delay variations on the arrival of the traffic at the receiver? and so on. But the key point is that knowing the raw capacity of any system (HFC, ADSL, etc.) is quite important. Equally important is knowing the characteristics of the traffic patterns of the users of the system. The former is easy to ascertain; the latter is not as easy, but certainly pliant to traffic analysis tools.

On another matter, the coding and modulation scheme follows the design philosophy of the ITU-T V Series modems by using simple integral multiples of the bits per symbol rate. This approach translates into the ability to build a cable modem that can support multiple schemes without making major changes to its architecture.

UPSTREAM AND DOWNSTREAM SYNCHRONIZATION

Since the upstream and downstream traffic may represent two-way traffic between the user applications, these streams must be synchronized together for synchronous transfer mode (STM) voice and video traffic. Yet, at the same time, the systems must also support asynchronous, delay-tolerant variable length (VL) data traffic.

In order to obviate echo cancellers, the round-trip delay for DSn traffic cannot exceed about 3 ms. Furthermore, the upstream direction operates in a burst mode in order to make efficient use of the facilities, and this direction requires more and different protocol control information (PCI, headers, and trailers) than in the downstream direction. Thus, the formats of the upstream and downstream frames (PDUs) differ.

In order to synchronize the upstream and downstream traffic, the downstream direction uses 125 µs frames (called subframes in ADAPt+) and allocates one byte for each DS0 connection. A fractional T1 transmission (say 384 kbit/s) uses n × DS0 bytes in each 125 µs subframe (for 384 kbit/s, 6 DS0s).

The upstream direction must complement the downstream direction (and vice versa). But, as stated earlier, an upstream DS0 slot will be associated with and accompanied by additional bytes. Consequently, the 125 µs length needs to be longer in the upstream direction.

The network (HE/BM) is responsible for providing timing through the downstream direction to the CM. The design of the upstream frame is such that it is 2 ms long (it is described later). As depicted in Figure 7–4, the synchronization between the HE/BM and the CM is achieved by forming sixteen 125 µs subframes into a frame of 2 ms. This approach produces 2 ms frames in each direction. As a consequence of this approach, 16 DS0 bytes (for each DSn transmission) are sent in each upstream transmission.

The ADAPt+ protocol is byte-oriented, and the 125 µs downstream subframes and 2 ms upstream frames yield an even integer number of bytes—all of which simplifies the synchronization of the PDUs.

With the 6 MHz downstream and 1.8 MHz upstream bandwidths, the 5.12 Msymbols per second and 1.28 Msymbols per second provide sufficient margin to prevent interference between adjacent channels with filtering operations.

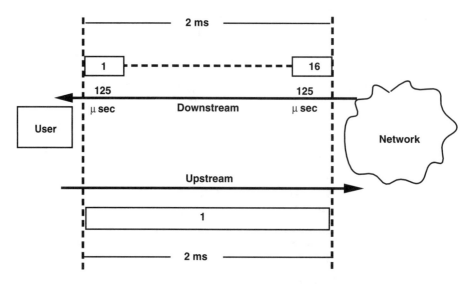

Figure 7–4   Upstream and downstream PDUs.

Upstream and Downstream Byte Rates

Given that the DS0 bytes are transmitted on the channels, a simple calculation will show how many bytes are available for each modulation technique:

Downstream

- QPSK: 10.24 Mbit/s /8 bits per byte/8000
             125 μs/sec = 160 bytes per 125 μs
- 16 QAM: 20.48 Mbit/s/8 bits-per-byte/8000
             125 μs/sec = 320 bytes per 125 μs
- 64 QAM: 30.72 Mbit/s/8 bits-per-byte/8000
             125 μs/sec = 480 bytes per 125 μs
- 256 QAM: 40.96 Mbit/s/8 bits-per-byte/8000
             125 μs/sec = 640 bytes per 125 μs

Upstream

- QPSK: 2.56 Mbit/s/8 bits-per-byte/8000
             125 μs/sec = 40 bytes per 125 μs

DOWNSTREAM AND UPSTREAM PDU STRUCUTURE

Because RBB technologies must support multiservice traffic, the network must be able to provide the CM with real-time control information. As discussed later, the upstream channel is managed with a contention protocol and the CM must have timely information about the results of access attempts on the upstream channel.

In addition to this "results" information, the HE/BM and CM must exchange signaling messages (to set up and tear down connections) and OAM messages (for overall network management). The signaling and OAM traffic is asynchronous and can tolerate considerably more latency than the real-time control information.

Downstream PDU Structure

Given these requirements, the downstream PDU structure is illustrated in Figure 7–5. This example is the 480 byte per 125 µs QAM signal. Each subframe begins with a 1-byte set of framing bits and 1, 2, or 3 sets of forward error correction (FEC) bits (each set is 4 bytes). For 64 QAM, 8 FEC bytes are used.

Framing

The framing operation is straightforward. The receiving CMs use the 1-byte framing bits to identify the beginning of the subframes.

As Figure 7–5 shows, the 16 125 µs subframes are organized into frames, which are organized into master frames. The frame structure is 7680 bytes over a 2 ms period. The master frame structure is 7,680n bytes over 2n ms.

Given this PDU structure, the byte capacity (less FEC and framing) of the downstream channel per 125 µs is:

- QPSK: 160 bytes – 1 framing byte – 4 bytes FEC = 155 bytes
- 16 QAM: 320 bytes – 1 framing byte – 8 bytes FEC = 311 bytes
- 64 QAM: 480 bytes – 1 framing byte – 8 bytes FEC = 471 bytes
- 256 QAM: 640 bytes – 1 framing byte – 8 bytes FEC = 627 bytes

Fast Control Field (FCF)

The FCF is used as a real-time control field for the MAC and PHY layers. It provides information on the boundaries between the STR/ATR1 and ATR1/ATR2 in the downstream direction and the STR/ATR in the

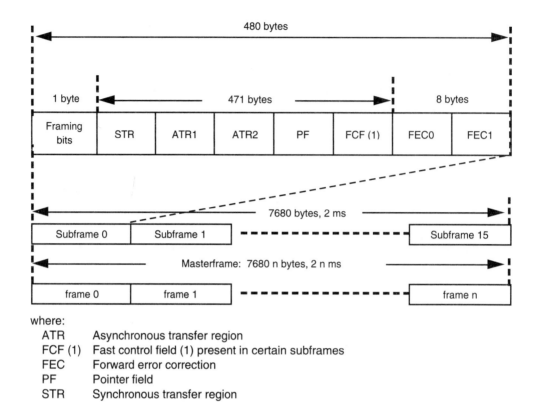

where:
ATR   Asynchronous transfer region
FCF (1)   Fast control field (1) present in certain subframes
FEC   Forward error correction
PF   Pointer field
STR   Synchronous transfer region

Figure 7–5   Downstream PDU structure (example is 64 QAM).

upstream direction (as explained later, the upstream direction has no separate ATR1/ATR2 boundaries).

The FCF also contains information on (1) the success or failure of the CM's contention access attempt in the last upstream PDU, (2) CM ATR slot information for the next upstream PDU, and (3) the status of each upstream slot in the next upstream PDU.

ATR1 AND ATR2 PDUs AND SDUs

The STR contains the DS0 channels discussed earlier. Two ATRs are present in the PDU. ATR1 contains ATM cells, and ATR2 contains variable-length PDUs, such as IP datagrams. The decision to use two ATRs was based on separating ATM traffic from other traffic to eliminate a type-of-traffic identifier.[3]

---

[3]More commonly known in the industry as an encapsulation header.

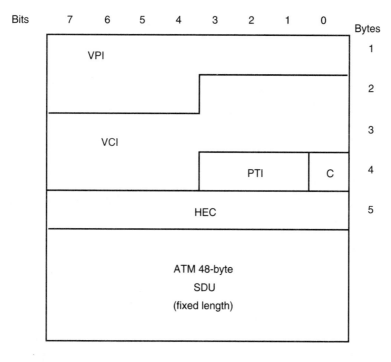

where:
  C   Cell loss priority
  HEC   Header error control
  PTI   Payload type ID
  SDU   Service data unit
  VPI   Virtual path ID
  VCI   Virtual channel ID

Figure 7–6   Cell format for ATR1.

Furthermore, the ATM NNI cell header format is employed (see Figure 7–6), which provides a 12-bit virtual path identifier (VPI) field. The VPI is used to identify the receiving CM. Consequently, the ADAPt+ PDU need not contain a separate CM identifier; the ATM VPI provides this information.

Other advantages accrue to the use of two ATRs (fixed and variable). The RBB system can configure the PDU as: (1) ATR1 and ATR2, (2) ATR1 only, or (3) ATR2 only. This crafting can be performed on channels whose traffic patterns are fairly predictable. The potential disadvantage to the two ATRs is that the approach might find one region overutilized and the other region underutilized. But the specification permits the HE/BM to alter the ATR1/ATR2 size periodically, if traffic conditions so-warrant.

The variable length SDU for the ATR2 is shown in Figure 7–7. The header is a 5-byte variation of the ATM cell header. The fields in the SDU are used as follows:

- Cable modem ID: A 12-bit address of the receiving CM
- C/U: Identifies the variable length SDU as containing user (1) or control (0) information
- B/C/E: Indicates if the traffic has been segmented into more than one 48-byte SDU, with beginning (B, with bits = 00) of a segment; continuation (C, with bits = 01) of a segment; end (E, with bits = 00) of a segment; or single (with bits = 11) variable length SDU. These bits are used at the receiving CM to assist in reassembling the segmented traffic.

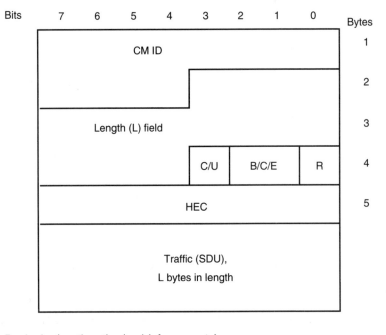

where:
B/C/E   Beginning/continuation/end (of segments)
CM ID   Cable modem ID
C/U   Control/user
HEC   Header error control
R   Reserved
SDU   Service data unit

Figure 7–7   Cell format for ATR2.

Forward Error Correction (FEC)

Figure 7–5 and related text identified the FEC bytes. The correction procedures are the conventional Reed-Solomon (RS) method where an RS interleaver/coder operates with:

- N = Number of coded bytes per block
- K = Number of precoded bytes per block
- T = A value that equals (N-K)/2 and is the number of errored bytes in the block that can be corrected
- I = Number of interleaved blocks, which enhance corrections

RS is effective in correcting an error burst of T × I, with an interleaving depth of I. However, for applications with tight timing requirements, the FEC operation may take too long, because the interleaving depth of I translates to a delay = N × I byte transmission time.

Other problems exist by attempting to use one FEC approach for all applications. Data do not need FEC because it can be retransmitted. Further, if an error burst exceeds T x I bytes, all I-interleaved blocks are in error, and data retransmissions are greatly affected by the spread of the error.

The compromise in ADAPt+ is to rely on an FEC at a higher layer that has deep interleaving and/or large error-burst protection. Additionally, the FEC might be tailored to the specific application.

The FEC operations in ADAPt+ are designed to handle short error bursts on signals like QAM. Numerous studies show: (1) error rates on high-quality fiber and coax are quite low (for example, 10^{-12} on fiber), (2) about 90% of errors deal with impulse noise (coax) or less than 1 µs, and (3) over 99% of errors on fiber affect only one bit in a block of 1 second duration. Consequently, the approach is to use the FEC to correct short error bursts. The ADAPt+ approach uses a FEC with T = 2 or 3 and I = 2.

Upstream PDU Structure

As shown in Figure 7–8, the HFC network topology is a branch-and-tree configuration. This arrangement means that the CM's traffic may collide on the shared media and the CMs are different distances to the HE. These differences are handled by a guard timer and a procedure to direct the CMs to send their transmission so that their bursts arrive at the HE without overlap.

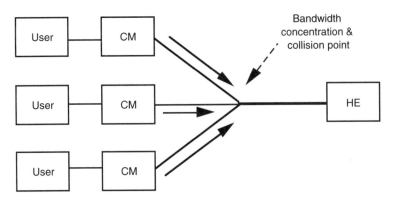

Figure 7–8   HFC branch and tree topology.

ADAPt+ supports synchronous and asynchronous transfer with an STR an ATR respectively, as depicted in Figure 7–9. Any synchronous traffic is placed in the fixed STR part of the PDU; the position is determined during the connection setup. Asynchronous traffic is placed in the ATR part of the PDU.

The reserved part of the ATR is used by a CM to request bandwidth for new asynchronous traffic (ATM or variable length traffic), which will be sent in the next PDU. The HE/BM replies to the request with information in the FCF, as explained earlier in this chapter.

The upstream frame is 640 bytes (2.56 Mbit/s × .002/8 = 640). The frames are organized into multiple master frames (n_{mf}) with 640 × n_{mf} bytes in length.

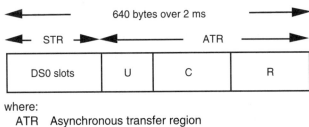

where:
  ATR   Asynchronous transfer region
  C   Contention
  R   Reserved
  STR   Synchronous transfer region
  U   Upstream slow control

Figure 7–9   Basic upstream frame format.

Upstream PHY Layer Requirements

Recall that the upstream direction is 2.56 Mbit/s (1.28 Msymbols/s) on each channel, with a 2 ms frame. Recall also that the upstream direction conveys synchronous and asynchronous traffic that, in turn, contains voice, video, and data payload as well as control signals (such as bandwidth requests, FECs, CM addresses, preamble, etc.). Given these diverse signals and traffic types, the upstream frame in Figure 7–9 is organized further into four formats, as shown in Figure 7–10:

- STR PDU
- Slot request PDU
- ATR fixed length PDU
- ATR variable length (VL) PDU

All PDUs in the upstream direction contain (1) guard time (10 bits at each end of the PDU), (2) a synchronization preamble (28 bits), and (3) FEC (which varies, based on PDU format). The carrier ramp time (turn-on time) is 4 µs (not shown in Figure 7–10), and there are no interburst gaps.

Figure 7–10a shows the STR PDU for synchronous upstream traffic. The complete PDU is 216 bits. The user payload is 16 bytes (128 bits) of DS0 traffic. Since the PDU is 2 ms, the user is provided a 64 kbit/s channel (128 bits $\times$ 500 PDU/sec. = 64,000). This format provides an 8-bit field for signaling information for each DS0 connection, which yields a 4 kbit/s signaling channel.

Figure 7–10b shows the format for the slot request PDU. The type field is set to one of four values: (1) 00 = ATM PDUs, (2) 01 = VL PDUs containing user payload, (3) 10 = VL PDUs containing control payload, and (4) 11 = reserved for future use.

The bandwidth request field (BWR) of 10 bits is used to request that the HE grant bandwidth to the CM. The request can take two forms. The first form is a request for 1-n ATM cells; the second is a request for 1-n VL slots. Nine bits are used for the request. The tenth bit is used to indicate if the request is for absolute units or units in addition to the present bandwidth allocation.

The bandwidth request field is used during the transmission of the other PDUs (Figure 7–10c and d to request additional bandwidth (for the same CM and the same traffic type).

This field uses 9 bits for the request itself, which allows for 1 to 511 ATM cells or variable length data units to be allocated. The s11 variable length data units translates into about 6000 bytes of bandwidth.

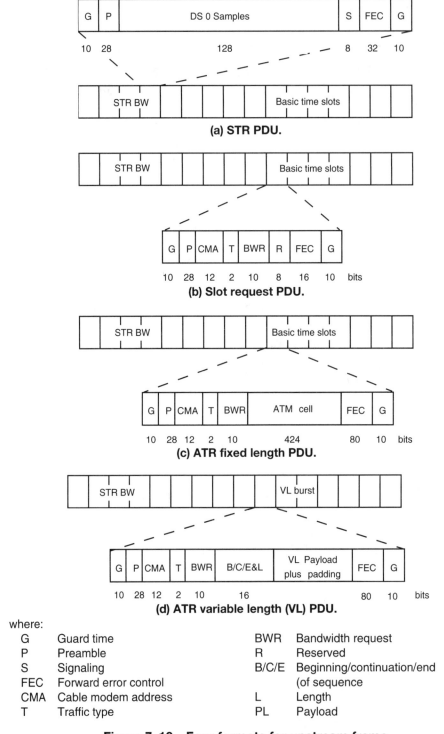

(a) STR PDU.

(b) Slot request PDU.

(c) ATR fixed length PDU.

(d) ATR variable length (VL) PDU.

where:

G	Guard time	BWR	Bandwidth request
P	Preamble	R	Reserved
S	Signaling	B/C/E	Beginning/continuation/end
FEC	Forward error control		(of sequence
CMA	Cable modem address	L	Length
T	Traffic type	PL	Payload

Figure 7–10   Four formats for upstream frame.

Figure 7–10c shows the format for carrying ATM cells in the PDU. Six successive slots are allocated by the HE/BM for the ATM cell.

Figure 7–10d shows the format for carrying variable length PDUs. The format is similar to the other PDUs, except a two-byte field is present to identify the relative portions of the segment's user traffic (if it is segmented) and the total length of the traffic. This field is labeled "B/C/E & L" in Figure 7–10d.

THE CONTENTION PROTOCOL

To begin the analysis of the protocol that manages the upstream bandwidth, refer back to Figure 7–5. The fast control field (FCF) contains the information for the CMs to burst their traffic in the correct part of a frame.

Figure 7–11 shows the format of the FCF. Earlier, the point was made that the upstream and downstream frames are synchronized with each other. The CM must act upon the information in the downstream FCF in the next upstream frame. To respond to frame n, ADAPt+ sets

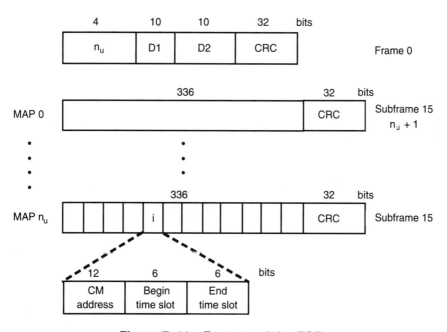

Figure 7–11   Formats of the FCF.

forth an O_u offset for the upstream byte time, and the time to process the FCF in the CM must be less than the O_u byte time. Therefore, the N+1 upstream frame transmission is delayed by O_u byte time after the last bit of the N+1 downstream frame is received.

The idea is for the CM to react to the contention information in the downstream frame that immediately follows its access attempt and then responds in the next frame. Thus, the CM reaction is one frame delay (one frame gap). This 1-frame delay assumes that processing operations (including O_u) and round-trip propagation delay do not exceed 2 ms, which is the length of one frame.

Referring back to Figure 7–5, the downstream traffic is organized into subframes, frames, and masterframes. The masterframe consists of an even integral number of frames. Figure 7–11 shows that the FCF is in the first subframe and the last n_u subframes of each frame. The value n_u = the number of upstream channels being supported. The subframes shown in Figure 7–10 contain one ATR MAP for each upstream channel.

The FCF in subframe O contains the following fields:

- n_u: Specified up to 15 upstream channels
- D1:   Defines boundary between STR and ATR1 in next downstream frame
- D2:   Defines boundary between ATR1 and ATR2 in next downstream frame
- CRC: Cyclic redundancy check

The MAP field indicates to the CM the i slots that are available for contention in the next upstream frame.[4] Based on this information, the CM generates a random number x that has a uniform distribution over i slots. The CM's message is sent in the xth slot in the upstream frame.

The HE detects if a collision has or has not occurred (by examining the RF energy in the slot). The CM is notified of the results of its access attempt in the MAP field. It either retries (based on a backoff algorithm) or gains access.

---

[4]This example explains contention in a basic slot in which bandwidth requests are made. Another contention operation is performed on another part of the message, and therefore is not discussed here.

BANDWIDTH REQUESTS AND ALLOCATIONS

The granting of bandwidth to the CM entails different operations for different types of traffic:

- STM DS0 slot traffic: Bandwidth is allocated and reserved during the connection setup.
- ATM constant bit rate (CBR) traffic: Bandwidth is allocated in a manner similar to STM slot traffic, since ATM CBR traffic is delay sensitive.
- ATM available bit rate (ABR) traffic: Bandwidth is allocated based on number of cells to be sent. The requests are stored as they arrive at the HE/BM, and all CM requests are treated equally, on a round-robin basis. Bandwidth is allocated for the ATM cell with six successive slots. Since ATM ABR traffic is more delay-tolerant than ATM CBR traffic, ATM ABR traffic is treated at a lower priority than ATM CBR traffic.
- Variable length (VL) traffic: Bandwidth is allocated on one SDU at a time. For example, one IP datagram or one Ethernet frame is sent at a time. The HE/BM or CM services the traffic on a first-come, first-served basis.

SUMMARY OF THE ADAPt+ OPERATIONS

This section provides a summary of the major ADAPt+ operations, and should tie together the procedures explained in this chapter. The summary is based on a downstream direction transmission. Figure 7–3 is a useful reference during this discussion.

At the HE/BM:

MSG function:
- VL, ATM, STM, and control traffic is assembled with appropriate headers.

HE/BM function:
- Traffic is multiplexed together, and FCF and PF are inserted. Idle PDUs are inserted, if necessary.

TCF function:
- Traffic is scrambled.
- Traffic is framed.
- FEC encoding and interleaving operations are performed.
- Traffic is modulated and transmitted.

At the CM:

TCF function:
- Traffic is received and demodulated.
- Signals are synchronized to the subframes.
- FEC decoding and interleaving operations are performed.
- Framing byte is removed.
- Descrambling operations are performed.

HE/BM function:
- Traffic is demultiplexed; FCF and PF are examined; idle PDUs are discarded.

MSG function:
- VL, ATM, STM, and control traffic is disassembled and passed to the appropriate traffic handler (TH).

SUMMARY

The ADAPt+ protocol represents the culmination of extensive work by Lucent Technologies (Bell Labs) and refinement by the 802.14 Working Group. It is designed to provide services to STM, ATM, and variable length traffic by taking advantage of the different characteristics (CBR, VBR, delay tolerance) of these traffic types.

8

Fixed Wireless Access

This chapter describes the use of wireless systems in RBB, known as fixed wireless access (FWA). The topologies for FWA are discussed first, followed by a comparison of time division multiple access (TDMA) and code division multiple access (CDMA). The LMDS and the MMDS, introduced in the first chapter, are explained in more detail as well. The chapter also includes a discussion on the DECT technology as a possible choice for an FWA protocol and concludes with a discussion on spectrum sharing issues.

TOPOLOGY OF FIXED WIRELESS ACCESS (FWA)

Fixed wireless access in the local loop provides yet another access alternative for RBB deployment. FWA both complements and competes with fixed wire access, such as telephone twisted pair (TTP), coaxial cable and optical fiber. To see why, Figure 8–1 shows several FWA configurations.

Connections to the customer dwellings are made through the wireless base station (BS). The RF transceivers at the customer's site may be antennas located outside or inside the dwellings. Direct attachments to the dwellings eliminate the need for external wiring to the homes (options (a) and (b) in Figure 8–1) and thus compete with the fixed wire offerings such as HFC and TTP/ADSL.

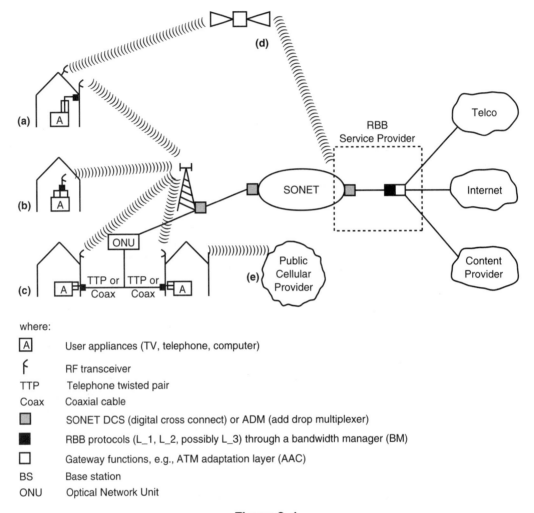

Figure 8–1.

where:

[A]	User appliances (TV, telephone, computer)
ʄ	RF transceiver
TTP	Telephone twisted pair
Coax	Coaxial cable
▦	SONET DCS (digital cross connect) or ADM (add drop multiplexer)
■	RBB protocols (L_1, L_2, possibly L_3) through a bandwidth manager (BM)
☐	Gateway functions, e.g., ATM adaptation layer (AAC)
BS	Base station
ONU	Optical Network Unit

With option (c), the wireless part of the loop extends into the neighborhood to an RF transceiver, which acts as a conduit to the dwellings. This option competes with fiber in the loop, yet provides a means to extend fiber (with SONET) into the distribution plant.

Option (c) retains the TTP/coax, which at first glance appears to be a redundant configuration. However, the wireless port of the system may be a one-way broadcast in the downstream direction, which necessitates using the TTP/coax for upstream communications. Notwithstanding, if the RF bandwidth is configured as two-way (which is technically feasible in LMDS, for example), then the requirement for the TTP/coax is illuminated.

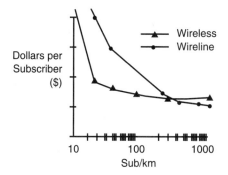

Figure 8–2   Capital Costs for Wireless and Wireline.

Option (d) is the direct TV (DTV) system introduced in Chapter 2. Recall that DTV can deliver 150 channels, but it is designed as a one-way system. The downstream direction uses the DTV media, but the upstream channel must use TTP on the POTS loop.

Option (e) obviates all wire-based systems in the local loop by using the conventional public mobile cellular provider.

FIXED WIRELESS VERSUS FIXED WIRE ACCESS

FWA's attraction over its fixed wire alternative is due to: (a) lower costs, (b) design flexibility, and (c) time-to-market.

Figure 8–2 compares the costs to deploy wireless and wireline systems, based on subscriber per km. For an access system in the distribution plant, the wireless alternative is the clear choice.

A wire-based system requires the service provider to dedicate substantial resources to upgrade the system as traffic demand increases, as shown in Figure 8–3. The tasks of laying more cable, installing more underground conduits, etc., is quite labor-intensive, and very expensive.

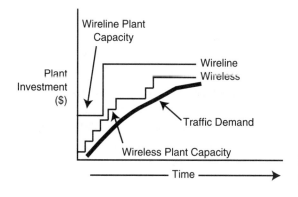

Figure 8–3   Adding Plant Capacity.

Wireless systems can be upgraded in a more incremental fashion. As traffic demand grows, wireless capacity can be added vis-á-vis the traffic demand.

The time-to-market aspect of the comparison stems from the fact that wireless systems can be deployed faster than their wire-based counterparts.

WIRELESS LOCAL LOOP (WLL) OPTIONS

Fixed wireless in the local loop is also called the wireless local loop (WLL). It is different from cellular because it is designed for the local loop and mobile cellular is not so designed. This discussion will focus on WLL with emphasis on (1) LDMS and MMDS, (2) CDMA, (3) DECT.

Local Multipoint Multichannel Distribution Service (LMDS) and Multipoint Multichannel Distribution Service (MMDS)

MMDS has been in place for several years, and operates between 2.150 GHz and 2.682 GHz and provides for 33 analog video channels. MMDS extends a cell to about 25 to 35 miles, depending upon the geographical region. It is a one-way technology and requires a separate channel (copper wire, for example) to communicate with a headend.

The LMDS technology uses smaller cells than MMDS (up to 5 miles for the cell radii). It supports two-way broadcast video, video-on-demand, data and telephony services. The proposed bandwidth spectrum for LMDS is between 27.5 and 28.35 GHz. This frequency band provides much bandwidth, but at these high frequencies, the radio wavelengths are very short and more susceptible to attenuation than waveforms operating at lower frequencies. Therefore, many LMDS systems employ digital repeaters to expand the distance of the cell. Line-of-sight is required for LMDS.

Both LMDS and MMDS are attractive for their bandwidths and their ease of installation. However, their deployment is dependent upon the amount of co-channel interference that may occur between nonadjacent cells using the same frequency. To help solve this problem, some operators are looking to spread spectrum and code division multiple access (CDMA), which allows adjacent cells to share the same spectrum spaces.

As mentioned earlier, LMDS operates in the 27.5 to 28.31 GHz spectrum, providing 850 MHz of bandwidth. An additional band has been allocated between 29.1 and 29.25 GHz for 150 MHz of bandwidth.

Table 8–1   LMDS and MMDS

Technology	Band	Pros	Cons
LMDS	27.5–28.35 GHz	• Bandwidth • Deployment ease	• Line of sight • 28 GHz electronics • Interference
MMDS	2.150–2.682 GHz	• Long range • Low cost • Deployment ease	• Spectrum is not contiguous • Interference

These high frequencies are severely attenuated by foliage, and a line-of-sight installation requires antenna at hubsites at least 75 to 90 feet above the ground. As stated earlier, these technologies also suffer from co-channel interference, and the FCC stipulates a 35-mile protection zone between MMDS service providers. Since LMDS cells are closely located, the LMDS service provider must deal with adjacent cell interference.

The advantages of LMDS and MMDS are the simplicity and ease of deployment and installation, especially in comparison with HFC systems. In addition, LMDS offers comparable capacity to HFC without the installation headaches. Table 8–1 provides a comparison of LMDS and MMDS (6).

CDMA AND TDMA

CDMA has been the subject of intense debate for several years. As of this writing, CDMA is now being deployed in commercial systems in several parts of the world (excluding Europe). In contrast, TDMA is well-entrenched. I will provide a brief introduction to TDMA and CDMA and then discuss some of the issues surrounding their use in RBB.

TDMA Concepts

Time-division multiplexing (TDM) provides a user the full channel capacity but divides the channel usage into time slots. In cellular systems the shared use of a TDM channel is called time division multiple access (TDMA). Each user is given a slot and the slots are rotated among the users. A pure TDM cyclically scans the input signals (incoming traffic) from the multiple incoming points. Bits, bytes or blocks of data are separated and interleaved together into frames on a single high-speed communications line.

In some systems, time division duplex (TDD) is used. With this approach, one frequency is used for both directions between the two stations and each station takes turns using the channel. TDD is also known by two other names: flip-flop and ping-pong. Essentially, it is a half-duplex system that gives the illusion of full-duplex operations.

If two separate FDM channels are available, one for each direction of transmission, the system is said to be operating in a frequency division duplex (FDD) mode, also known as full-full duplex (FFD). This latter operation (FDD) is more prevalent in wireless systems today.

TDMA is well understood and widely used throughout the world. In one form or another, it plays a role in FWA. The still unknown factor in FWA is the role of CDMA.

CDMA Concepts

Code division multiple access (CDMA) is quite different from TDMA. First, CDMA uses a single spectrum of bandwidth (not slices of bandwidth) for all users in a cell. It transmits all the users' signals onto the channel at the same time, which allows the users' signals to "interfere" with each other.

Like TDMA, the analog speech is coded into digital signals, but unlike TDMA, each conversation is assigned a unique code (a "signature" for each individual transmission). The coded signal is extractable at the receiver by the use of a complementary code. The codes of different users on the channel are designed to be as different from each other as possible (the codes are *orthogonal* to each other).

Each speech signal is modulated ("spread") across an entire band (e.g., a 1.25 MHz band). The respective receiver demodulates and interprets the signal using the relevant code that is embedded in the signal. The final signal contains only the relevant conversation. Any other signals (other users' coded signals) are picked-up as noise.

Other aspects of CDMA are noteworthy. Multipath receptions of signals are coherently combined at the receiver, which enhances the quality of the signal. A power control system adjusts transmit power to enhance the quality of the signal. As a general practice, hand-off is soft in that two cells share the call during hand-off.

In the IS-95 CDMA system, the uplink channel (MS to BS) is set up so that each MS uses the same code, but with a different time shift. This shift allows the BS to decode the information from each MS. The traffic on the uplink channel is grouped into 20 ms frames. The downlink channel (BS to MS) consists of control and user information, which are also called channels. All information is modulated by a Walsh function then modulated by a pair of pseudo number (PN) code sequences at a fixed chip rate of 1.2288 Mcps. Therefore, Walsh functions are used to identify the downlink channels, and a long PN code with the 20 ms time shifts is used to identify the uplink channels. The uplink channels are identified also by an access number.

CDMA: Pros and Cons

Various studies of CDMA capacity conclude that a 3-sector CDMA cell can provide as many as 945 voice channels for mobile stations, and high capacity has been the cornerstone of CDMA. A study by Palmer (7) states that CDMA provides substantial capital cost savings over TDMA technologies such as DECT, as depicted in Figure 8–4.

These studies may indeed bear out as CDMA is placed into the fixed-wire local loop, and comparing fixed-based CDMA to mobile-based CDMA requires a different set of variables. Nonetheless, a good dose of skepticism is recommended when analyzing the capacity of CDMA.

CDMA is an effective technology. The principal problem in the past has been overestimating CDMA's capacity, specifically the TIA standard, IS-95. Recent experience (8) demonstrates that IS-95: (a) does not offer as much bandwidth as initial estimates claimed, (b) is difficult to calibrate, and (c) is still not a mature technology.

Some of CDMA's mobile-based problems will not exist with the fixed-based access. But capacity management remains a problem. The CDMA–TDMA debate continues into the FWA world, and we must move on. For excellent views of the issue, I refer you to Palmer (7) and Titch (8).

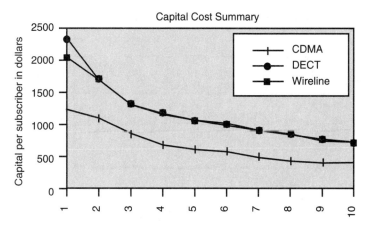

Figure 8–4   Comparison of CDMA, DECT, and wireline (see Palmer [7]).

DECT: AN ALTERNATIVE FOR FWA

As we will see in this section, DECT provides a flexible and efficient wireless technology for RBB. In North America, the TIA Personal Wireless Telecommunication Standards (PWT) are based on DECT and uses the same MAC layer and frame structure of DECT (discussed shortly). The North American version uses a different physical layer to meet U.S. regulatory requirements.

In the United States, PWT operates in the unlicensed band at 1910 to 1920 MHz. PWT/Extended (PWT/E) is an extension into the 1850 to 1910 and 1930 to 1990 MHz spectrum.

DECT Architecture

DECT architecture is organized around the lower layers of the Open Systems Interconnection (OSI) Model. Figure 8–5 illustrates this architecture. The physical layer concerns itself with the radio interface. This interface operates with time division multiple access (TDMA) on multiple RF carriers. The MAC layer operates at both the physical and data link layers and is responsible for selecting physical channels and managing the connections on these channels. It is also responsible for multiplexing information into slot-sized packets. The MAC functions provide for three types of services: (1) a broadcast service, (2) a connection-oriented service, (3) a connectionless service.

The data link control layer (DLC) is a conventional layer 2 protocol that is responsible for the reliable transmission of traffic across the air interface. It is divided in two planes of operation, the C-plane and the

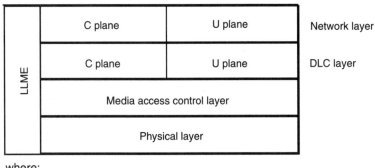

where:
    LLME   Lower layer management key

Figure 8–5   DECT layered architecture.

U-plane. The C-plane is applicable to all applications and is responsible for the transmission of internal control signaling and a limited amount of user information. This procedure is provided with a protocol called link access procedure for the C-plane (LAPC). The U-plane is specific to an application, although the services can be tailored for a particular service need. For example, the U-plane can offer unacknowledged and unsequenced transfer for speech traffic. It also offers options for circuit-mode and packet-mode data transmission.

The network layer operates at OSI layer 3. It has many functions similar to the ISDN layer 3 protocol called Q.931. Its principal function is the establishment and release of connections between two devices, although it also provides other services such as a connectionless service and a variety of supplementary services.

Finally, the lower layer management entity (LLME) is used to manage local MAC, DLC, and network layers. By local, I mean that the operations are not made visible outside the machine on which LLE operates.

The C Plane. The C plane of the network layer (Figure 8–6) is invoked through service access points (SAPs). The SAPs are used to move the traffic into and out of specific entities in the C plane. At the top of the C plane are the following SAPs (and services):

CC   Call control: Management of circuit switched calls.
CISS   Call independent supplementary services. Support of all calls.
COMS Connection-oriented message service: Support of connection-oriented messages.
CLMS Connectionless message service: Support of connectionless messages. The SAR entity will segment and reassembly traffic, if necessary.
MM   Mobility management: Support of location updating, authentication, and key allocation.

The link (also called layer) control entity (LCE) routes messages to the appropriate data link layer endpoints through the SAPs shown at the bottom of the figure. It also routes the traffic up to the proper entity with a protocol discrimination function and a transaction identifier. Each of the entities is identified with a unique protocol identifier (e.g., CC messages = 2, MM messages = 5, etc.). The transaction identifier distinguishes multiple activities associated with one portable terminal (PT).

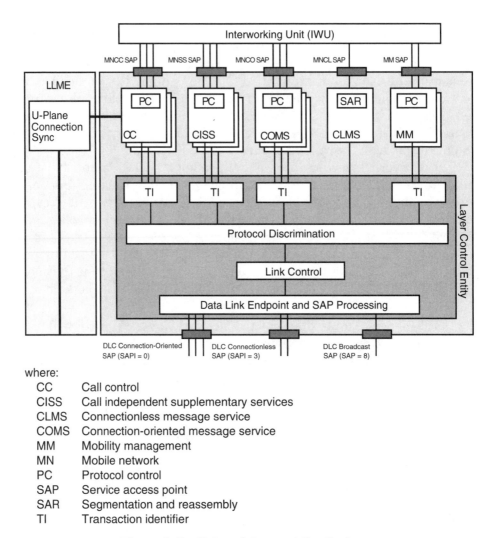

where:
CC   Call control
CISS   Call independent supplementary services
CLMS   Connectionless message service
COMS   Connection-oriented message service
MM   Mobility management
MN   Mobile network
PC   Protocol control
SAP   Service access point
SAR   Segmentation and reassembly
TI   Transaction identifier

Figure 8–6   Network layer at the C plane.

The data link layer C plane (Figure 8–7) is divided into three protocol entities, LAPC, Lc, and Lb. Taken as a whole, LAPC + Lc are accessed
through the S SAP, and provide for three classes of service (Lb is a broadcast service):

• Class U: Unacknowledged service
• Class A: A single-frame acknowledged service
• Class B: A multiple-frame acknowledged service

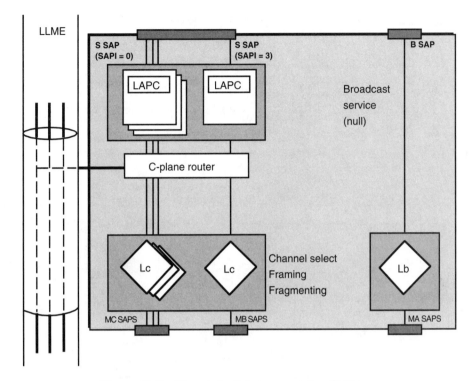

Figure 8–7   The data link layer at the C Plane.

LAPC provides for the following types of service:

- Provisioning of one data link
- Control of one data link
- Error detection and error recovery
- Flow control
- Suspending or releasing the connection

Lc provides for the following types of service:

- Provisioning of one or more data links
- Frame delimiting
- Checksum generation and checksum checking
- Frame fragmentation (if appropriate)
- Frame routing to and from logical channels
- Connection handover

The major aspect of the data link layer U plane (see Figure 8–8) is its use of link user plane (LU) service access points (SAPs). They are used to provide for the following services:

LU1:   TRansparent UnProtected service (TRUP)
             This is the simplest service and is designed for speech transmission.

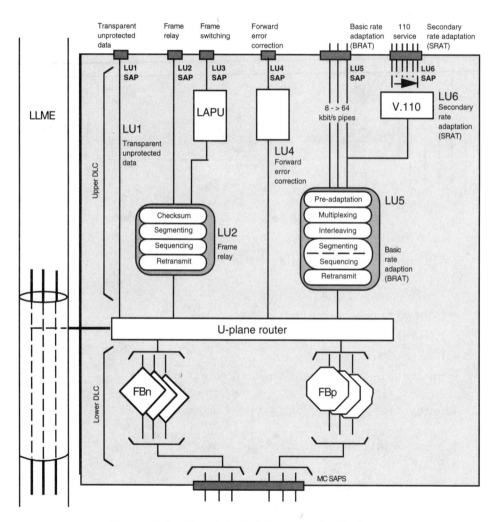

Figure 8–8   The data link layer at the U plane.

LU2:   Frame RElay service (FREL)
        Support of single user service data unit (SDU); very simple
        with no ACKS or NAKS.

LU3:   Frame SWItching service (FSWI)
        Supports a full, conventional data link protocol, such as
        ACKS, NAKS, sequencing. It is based on the V.42 protocol,
        which is an HDLC-based protocol.

LU4:   Forward Error Correction (FEC)
        When finished, will perform forward error correction opera-
        tions.

LU5:   Basic Rate AdapTation service (BRAT)
        Used for ISDN interworking, it supports the continuous
        sending of data at 8, 16, 32, or 64 kbit/s.

LU5:   Secondary Rate AdapTation service (SRAT)
        Based on ITU–T V.110, this is also used with ISDN inter-
        faces and supports conventional V Series rates (50 to 19200
        bit/s).

The U plane router is an internal router that routes traffic to and
from the upper DLC and MAC.

Figure 8–9 shows an example of how layer 3 of DECT sets up a connection. I have added another aspect of layer 3 to this example: the use of
states. Connection-oriented interfaces use states and state tables to control and govern how a connection is established and released. In addition,
timers (not shown here) are turned on when the machine sends a message. Typically, when the machine sending a message, it progresses from
one state to another (and turns on a timer). If the other machine does not
respond with a specific message within the maximum bound of the timer,
the machine takes remedial actions (usually, sending the message again
or invoking some other error-correction procedure).

Figure 8–7 shows the states and state transitions on the mobile side
(called a portable terminal [PT]) as it interworks with the base station
(called a fixed terminal [FT]) to set up and clear down a connection.

DECT's Future in RBB?

It is too early to know if DECT will be a choice for the RBB FWA
technology. The DECT technology has many supporters, principally in
the European marketplace. At this time, it has an inside track, but we
shall have to wait and see what the marketplace decides.

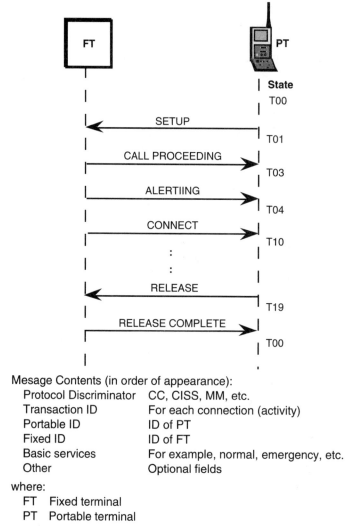

Figure 8–9   Example of a connection set up (and state transitions).

CURRENT ISSUES WITH SPECTRUM ALLOCATION

In the United States, the FCC in 1992 reallocated the 1850–1990, 2110–2150, and 2160–2200 MHz spectrum space for Personal Communication Systems (PCSs). The FCC rules established procedures to relocate existing users (common carrier and fixed microwave services) of these spectra to comparable facilities. The basic approach involves voluntary negotiations between the PCS licensees and the microwave incumbents. This section provides a summary of the issues, based on a study by Luther (5).

The voluntary negotiation period between PCS licensees and microwave incumbents is two to three years, depending on the type of microwave incumbent.

The relocation process for Blocks C, D, E, and F licensees now consists of a one-year voluntary negotiation period (three years for some incumbents) and a one-year mandatory negotiation period (two years for some), after which the incumbent becomes subject to involuntary relocation provided that the PCS licensee pays for comparable facilities.

Cost-Sharing Formula

A PCS licensee who relocates an interfering microwave link, that is, one that is in all or part of its market area and in all or part of its frequency band, or a voluntarily relocating microwave incumbent, is entitled to pro rata reimbursement based on the following formula:

$$R_N = (C/N) \times [120 - (T_m)]/120$$

where:

R_N = the amount of reimbursement

C = actual cost of relocating a microwave link

N = number of PCS entities that would have interfered with the microwave link (For the PCS relocated, N = 1. For the next PCS entity that would have interfered with the link, N = 2, and so on.)

T_m = number of months that have elapsed between the month the PCS relocator obtains reimbursement rights and the month that the Clearinghouse notifies a later-entrant of its reimbursement obligation. A PCS relocator obtains reimbursement rights on the date that it signs a relocation agreement with a microwave incumbent.

Effect of the Spectrum Allocation Plan in RBB

Fortunately for the RBB market, these contentionuous issues are not a major factor in RBB FWA deployment, since the spectrums differ between the unlicensed PCS frequencies and the LMDS/MMDS frequencies.

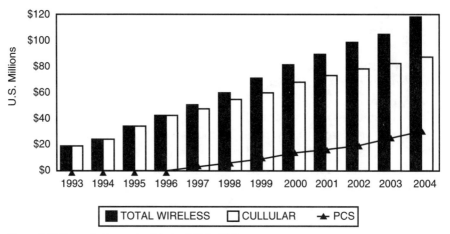

Figure 8–10   U.S. wireless market forcast.

U.S. MARKET FORECAST

Without question, the wireless technology has enjoyed great success and all predictions are that it will continue to penetrate into businesses and households. Figure 8–10 shows a prediction into 2004, based on a study by Donaldson, Lufkin, and Jeanette and cited in (5).

The exact role and place of FWA in residential broadband is not yet known, but this statement reflects the state of the RBB marketplace and technology at this time. After all, as we have learned in this book, the role and place of the RBB wire-based systems is still undecided.

SUMMARY

The fixed wireless access (FWA) technology for residential broad-band (RBB) is in its early stages of development and deployment. It is expected that FWA will co-exist with the wire-based alternatives, and that LMDS and MMDS will be part of the system. The issues pertaining to using physical layer technologies such as CDMA remain open, as does the use of MAC layers, such as DECT. Most of the spectrum allocation issues are now resolved by the FCC.

Appendix A

Signaling Basics

This appendix provides a brief explanation of several control signals used with in-band analog signaling systems. Many other signals are used by the telephone network, but those described provide sufficient background to understand this type of signaling in the context of this book.

COMMON TERMS AND OPERATIONS

The terms *on-hook* and *off-hook* were derived from the old telephones that used a hook to hold the telephone. When the handset was removed to make or answer a call, it was off-hook. Otherwise, it was on-hook. In modern networks, a station is on-hook if the conductor loop between the user station and the end office is open, with no current flowing. The off-hook has a dc shunt across the line, and current is flowing between the station and the end office.

For the discussion in this section, we use these terms to designate the two signaling conditions of a trunk. Typically, if a trunk between these offices is idle (not in use) the offices send on-hook signals to each other. Trunk seizure occurs at the calling end by sending an off-hook signal to the called end. If the trunk then is awaiting an answer from the called end, the called end sends on-hook signals to the calling end. The calling end receives an off-hook signal when the called end answers the call.

Off-hook and on-hook signals are used to convey a wide variety of control signals, which are identified by the duration of the off-hook/on-hook conditions.

Connect (seizure) is a sustained off-hook signal that is sent from the calling end of a trunk to the called end following the trunk seizure. The purpose of this signal is to provide a means for the calling end to request service. As long as the connection is up, this signal continues to exist.

The *disconnect,* as its name implies, is used to terminate the call. Several forms of disconnect operations are available. The first disconnect described is known as *calling-customer control of disconnect.* This is also known as *forward control of disconnect, forward disconnect,* or *calling-party control.* It is used by the calling end to signify that the connection is no longer needed. Forward disconnect is an on-hook signal. In order to distinguish this on-hook signal from other on-hook signals, the forward-disconnect signal must exceed 150 ms. Typically, this signal ranges from 150 to 400 ms.

The second form of disconnect is called *calling-customer control of disconnect with forced disconnect.* As this name implies, even though the customer may disconnect at any time, the call may also be disconnected when an on-hook signal is received from the network.

Yet another form of disconnect is known as *operator control of disconnect.* Once again, as the name implies, the operator controls the disconnect on outgoing trunks to operator-services systems. The end-offices are designed to support customer control of disconnect, until the operator office returns off-hook supervision to indicate that the operator office is ready to accept the call. For the duration of the call, this off-hook signal remains in the system, which essentially locks the calling customer to the operator office. Eventually, the operator office recognizes an on-hook from either a called or calling party and reverts to on-hook toward the end office. And this forces a disconnect of the customer.

During the call setup, the network performs a *signaling integrity check* to test the ability of the trunk to handle the connection. The test detects, identifies, and records troubles and ensures a caller is not "suspended" with no activity from the service provider.

While the exact type of check varies between systems, the most common types are a *delay-dial* or *wink start signal,* which is called an integrity check. The second type, used on wire trunks only, is called a *continuity and polarity check.* SS7 uses the initial COT to describe a continuity check. The integrity check is some form of a wink start signal or delay-dial signal. The COT requires circuit continuity and the correct polarity on the tip and ring of the trunk.

Wink start and delay-start signals are off-hook signals of varying durations. They are used from the called end to control the calling end's operations, usually the beginning of pulsing the address digits of a called party number. The duration of the wink ranges between 140 ms and 290 ms, but due to transmission delays and distortion occurrences, the wink may range between 100 ms and 350 ms in duration.

ACCESS AND SUPERVISORY SIGNALING

Access line signaling defines the operations to connect the CPE to the switching system. The signaling can take place across a two-wire or four-wire interface, and signaling is transmitted in various modes, depending on the specific implementation by the network provider. Regardless of the mode of operation, six classes of signals are used during access line operations:

- Supervisory: These signals are used to initiate or terminate connections. From the sending customer, the initiator requests a service. From the standpoint of the receiver, the signals represent the initiation of a connection.
- Address: These signals provide information to the network about the destination user. In so many words, they are the called party (and maybe the calling party) numbers.
- Alerting: These signals are provided by the network to the receiving customer that an incoming call is taking place, or to alert that some need is being signaled (flashing, recall, etc.).
- Call progress: These signals inform the user about the progress or lack of progress of a call that has been initiated by this user.
- Control: These signals are used for functions that usually remain transparent to the end customer. They are usually associated with network connections to the point of termination (POT) or the demarcation point. One example of a control signal is the requirement for party identification.
- Test: These signals are used for a wide array of circuit validation and quality checks.

The supervisory signals convey the following service conditions:

- Idle circuit: Indicated by the combination of an on-hook signal and the absence of any connection in the switching system between loops.

- Seizure (request for service): Indicated by an off-hook signal and the absence of any connection to another loop or trunk.
- Disconnect: Indicated by an on-hook signal in the presence of a connection to a trunk or another loop.
- Wink start: Indicated by an off-hook signal from the called office after a connect signal is sent from the calling office.

SIGNALING ARRANGEMENT (LOOP START)

Access line signaling can be implemented in a number of ways. The most common scheme used in the public telephone network is known as *loop-start signaling.* It is employed in the BOC's Message Telecommunications Service (MTS) for residence and business lines, the public tele-

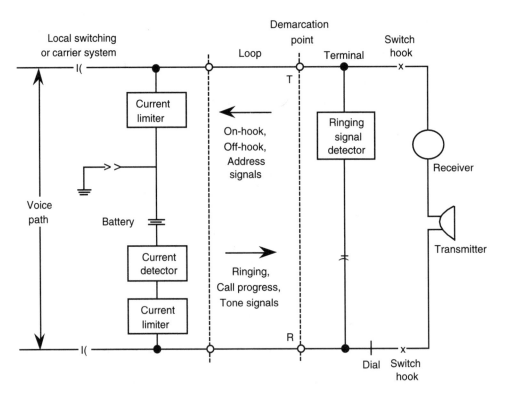

Figure A–1   Signaling arrangement (loop start).

phone service, data/facsimile service, and private branch exchange (PBX) or automatic call distributor (ACD) service.

Loop-start signaling requires that the network connect the tip connector to the positive end and the ring connector to the negative end of the power supply for an on-hook (idle) state. The voltage supply is usually 48 volts (V), but different line conditions may cause the voltage to vary from as low as 0 V to as high as 105 V.

The Bell system imposes stringent requirements on vendors' systems with regard to access line signaling. Nonetheless, within the confines of the standards, variations do exist. The variations are well documented and well understood and do not usually present a major problem to the end user. Figure A–1 shows a schematic representation of loop-start signaling and the directions of the major signals that are sent from the user equipment or the network. The following material explains Figure 2–1 in more detail.

GROUND START SIGNALING

The ground start signaling for a two-way dial system is an old technology (introduced in the 1920s). It is used typically on two-way PBX central office trunks with direct outward dialing (DOD) and attendant-handled incoming call service. The ground-start line conductors transmit common battery-loop supervision, dual-tone multifrequency (DTMF) address signaling or loop dial pulses, alerting signals, and voiceband electrical energy.

Even though ground-start lines are an old technology, they may be used in place of loop-start because: (1) They provide a signal that can act as a start-dial signal (it is not necessary to detect dial tone in most situations), (2) they provide a positive indication of a new call, (3) they help prevent unauthorized calls, and (4) they provide an indication to the calling or called party of distant-end disconnect under normal operation.

WINK START SIGNALING

Figure A–2 shows an example of the use of wink start signaling. Notice that it is sent by the receiving end. The end of the wink start signal must not occur until 210 ms after the receipt of the incoming seizure signal.

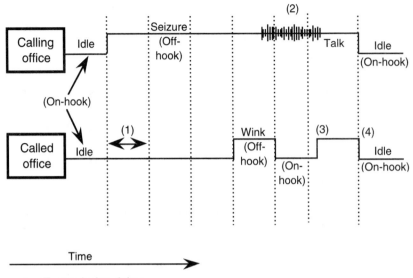

Time

1. Transmission delay
2. Multifrequency pulses
3. Answer
4. Disconnect

Figure A–2   Wink start signaling.

MULTIFREQUENCY CODES

To this point in the appendix, we have discussed several types of signals and tests that are used in in-band, analog systems. Most of these signals are represented with the off-hook/on-hook operations or the measurement of a voltage level on the circuit.

In addition to these simple arrangements, most analog telephone systems in use in modern countries use multifrequency (MF) pulsing. This type of signaling consists of combinations of frequencies to send other kinds of information over trunks. The combinations of two frequencies represents a pulse and as depicted in Table 2–1, each combination represents a digit. These signals fall within the speech bandwidth, so they can be sent over regular voice channels. MF pulses are used to transfer information to the control equipment that sets up the connections through the switches.

MF pulsing is also used to send information on the call in a BOC Centralized Automatic Message Accounting-Automatic Number Identification (CAMA-ANI) procedure. The calling number is transmitted from

Table A–1   Multifrequency Codes

Frequencies (in Hz)	Digit and Control
700 + 900	1
700 + 1100	2
700 + 1300	4
700 + 1500	7
700 + 1700	
900 + 1100	3
900 + 1300	5
900 + 1500	8
900 + 1700	
1100 + 1300	6
1100 + 1500	9
1100 + 1700	KP
1300 + 1500	0
1300 + 1700	
1500 + 1700	ST

the originating end office to the CAMA office after the sending of the called number. For equal access arrangements to an IC, the calling number is sent first, followed by the called number.

Two control signals listed in Table A–1 are of particular interest because they must be interpreted by an SS7 gateway and mapped into SS7 messages (signaling units). They are the key pulse signal and the start signal.

A key pulse (KP) signal is a multifrequency tone of 1100 + 1700 Hz ranging form 90 to 120 ms. Its function is to indicate the beginning (the start) of pulsing—that is, the dialed number follows the KP signal. The start (ST) signal does not mean the start of the signal. It indicates the end of the pulsing—that is, the end of the dialed telephone number. From the perspective of the telephone exchange, it represents the beginning of the processing of the signal.

DTMF PAIRS

For customer stations, another signaling arrangement is used called dual-tone multifrequency (DTMF) signaling. DTMF is provided for the

Table A–2   DTMF Pairs

Low Group (Hz)	High Group (Hz)			
	1209	*1336*	*1477*	*1633*
697	1		3	A
770	4	5	6	B
852	7	8	9	C
941	*	0	#	D

push buttons on the telephone set. This form of signaling provides 16 distinct signals, and each signal uses two frequencies selected from two sets of four groups. Table A–2 shows the arrangement for the DTMF pairs.

EXAMPLE OF TRUNK-SIDE ACCESS ARRANGEMENT

Earlier, I stated that digital signaling systems must support (interwork with) the older analog signaling systems because analog is still the pervasive technology used in the local loop. There are a variety of options and scenarios that exist in the network, and I provide two examples in the remainder of this appendix.

These examples are not all-inclusive, but they represent common implementations. For the reader who needs information on each service option offered by the U.S. BOCs, I refer you to Bellcore Document SR-TSV-002275, Issue 2, April 1994.

The BOCs classify several of their access arrangements with the title "Feature Group." This example is feature group B, which specifies an access agreement between an LEC end office (EO) and an interexchange carrier (IC).

With this arrangement, the calls to the IC must use the initial address of:

$$(I) + 950 + WXXX$$

where: $W = 0/1.$

Figure A–3 is largely self-descriptive, but some rules for the signaling sequences shown in the figure should be helpful. For calls from

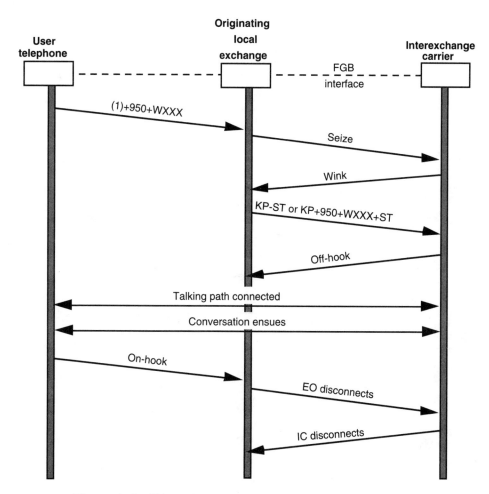

Figure A–3   Example of trunk-side access arrangement.

EOs or an access tandem: (1) The carrier returns a wink signal with 4 seconds of trunk seizure, and (2) the carrier returns an off-hook signal within 5 seconds of completion of the address outpulsing. For calls from a carrier to an EO or access tandem: (1) The end office or access tandem returns the wink start signal within 8 seconds of trunk seizure, (2) the carrier starts outpulsing the address with 3.5 seconds of the wink, and (3) the carrier completes sending the address sequence within 20 seconds.

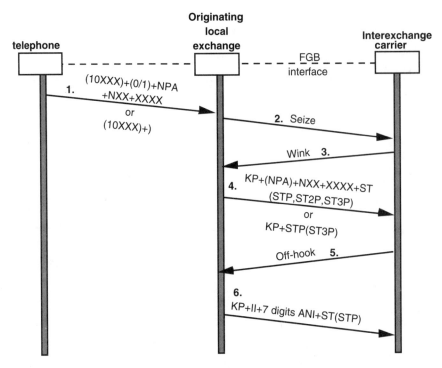

Figure A–4   Operator service (SO) signaling.

OPERATOR SERVICE SIGNALING (SO)

SO signaling is similar to one of the feature groups (FGC, not ex-plained in this book), but it has some characteristics that may be more familiar to the reader. Figure A–4 shows these operations, with six events.

In event 1, the customer dials 10XXX+(1)+7 or 10, or 10XXX+0+7 or 10. Upon receiving these signals, the EO (event 2) seizes an outgoing trunk. In event 3, the OS facility responds with a wink. Upon receiving the wink signal, the EO outpulses in event 4 the called number after a delay of 40 to 200 ms. The outpulsing is KP + 7/10 digits + ST (STP, ST2P, ST3P), or KP+STP(ST3P). In event 5, the OS facility will go off-hook (any time after the start of the ST pulse. Off-hook indicates its abil-ity to receive ANI. In event 6, the EO sends the ANI (after a delay of 40 to 200 ms). The signals are KP + 02 + ST (STP).

Appendix B

Media

$\mathbf{F}$or the newcomer to the industry, this appendix provides a tutorial on prevalent communications media, most of which are used in residential broadband. The material is not intended for the more experienced reader.

IMPORTANCE OF COMMUNICATIONS MEDIA

In many instances, the data communications user has no option in choosing the media for the communications link. For example, when a user dials a computer, the user does not instruct the telephone phone company to use microwave, coaxial cable, or optical fiber. Ideally, the user does not care. The media type should remain transparent to the communications process, and it usually does.

In many situations, one does not care about the transmission media. For example, an applications programmer is not concerned if the effect of a "WRITE" statement from a program finds its way onto a wire or an optical fiber.

In other situations, the media choice is important. The communications programmer is indeed concerned with the media because it affects throughput, delay, and cost of the transmission. In addition, the network administrator is quite concerned with what type of media is used in the network for the same reasons.

LOCAL LOOPS

The telephones in our homes and offices are connected through local loops to a local facilities network. This network consists of switching gear located at office centers. The actual building is called a wire Center. It services a wire Centre area. The customers in a wire Center area can communicate with each other through the wire Centre.

The telephones in our homes and offices carry the voice, data, and other images to and from the telephone network in the format of analog signals. Increasingly, digital techniques are being used both within the telephone network and at the local loop interfaces.

The connections from residences to the telephone system are through simple twisted pair cable, usually called a two-wire loop. With very few exceptions, these lines are designed for analog transmission.

The local loops emanating from businesses and buildings that have many tenants are configured for either analog or digital transmission. Typically, the lines are analog if conventional dial-up services and digital if dedicated lines are leased from the local exchange carrier. Twisted pair cable is gradually being replaced with optical fiber in many buildings.

With very few exceptions, the "long-haul trunks" that comprise the media between telephone switching facilities use digital transmission technology. In addition, optical fiber has become the preferred method for sending traffic, due to its large information-carrying capacity. Microwave is also widely used for long-haul transmissions between the switching facilities.

TWISTED-PAIR CABLE

The early communications systems used open-wire pairs (see Figure B–1). They consisted of uninsulated pairs of wires strung on poles about 125 feet apart. The air space between the wires provides insulation (isolation) from each other. With the early systems, a limited number of wires could be accommodated on a pole and the wires were very susceptible to corrosion, storm damage, and interference from power lines.

In 1883, the first underground cables were laid. Two years later, lead sheathing was placed around cables to provide protection. Prior to

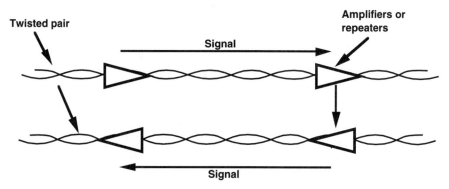

Figure B–1   Twisted-pair cable.

the use of the lead sheath, oil was used to provide insulation to the wires. It now was possible to use dry paper for insulation, and it rapidly became the industry standard.

Later, the pairs were twisted around each other to compensate for (and cancel) the effects of pair-interference. These circuits are pervasive today and are called twisted-pair cable. They can be used to support both analog and digital signals.

The twisting of each pair (in a multipair cable) is staggered. Radiated energy from the current flowing in one wire of the pair is largely canceled by the radiated energy of the current flowing back into the return wire of the same pair. This approach greatly reduces the effect of crosstalk. Moreover, each pair in the cable is less acceptable to external noise; the pair cancels out much of the noise because noise is coupled almost equally in each wire of the pair.

These characteristics describe a balanced line. Both wires carry current; the current in one wire is 180° out of phase with the current in the other wire. Both wires are above ground potential. In contrast, an unbalanced line carries the current on one wire and the other wire is at ground potential.

Shielded and Unshielded Cable

Unshielded wire has no metallic cover around it. These wires are inexpensive and offer reasonable performance over a long distance. However, they are quite susceptible to crosstalk and interference from external power sources.

Shielded twisted pairs (also called data-grade media) improve the resistance to crosstalk and external noise. The shield surrounds the wire with a metallic sheathing or braid. Several analyses reveal that a shielded pair system improves crosstalk and noise resistance by a factor of 1000 or more. Attenuation of TTP is about 2.3 times more severe than shielded pairs. (It is suggested that each copper conductor be made from the same production run to ensure the pair is balanced. Also, the insulation must be carefully crafted and a low dielectric-constant material must be used.)

One might think that unshielded cable is not a good choice for a media. However, TTP is quite effective for data communications links of relatively short distances of a few hundred feet in an electrically benign environment. By limiting the high-frequency signal components with a filter (also, to stay within FCC regulations), a TTP can support transmission speeds of up to 10 Mbit/s.

Moreover, TTP is there—it is already installed. The question is: Are you allowed to use it? The answer is not a definite yes or no. It depends on a user's decision to "acquire" ownership of the existing wire inside the user premises or to have the telephone company continue to maintain the media. The user should check with the local telephone company to determine the options.

Electronics Industries Association (EIA) Cable Categories

The Electronics Industries Association (EIA) has established a procedure for describing twisted-pair cable. The procedure entails the description of the electrical characteristics of the media and its recommended pull-length, for example. Table B–1 shows EIA categories 1 through 5.

Much of the recent activity in the industry has focused on category 5 cable. For example, it is being deployed with some of the new local area network (LAN) Ethernets for 100 Mbit/s wire speeds.

It is anticipated that some of the emerging technologies, such as the asynchronous transfer mode (ATM) will utilize category 5 cable. Some of

Table B–1   Electronics Industries Association (EIA) Cable Categories

Category	Description	Typical Use
1	Basic media for low power needs	Not rated
2	Media for low-speed data or voice	PBXs, alarm systems
3	Media for higher-speed LANs	10 BASET, 4 Mbits/s token ring
4	Media for still higher-speed LANs up to 20 Mbits/s	16 Mbits/s token ring
5	Media for new LANs (100 Mbits/s)	ATM, Fast Ethernet, CDDI, etc.

the other categories have been used for many years for other applications, some of which are listed in Table B–1.

COAXIAL CABLE

Coaxial cables (coax) have been in existence since the early 1940s and are another very widely used medium (see Figure B–2). They are employed extensively in long-distance telephone toll trunks, urban areas, and local networks. The coax consists of an inner copper conductor held in position by circular spacers (insulating disks). The inner wire and disks are surrounded by an outer conductor that forms a cylinder around the inner conductor and disks. The covering acts as a shield to protect the conductor and prevent interference from signals from other media. The center copper conductor ranges from 10 AWG used on long distance transmission to very small sizes of only .1 inches.

Coaxial cables provide for greater bandwidth and faster bit rates than wire cables. Typical coaxial cable systems can carry as many as 10,800 voice-grade channels. The technology is somewhat limited due to repeater design and signal loss at higher frequencies. In fact, the attenuation of coaxial cable increases as the square root of frequency.

OPTICAL FIBER

Today, the use of light for transmitting data, voice, and video has become a pervasive technology (see Figure B–3). Cables (optical fibers) are used for the transmission. Without question, optical media have a bright future (no pun intended) for several reasons.

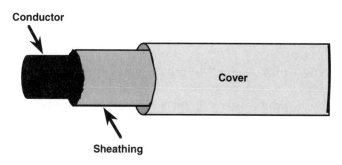

Figure B–2   Coaxial cable.

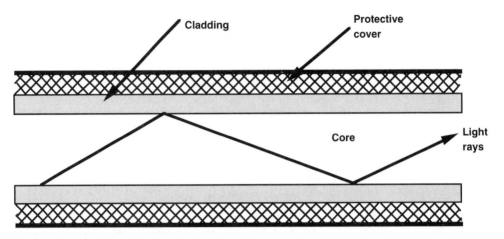

Figure B–3   Optical fiber.

Optical transmission has a very large information capacity. Bell Laboratories has successfully placed 60,000 simultaneous telephone calls on one optical fibber. Optical fibers have electrically nonconducting photons instead of the electrons found in metallic cables such as wires or coaxial cables. This is attractive for applications in which the transmission path traverses environments that are subject to fire and gaseous combustion from electricity.

Optical fibers have less loss of signal strength than copper wire and coaxial cables. The strength of a light signal is reduced only slightly after propagation through several miles of cable. Optical fibers are more secure than copper cable transmission methods. Transmission of light does not yield residual intelligence that is found in electrical transmission.

Optical cables are very small (roughly the size of a hair) and weigh very little. For example, 900 copper wire pairs pulled through 1000 feet in a building would weigh approximately 4800 pounds. Optical fibers are relatively easy to install, and operate in high and low temperatures.

Due to the low signal loss, the error rate for optical fibers is very low. For example, a typical error rate on an optical fiber is 10^{-9} versus 10^{-6} in metallic cables.

Semiconductor technology has been refined to provide transmitting and receiving devices for the system. The rapidly decreasing costs of solid state chips have further spurred the optical fiber industry.

Typically, the optical fiber light signal is transmitted down the fiber in the form of on/off pulses representing a digital bit stream. The fiber consists of concentric cylinders of dielectric material, the jacket, the cladding and the core. The core and cladding are made up of transparent glass (some systems use plastic) that guides the light within the core and reflects it as it travels between the core and the cladding.

The core and the cladding have different refractive indices (refraction is the ratio of the velocity of a lightwave in free space to its velocity in a medium, such as core and cladding). Since the refractive index of the two differ, light in the cladding propagates faster than it does in the core. As the light moves toward the cladding (a region of higher velocity), it is bent back toward the core and guided along the fiber (hence, another name of optical fiber is lightguide cable).

RADIO FREQUENCY BANDS

Electromagnetic radiation is created by inducing a current of sufficient amplitude into an antenna whose dimensions are approximately the same as the wavelength of the generated signal. The signal can be generated uniformly (like a light bulb) or can be directed as a beam of energy (like a spotlight).

Radio signals are radiant waves of energy transmitted into space. The signals are similar to that of heat or light. In a vacuum, they travel at the speed of light (186,000 miles per second or 297,000 kilometers per second). Due to the resistance of media (such as cable, air, and water), waves travel

Table B–2   Radio Frequency Bands

Classification Band	Initials	Frequency Range
Extremely low	ELF	Below 300 Hz
Infra low	ILF	300 Hz–3 KHz
Very low	VLF	3 KHz–30 KHz
Low	LF	30 KHz–300 KHz
Medium	MF	300 KHz–3 MHz
High	HF	3 MHz–30 MHz
Very high	VHF	30 MHz–300 MHz
Ultra high	UHF	300 MHz–3 GHz
Super high	SHF	3 GHz–30 GHz
Extremely high	EHF	30 GHz–300 GHz
Tremendously high	THF	300 GHZ–3000 GHz

Where:
 GHz   Gigahertz
 MHz   Megahertz

at a reduced rate from the theoretical maximum. The radio frequency spectrum is divided and classified by frequency bands (see Table B–2).

A MICROWAVE SYSTEM

Microwave is a directed line-of-sight radio transmission (see Figure B–4). It is used for radar and wideband communications systems and is quite common in the telephone system. In fact, well over half of the toll and long-distance telephone trunks use microwave transmission. The

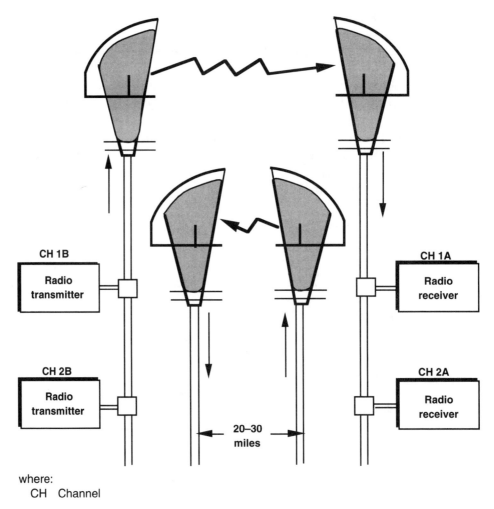

where:
CH   Channel

Figure B–4   A microwave system.

first commercial microwave system was used across the English Channel. In 1931 in Dover, England, the International Telephone Company implemented this microwave system.

Microwave covers a wide range of the frequency spectrum. Typically, frequencies range from 2 to 40 GHz, although most systems operate in the range of 2 to 18 GHz. The data rate is greater at the higher frequencies. For example, a data rate of 12 Mbit/s can be obtained on a 2 GHz band microwave system, yet a data rate of 274 Mbit/s is possible on a 18 GHz band system.

Television transmission also utilizes microwave transmission, because microwave provides the capacity required for video transmission. The high bandwidth gives a small wavelength—the smaller the wavelength, the smaller one can design the microwave antenna. Microwave is very effective for transmission to remote locations. For example, Canada has one of the most extensive systems in the world, and Russia has placed microwave systems in such remote areas as Siberia. Several U.S. carriers' primary product line is the offering of voice-grade channels on their microwave facilities.

SATELLITE COMMUNICATIONS

Satellite communications are unique from other media for several reasons:

- The technology provides for a large communications capacity. Through the use of the microwave frequency bands, several thousand voice-grade channels can be placed on a satellite station.
- The satellite has the capacity for a broadcast transmission. The transmitting antenna can send signals to a wide geographical area. Applications such as electronic mail and distributed systems find the broadcast capability quite useful.
- Transmission cost is independent of distance between the earth sites. For example, it is immaterial if two sites are 100 or 1000 miles apart as long as they are serviced by the same communications satellite. The signals transmitted from the satellite can be received by all stations, regardless of their distance from each other (see Figure B–5).
- The stations experience a significant signal propagation delay. Since satellites are positioned 22,300 miles above the earth, the

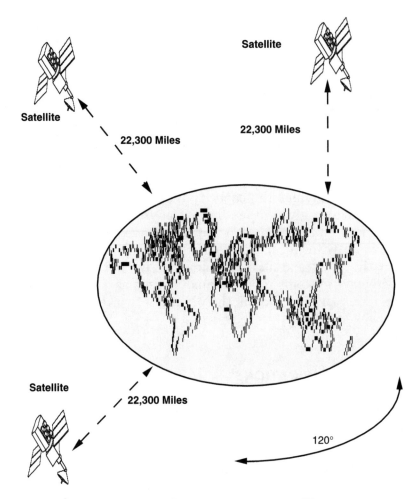

Figure B–5   Geosynchronous satellites.

transmission has to travel into space and return. A round trip transmission requires a minimum of about 240 milliseconds (ms) and could be greater as the signal travels through other components. This may affect certain applications or software systems.

• The broadcast aspect of satellite communications may present security problems, since all stations under the satellite antenna can receive the broadcasts. Consequently, transmissions are often changed (encrypted) for satellite channels.

Geosynchronous Satellites

Many satellites are in a geosynchronous orbit. They rotate around the earth at 6900 miles/hour (11040 km/hour) and remain positioned over the same point above the equator. Thus, the earth stations' antenna can remain in one position since the satellite's motion relative to the earth's position is fixed. Furthermore, a single geosynchronous satellite with nondirectional antenna can cover about 30% of the earth's surface. The geosynchronous orbit requires a rocket launch of 22,300 miles (35680 Km) into space. Geosynchronous satellites can achieve worldwide coverage (some limited areas in the polar regions are not covered) with three satellites spaced at 120° intervals from each other.

CELLULAR RADIO

Cellular radio was conceived as a terrestrial voice telephone network. Its purpose is to upgrade the existing mobile radio-telephone system. The idea goes back to 1972 when the FCC recognized that the demand for mobile telephones was exceeding the frequencies available.

The FCC then opened up frequencies initially in the 800 to 900 MHz band and schemes were developed to reuse the same frequencies in the same geographical vicinity. In 1979, a prototype network was built in Chicago by AT&T. In a few short years, cellular radio has grown to reach all metropolitan areas, and systems are being developed for nationwide service.

A cellular radio network is structured around the concepts of "cells" (see Figure B–6). Each cell is a geographical area with a low-power transmitter. The mobile telephone in the automobile or truck communicates with the transmitter, which in turn communicates with the Mobile Telephone Switching Office (MTSO). The MTSO is an extension of the telephone central office, and the mobile channel appears to be the same as a wire line to the stored program control logic (SPC) at the telephone office.

As the mobile unit passes through the network, the user is assigned a frequency for use during transit through each cell. Since each cell has its own low-power transmitter, the signals for nonadjacent cells do not interfere with each other. As a consequence, the noncontiguous cells can use the same frequencies.

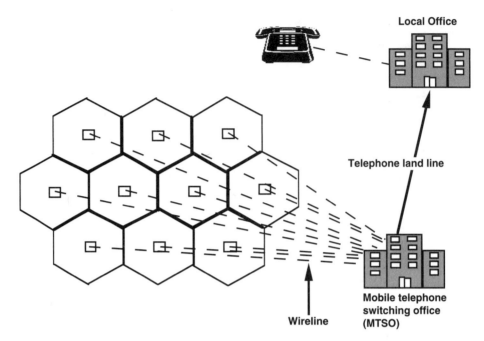

Figure B–6   Cellular radio.

UPCOMING WIRELESS NETWORKS

An emerging communications media that is focused on the local area network industry is called wireless networks or wireless LANs. Presently, most local area networks are configured with coaxial cable, twisted pair, or optical fiber. While these media have proven to be beneficial to organizations, they do require considerable installation costs, as well as ongoing maintenance. Additionally, some buildings are difficult to wire. Old buildings with asbestos components present problems. Some historic sites have restrictions on what can be done to the buildings. Moreover, many organizations have projects and people that move frequently; this presents some problems for hardwired systems.

The wireless LAN industry is based on a Federal Communications Commission ruling that certain frequency bands need not be licensed if they use low power transmitters and spread spectrum techniques (spread spectrum uses a number of frequencies to transmit a signal).

The products emerging in the wireless marketplace transmit to a relatively limited area—a few thousand feet only. Ideally, the signal does not emanate from the building. These products are often used to connect to Ethernet LANs.

Another approach to wireless LANs is the use of infrared frequencies. These products provide point-to-point configurations with a single beam. A diffused beam provides broadcast capabilities. Some of these products interface into AppleTalk for interconnecting Macintosh computers. A number of products also connect to IEEE 802.5 token rings.

The IEEE has formed the IEEE 802.11 committee to address this technology, although it is not expected to finish the standard for several years.

Appendix C

V.34

$\mathbf{V}$.34 is the basic architecture used in high-speed modems, such as V.34+ and part of the 56 kbit/s modem. This appendix provides an analysis of the V.34 architecture, as published in the ITU-T Recommendation. The seasoned user of V Series modems will find V.34 a diversion from the V Series architectures that have been in the industry since 1988.

FEATURES OF V.34

In the continuing quest to gain more bandwidth from the local subscriber loop, the ITU-T has been publishing specifications for higher speed modems for many years. The latest entry is V.34, which was approved in 1995, but has seen use since 1993. This technology is analog-based.

V.34 retains some of the features of V.17, V.29, V.32, V.32 bis, and V.33 and at the same time adds many of its own unique characteristics. This list explains some of its major attributes.

Features of V.34

- Operates on 2-wire, point-to-point telephone circuits (or circuits that meet PSTN specifications)
- Operates on dial-up (switched) or leased circuits

- Operates in half-duplex or duplex modes
- Achieves channel separation by echo cancellation
- Utilizes QAM on each channel
- Operates in synchronous mode
- Employs trellis coding
- Provides for an optional 200 bit/s asynchronous secondary channel
- Provides adaptive signaling (in bit/s) through line probing by adjusting to channel quality/capacity
- Uses conventional V.24 interchange circuits
- Supports the following signaling rates (bit/s):

2400	12000	21600
4800	14400	24000
7200	16800	26400
9600	19200	28800

SYMBOL RATES AND CARRIER FREQUENCIES

Unlike the previous high-speed V Series modems, V.34 uses symboling rates other than 2400. The following symbol rates are supported: 2400, 2743, 2800, 3000, 3200, 3429, with symbol rates of 2400, 3000, 3200 mandatory. Furthermore, the carrier frequencies can also vary, ranging from 1600 to 2000 Hz.

Both the symbol rate and the carrier frequency are selected during the modem startup and handshaking procedure. During this procedure, the modems can select one or two carrier frequencies for each symbol rate.

Table C–1 is an extraction of several tables in the V.32 Recommendation. (I will be using the 2400 and 3200 symbol rates and high-carrier throughout this discussion).

The symbol rate is S = (a/c) × 2400 ± 0.01% two-dimensional (2D) symbols per second. Therefore, using Table C–1, the symbol rate of 3200 is derived by (4/3) × 2400 = 3200.

The carrier frequency is C = (d/e) × S. Therefore, using Table C–1 once again, a carrier frequency of 1800 is derived by (3/4) × 2400 = 1800. A carrier frequency of 1920 is derived by (3/5) × 3200 = 1920.

V.34 alternates between sending b–1 or b bits per mapping frame based on a switching pattern SWP (of period P in Table C–1). The result is that the transmission of a fractional number of bits per mapping frame is N/P. The value of b is the smallest integer not less than N/P.

Table C–1   Symbol Rates and Carrier Frequencies

			High Carrier			Framing Parameter	
Symbol Rate,S	a	c	Frequency	d	e	J	P
2400	1	1	1800	3	4	7	12
3200	4	3	1920	3	5	7	16

SWP,b.

	S = 2400 P = 12		S = 3200 P = 16	
Signaling Rate	b	SWP	b	SWP
2400	8	FFF	–	–
28800	–	–	72	FFFF

Note: Partial examples, see V.34 for complete tables

SWP consists of 12- to 16-bit binary numbers. V.34 contains information on all combinations of signaling rate and symbol rate. For our examples of S = 2400 and 3200, the second part of Table C–1 gives some partial examples of b, SWP. The value of SWP is shown as a hex value.

THE V.34 USE OF V.24 INTERCHANGE CIRCUITS

As with all V Series modems, V.34 uses a subset of the V.24 interchange circuits (see Table C–2). This table provides a summary of these circuits. As discussed earlier in this book, V.24 is a "superset" recommendation, and all the V Series modems utilize a subset of the V.24 interchange circuits.

V8 AND V.34 SIGNALS AND THEIR USE

V.34 executes four phases before it begins sending user data (in superframes). Some of these procedures are defined in V.8. This section examines each phase. For purposes of clarity, I describe some of the V.8 and V.34 terms with a general description that you should be able to follow without having to read (at least, initially) the V.8 and V.34 recommendations. Table C–3 defines the V.8 and V.34 signals that I use in this discussion. The table does not show this bit structure for each signal. The reader should study V.8 and V.34 if this level of detail is needed. The sig-

Table C–2   The V.34 Use of V.24 Interchange Circuits

Interchange Circuit	Description
102	Signal ground or common return
103	Transmitted data
104	Received data
105	Request to send
106	Ready for sending
107	Data set ready
108/1 or 108/2	Data terminal ready
109	Data channel received line signal detector
113	Transmitter signal element timing (DTE source)[1]
114	Transmitter signal element timing (DCE source)[2]
115	Receiver signal element timing (DCE source)[2]
125	Calling indicator
133	Ready for receiving[3]
140	Loopback/maintenance
141	Local loopback
142	Test indicator
118	Transmitted secondary channel data[4]
119	Received secondary channel data[4]
120	Transmit secondary channel line signal[4,5]
121	Secondary channel ready[4,5]
122	Secondary channel received line signal detector[4,5,6]

[1]When the modem is not operating in a synchronous mode at the interface, any signals on this circuit shall be disregarded. Many DTEs operating in an asynchronous mode do not have a generator connected to this circuit.

[2]When the modem is not operating in a synchronous mode at the interface, this circuit shall be clamped to the OFF condition. Many DTEs operating in an asynchronous mode do not terminate this circuit.

[3]Operation of circuit 133 shall be in accordance with 7.3.1/V.42.

[4]This circuit is provided where the optional secondary channel is implemented without a separate interface.

[5]This circuit need only be provided where required by the application.

[6]This circuit is in the ON condition if circuit 109 is in the ON condition and the optional secondary channel is enabled.

Table C–3 Key V.8 and V.34 Signals and Their Use

Notation	Name	Function
CI	Function indicator signal	Indicates a session
ANSam	Modified answer tone	Response to a CI signal
Te	——	A silent period, which begins with the termination of the call signal or after detection of ANSam. Can be used for echo canceller disabling, if necessary
CM	Call menu signal	Initiates modulation-mode selection[1,2,3]
JM	Joint menu signal	Response to the CM signal[1,2,3]
CJ	CM terminator	Acknowledges JM signal and terminates CM signal
INFO	Information sequence	Exchanges modem capabilities, results of line probing, and data mode modulation parameters[4]
A, $\underline{A}$	2400 Hz tone	Transmitted by answer modem, with A and $\underline{A}$ representing 180° phase reversals of 2400 Hz tone
B, $\underline{B}$	1200 Hz tone	Transmitted by call modem, with B and $\underline{B}$ representing a 180° phase reversal of the 1200 Hz tone
L1, L2	Line probing signals	Used to analyze channel characteristics
S, $\underline{S}$	——	S and $\underline{S}$ sent as part of quarter-super constellation rotation
MD	Manufacturer-defined signal	Used to train a vendor-specific echo canceller
PR	——	Used to train equalizer
TRN	——	A sequence of symbols chosen from 4- or 16-point 2D constellation
J	——	Indicates 4- or 16-point constellation size used by remote modem
J'	——	Terminates the J sequence
MP, MP'	Modulator parameter sequences	Contains parameters to negotiate: signaling rate, trellis code choice, auxiliary channel enable, amount of constellation shaping
E	——	Signals end of MP
B1	——	Sent at the end of start-up

[1]Part of the signal is used to indicate the V Series modulation modes: (a) V.34 half-duplex or duplex, (b) V.32/V.32 bis, (c) V.22/V.22 bis, (d) V.17, (e) V.29 half duplex, (f) V.27 ter, (g) V.26 ter, (h) V.26 bis, (i) V.23 half duplex or duplex, and (j) V.21. For CM, it indicates the suggested signaling mode; for JM, it indicates the lowest signaling mode.

[2]Part of the signal is used to indicate the use of LAPM (V.42).

[3]Part of the signal is used to indicate the use of cellular access.

[4]Two sets of INFO messages are used (where a = answer modem and c = call modem): $INFO_{0a}$, $INFO_{0c}$ and $INFO_{1a}$ and $INFO_{1c}$.

nals in the table are listed according to the order of their invocation by the V.34 modem.

V.36 PHASES

A V.34 modem executes four phases of operations before it is ready for data transfer. These phases are listed here and described in more detail in this section.

- Phase 1 Network interaction
- Phase 2 Probing/ranging
- Phase 3 Equalizer and echo canceller training
- Phase 4 Final training

Table C–3 should be used during this analysis. Additionally, the next four sections provide a general depiction of the four phases. Be aware that these figures do not show exact timing relationships and do not show the overlapping of the signals on the duplex channel. They show typical (but not all) sequences. This other information can be found in Section 11 of V.34.

Phase 1: Network Interaction

Figure C–1 shows the signal exchange for phase 1, network interaction. The call modem conditions its receiver to accept ANSam and then transmits CI to the answer modem. The answer modem, after it is con-

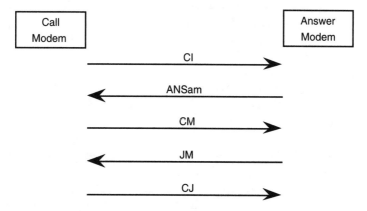

Figure C–1   Phase 1: Network interaction.

nected to the line, remains silent for 200 ms and then transmits ANSam to the call modem, and conditions its receiver to detect CM.

When the call modem receives ANSam, it remains silent for the period T_e and conditions its receiver to detect JM and sends CM to set up the categories to be used during this session (see footnotes of Table C–3).

The answer modem receives CM, and since CM indicates the V.34 operations, the modem sends JM and conditions its receiver to detect CJ.

At the call modem, after it has sent CJ, it remains silent for 75 ± 5 ms and enters phase 2. At the answer modem, after receiving CJ, it remains silent for 75 ± 5 ms and enters phase 2.

Phase 2

Phase 2 is concerned with channel probing and ranging (see Figure C–2). These operations begin with the exchange of $INFO_{0c}$ and $INFO_{0a}$, which contain the following negotiated parameters: (1) symbol rate, (2) the use of a high or low carrier, (3) maximum allowed symbol rate in the transmit and receive directions, and (4) transmit clock source.

Next, the receivers are conditioned to each other. Then, round trip delay is calculated between the two machines by the alternate sending and receiving of Tone A and Tone B. A an B are 2400 and 1200 Hz tones, respectively, while $\underline{A}$ and $\underline{B}$ are 180° phase reversals, respectively.

The next part of phase 2 deals with sending and receiving of L1 and L2, which are line probing signals. They are used by the two modems to analyze the characteristics of the channel. Both L1 and L2 are a defined set of tones that enable the receiver to measure channel distortion and noise.

The final part of phase 2 deals with the exchange of $INFO_{1c}$ and $INFO_{1a}$ (see footnote 4, Table C–3). These signals provide the following functions: (1) permissible power levels for the session and minimum power reduction that can be accepted; (2) length of MD (for phase 3); and (3) final symbol rate selection as a result of the previous probing.

Phase 3

Phase 3 is concerned with training both modem's equalizers and echo cancellers (see Figure C–3). The answer modem begins these procedures by sending S and $\underline{S}$. Signal S is sent by alternating between point 0 of the quarter-superconstellation and the same point rotated counterclockwise by 90°. Signal $\underline{S}$ is sent by alternating between point 0 rotated by 180°, and point 0 counterclockwise by 270°.

Next MD is sent, following (once again) by S and $\underline{S}$, and then PP is transmitted, which is used to train the receiver's equalizer. The answer

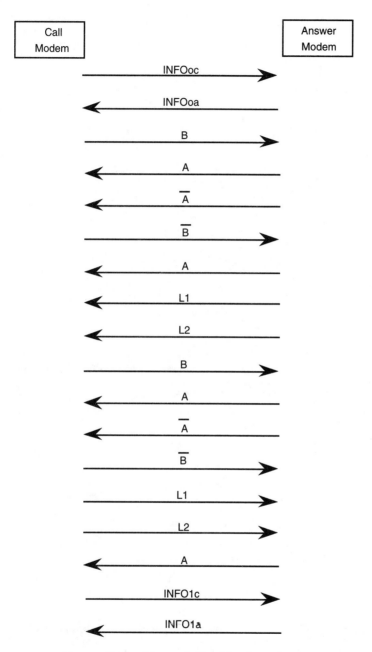

Figure C–2   Phase 2: Probing/ranging.

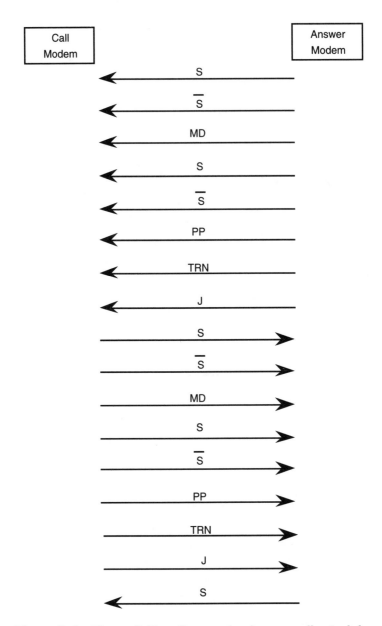

Figure C–3   Phase 3: Equalizer and echo canceller training.

modem completes its phase 3 by sending TRN and J. It can be seen that the call modem's phase 3 procedures are identical to those of the answer modem.

Phase 4

After the two modems have moved from phase 3 to phase 4 by exchanging J, J' and S, S̲, both modems send TRN signals (discussed earlier) (see Figure C–4). Next, MP and MP' are exchanged, which contains parameters used to negotiate a variety of options explained in Table C–3. The E signals end the MP sequence, and the B1 signals end this phase and the overall startup procedure.

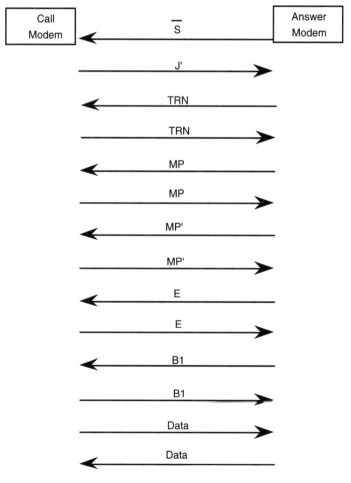

Figure C–4 Final training.

Appendix D

Channel Performance and Measurements

This appendix has been prepared for the newcomer who is unfamiliar with the terms and concepts associated with channel performance. The decibel is examined as a descriptor of channel power and power loss. Next, the signal-to-noise ratio is discused in the context of the decibel. For wireless systems, the co-channel interference ratio is explained, and several cellular systems are compared in relation to their co-channel interference performance. The tutorial concludes with a look at bandwidth performance, and a review of Nyquist's theory and Shannon's Law.

DECIBEL LOSSES AND POWER RATIO

The engineers who design and maintain communications systems must be concerned with the quality and strength of the signals on the communications channels (links) in the system. Typically, a communications link consists of more than the link itself—a number of different components such as amplifiers, communications lines and switches are also included. Each component on the link introduces a signal loss or gain into the signal.

These losses and gains are described as a ratio of power into and out of the component:

$$\text{Power ratio} = \text{Power In/Power Out}$$

A tandem link (in which several components connect the two communicating devices) necessitates a calculation of loss/gain at each component and the multiplication of these ratios together. For example, assume five components introduce the following losses or gains:

$$1/2 * 1/10 * 1/50 * 1/50 * 10000/1 = 2.$$

Thus, the signal is twice as strong at the end of the tandem link as it was at the beginning.

This multiplication process can be tedious and the numbers can be very small or very large. Instead of multiplying the numbers together, the same result can be obtained by adding the logarithms of the numbers. Today, the standard practice is to use the logarithms of the ratios, rather than the ratios themselves (see Figure D–1).

The term decibel (dB) (named after the inventor of the telephone, Alexander Graham Bell) is used in communications to express the ratio of two values. The values can represent power, voltage, current, or sound levels.

The decibel (1) is a ratio and not an absolute value, (2) expresses a logarithmic relationship and not a linear one, and (3) can be used to indicate either a gain or a loss.

The logarithm is useful because a signal's strength falls off logarithmically as it passes through a cable. A decibel is 10 times the logarithm (in base 10) of the ratio:

Decibel Losses	Power Ratio: Out/In
−1 dB	0.790
−2 dB	0.630
−3 dB	0.500
−4 dB	0.398
−5 dB	0.316
−6 dB	0.215
−7 dB	0.200
−8 dB	0.158
−9 dB	0.126
−10 dB	0.100

Figure D–1   Decibel losses and power ratio.

$$dB = 10 \log P1/P2$$

where: dB = number of decibels; log = logarithm to base 10; P1 = one value of the power; P2 = comparison of value of the power.

Decibels are often used to measure the gain or loss of a communications signal. These measurements are quite valuable for testing the quality of lines and determining noise and signal losses, all of which must be known in order to design a communications system. The decibel is a very useful unit because it can be added or subtracted as a signal is cascaded through a communications link. For example, if a line introduces 1dB of loss in a span of one mile, a three mile length will produce a loss of 3 dB. If the line is connected to an amplifier with a gain of 10 dB, then the total gain is 7 dB.

Suppose a communications line is tested at the sending and receiving ends. The P1/P2 ratio yields a reduction of the signal power from the sending to receiving end by a ratio of 200:1. The signal experiences a 23 dB loss (23 = 10 log 200). The log calculations are readily available for tables published in math books.

Table D–1 shows some examples of decibel loss in relation to power loss. The dB figures represent a loss of power. The table was sourced from *Telecommunications Wiring,* by Clyde N. Herrick and C. Lee Mckim, Prentice Hall, 1992, Englewood Cliffs, NJ 07632. I recommend this book if you want to delve into the details of wiring communications systems.

DECIBELS AND SIGNAL-TO-NOISE RATIOS

The decibel is often used to describe the level of noise on the circuit by a signal-to-noise ratio (see Figure D–2). A signal-to-noise ratio of 23 dB (poor, but acceptable) to 26 dB (good) is normal for relatively high-quality telephone lines. It is calculated as:

$$dB = 10 \log S/N$$

So, for a low 23 dB ratio, the ratio is: 23/10 = log S/N = 199.5. For the high 26 dB ratio, the ratio is: 26/10 = log S/N = 398. The 3 dB difference represents the doubling of the power. In fact, any increase of 3 dB is a doubling of power and a decrease is a halving of the power, for a 50% power loss.

Given the formula: dB = 10 log S/N

S/N Ratio in Decibels (dB)	Signal-to-Noise Power
0	1:1
+3	2:1
+6	4:1
+9	8:1
+10	10:1
+13	20:1
+16	40:1
+19	80:1
+20	100:1
+21	126:1
+22	158:1
+23	199:1
+24	251:1
+25	316:1
+26	398:1
+27	501:1
+28	631:1
+29	794:1
+30	1,000:1
+33	2,000:1
+36	4,000:1
+39	8,000:1
+40	10,000:1

Figure D–2   Decibels and signal-to-noise ratios.

dB Losses in Relation to Power Losses in Electrical Circuits

Table D–1 provides some examples of dB losses compared to power losses for typical electrical circuits.

THE CARRIER INTERFERENCE RATIO
(CO-CHANNEL INTERFERENCE)

Interference from other signals is a constant source of concern in any system that has multiple circuits. Examples are multiple twisted-pair cables in a sheath or adjacent channels in a wireless system. This

Table D–1 Examples of dB Losses in Relation to Power Losses in Electrical Circuits

Decibel Values	Power Ratio (Input/Output)
1 dB	0.790
2 dB	0.530
3 dB	0.500
5 dB	0.398
6 dB	0.316
7 dB	0.251
8 dB	0.200
9 dB	0.126
10 dB	0.100

From: *Telecommunication Wiring,* 1992, by Clyde N. Herrick and C. Lee Mckim. Englewood Cliffs, NJ: Prentice Hall.

type of interference is measured in a variety of ways. One method is to calculate the ratio of the power of the desired signal (carrier, or C) to that of the interfering signal (interference, or I), calculated as C/I. This ratio is measured in dB.

Different systems tolerate different amounts of interference. For example, the AMPS (Advanced Mobile Phone System) and TACS (Total Access Communications System) can tolerate a C/I ratio of 17 to 18 dB. A degradation to around 10 to 14 dB is unacceptable.

As other examples, the Global System for Mobile Communications (GSM) can tolerate a C/I ratio of around 9 to 6.5 dB. The IS-54 and IS-136 systems can tolerate a C/I ratio of around 14 dB. For this latter system, most designs attempt to maintain the same quality as AMPS, since IS-54 and IS-136 operate over the AMPS frequency spectrum.

In cellular systems frequencies are reused, and therefore careful consideration of potential channel interference must be made. For example, in an AMPS network, cells using the same frequencies must be spaced far enough apart that the 17 to 18 dB C/I ratio is maintained.

The Carrier-Interference Ratio (Co-channel Interference)

- Interference from other signals is a source of concern in a system that has multiple circuits.
- Interference is measured as the ratio of the power of the desired signal (carrier, or C) to that of the interfering signal (interference, or I), calculated as C/I.

Examples

- The AMPS (Advanced Mobile Phone System) and TACS (Total Access Communications System) can tolerate a C/I ratio of 17 to 18 dB.
- The Global System for Mobile Communications (GSM) can tolerate a C/I ratio of around 9 to 6.5 dB.
- The IS-54 and IS-136 systems can tolerate a C/I ratio of around 14 dB.

DECIBEL 1 MILLIWATT

In the early days of the development of the telephone system, it was recognized that since the decibel is a ratio and not an absolute unit, it is meaningless to use if there is no reference point by which to apply the ratio. For example, a 30 dB increase of one watt of power is considerably different from a 30 dB increase in one milliwatt of power. It is common practice to use a reference level of 1 watt or 1 milliwatt. Most companies have chosen 1 milliwatt, which is the output level of a voice signal from the telephone transmitter.

The decibel in 1 milliwatt (dBm) is used as a power measurement in which the reference power is 1 milliwatt (0.001 watt) taken across 600 ohms. It is expressed as:

$$dBm = 10 \log P/0.001 \text{ [i.e., 1 milliwatt]}$$

where P = signal power in milliwatts (mW).

This approach allows measurements to be taken in relation to a standard. A signal of a known power level is inserted at one end and measured at the other. A 0 dBm reading means 1 mW.

For a 1 watt benchmark, the microwave industry uses the dBW (decibel-watt):

$$dBW = 10 \log P \text{ (W)}/1W$$

As stated earlier, carriers (such as telephone companies) use a 1004 Hz tone (referred to as a 1 kHz test tone) to a test a line. The 1 kHz tone is used as a reference to other test tones of a different level. The test tone is used to establish a zero transmission level point (TLP). The TLP is a convenient concept for relating signal or noise levels at various points in the communications system. It is common practice to consider the outgoing 2 wire class 5 system as the 0 dB TLP reference point. All gains/ losses are compared to this value.

A reading of 0 dBm at the frequency of 1004 Hz means there is no gain or loss.

Decibel 1 Milliwatt

- Decibel is a ratio and not an absolute unit.
- Common practice is to use a reference level of 1 milliwatt.
- Most companies have chosen 1 milliwatt, which is the output level of a voice signal from the telephone transmitter.

$$dBm = 10 \log P/0.001 \text{ [i.e., 1 milliwatt]}$$

- A signal of a known power level is inserted at one end and measured at the other.
- Operators use a 1004 Hz tone (referred to as a 1 kHz test tone) to a test a line.

Example

- An AMPS network is designed to have a signal exhibit a loss of no more than −95 dBm at the edge of the cell. Assume another cell using same frequencies delivers −112 dBm. The minimum −17 dB is just preserved.

NYQUIST MODEL

One of the most important works regarding bandwidth deals with how a certain bandwidth can carry a certain amount of traffic. To understand this concept more fully, we must examine the classical work performed by Harry Nyquist in the 1920s concerning the capacity of a noiseless channel.

Nyquist showed that a channel with bandwidth B (in hertz) can carry 2B symbols per second. However, if a signal change takes the form of more than two states (for example, four voltage levels), then the channel capacity is 4B symbols per second. Four symbols can represent any combination of 0 and 1: (1) 00: first symbol possibility; (2) 01: second symbol possibility; (3) 10: third symbol possibility; and (4) 11: fourth symbol possibility.

In a simple baseband system, eight alternative voltages per signal change (i.e., baud) can be used to provide any possible combination of 3 bits ($2^3 = 8$). Sixteen voltages per baud represent any combination of 4 bits ($2^4 = 16$) and so on.

From the above discussion, it follows that in the absence of noise, channel capacity (C) in bits per second in relation to bandwidth (B) and signaling levels (L) is stated as:

$$C = 2B \log_2 L$$

Generally speaking, n bits can be transmitted by 2n possible signaling levels. A signal with a signaling rate of 2nB bit/s can be sent through a noiseless channel with B Hz of bandwidth. The following relationship exists:

$$2n = L \text{ therefore:}$$
$$n = \log_2 L$$

Remember, L is the number of signaling levels (for example, multiple amplitude levels or multiple combinations of phase changes). An 8-level transmitter (for example, a modem) yielding 3 bits per baud provides a C of 18,300 bit/s on a noiseless channel.

We now know that modern systems achieve such a high bit rate across a seemingly low capacity voiceband telephone line by multilevel signaling.

The inquiring reader might wonder if this equation restricts the volume of L. Indeed, why not make L very large and achieve a very high data rate? Several factors restrict the magnitude of the L value. First, the electrical properties of the line restrict L (resistance, capacitance, attenuation, etc.). Second, the larger the value of L, the smaller the increments must be between the levels within the signal. If a signal is restricted to 5 volts, for example, a large L value means the signal voltage differences are quite small. As a result, the receiver must be very sophisticated (and expensive) to discern the small differences between the small voltages. Moreover, any slight distortion on the channel makes the voltage differences indistinguishable from each other. Third, the channel is not noiseless; the signal must manifest itself in the presence of noise, which limits C rather dramatically.

NOISE AND SHANNON'S LAW

With these thoughts in mind, we now examine the characteristics of one type of noise, then we can understand the implications of the works of Shannon and Hartley, as well as the concepts of entropy and data encoding.

The noise to which we refer is the thermal noise, and all communications conductors and electronic circuitry possess it. It cannot be eliminated. Thermal noise is called Gaussian noise because its amplitude varies randomly around a certain level. It is also called white noise because the noise is distributed uniformly (i.e., averaged) across the frequency spectrum, just as white light is an average of all the color frequencies.

In a conductor such as a wire or cable, the nonrandom movement of electrons creates an electric current that is used for the transmission signal. Along with these signals, all electrical components also experience the vibrations of the random movement of electrons. These vibrations cause the emission of electromagnetic waves of all frequencies. Other kinds of noise exist that can affect transmission quality. For example, space noise results from the sun and other stars radiating energy over a broad frequency spectrum. Atmospheric noise comes from electrical disturbances in the earth's atmosphere.

The thermal noise (N) present in an electrical conductor is calculated as:

$$N = k \, TB$$

where: k is Boltzmann's constant (1.37 * 10–23 joules per degree), T is temperature in degrees (Kelvin), and B is bandwidth (note that bandwidth (B) is one determinant of thermal noise).

Some twenty years after the work of Nyquist, Claude Shannon developed a set of theories that have become know as Shannon's Law (published in 1948). It is best known by the concept that the capacity of a channel (C) (in bit/s) is determined by its bandwidth (B) and the ratio of the power in the signal to the power in the noise:

$$C = B \log_2 (1 + S/N)$$

where: S is the power in the signal and N is the power in the thermal noise.

We can certainly achieve faster data rates by increasing the bandwidth, increasing the signal power, or both. More bandwidth means more information can be passed over the channel. Nonetheless, Shannon's Law sets the transmission rate that can be achieved at baseband. For this discussion, however, Shannon's equation is also applicable to radio frequency (RF) if certain operations are undertaken on the communications channel (the use of filters, error correction schemes, etc.).

A typical voice grade line yields a S/N ratio of 1000 to 1. Given a bandwidth of 3100 Hz, the channel could theoretically support a data transmission rate of 30.8 Kbit/s (C = 3100 $\log_2$ (1 + 1000/1) = 38,894). Many user devices do not utilize the full voice band spectrum and are much slower. This theoretical rate is further constrained by other factors such as signal decay (attenuation) and other types of noise.

As an example of a use of the S/N ratio, an analog cellular system is designed to have a S/N ratio of 17 dB or more. Other systems (such as CDMA) can be designed to operate with at much lower S/N ratio. In CDMA, which uses a very large bandwidth, this extra bandwidth is used to provide high-quality signals with a low S/N ratio.

We can rewrite Shannon's equation as:

$$C/B = 1.44 \log_e (1 + S/N)$$

By assuming signal-to-noise ratio is small (for example, less than or equal to 0.1), we can rewrite the above equation to:

$$B = C/1.44 \times N/S$$

From the above equations, and with a given S/N ratio, it is possible to increase the bandwidth on a channel and maintain a low error rate. For example, assume the system is to operate on a channel of 10 Kbit/s with a given S/N ratio of 0.01, then:

$$B = 10/1.44 \times 10^3/0.01 = 0.69 \times 10^6 \text{ Hz or 690 kHz}$$

Appendix E
TR-57, TR-507, TR-08

The TR-57, TR-507, and TR-08 specifications are cited in the main body of this book, without any explanations of their functions. This appendix provides the reader with enough information to understand these specifications in the context of their use in residential broadband. Be aware that this appendix is a broad overview of TR-57, TR-507, and TR-08. Details are available in the original documents, whose full titles are cited in the descriptions that follow.

ASPECTS OF TR-57

The present generation of residential broadband systems use Bellcore's specification TR-NWT-000057 in their products. This specification is titled, *Functional Criteria for Digital Loop Carrier Systems,* hereafter referred to as TR-57. The DLC specifications define the features for the local exchange carrier (LEC) network, which consists of the central office terminal (COT), the remote terminal (RT), and the transmission facility that connects the COT and RT. The COT is located at the central office near the digital switch and the RT is located in the neighborhood of the served customers.

Generic Layout:

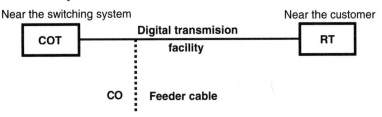

Figure E–1   Aspects of TR-57.

TR-57 defines the interfaces between the COT and RT but confines itself to the physical layer features of the interface.

The actual transmission links may be conventional twisted pair, optical fiber, or a combination of the two, if necessary. The distribution cable facilities connect individual subscriber network interfaces with a cross-connect interface, known as a feed-distribution interface (FDI). The distribution facilities consist of cables that are relatively short within the neighborhood of the subscriber. On the other side of the FDI are the feeder facilities, which link the FDIs to the central office.

Interestingly, DLCs were first employed to provide feeder relieve in the loop plant. They were placed in subscriber routes in rural areas where the cable had to be relatively long in distance. As their cost decreased, they were then employed in suburban areas.

The concept of the carrier serving area (CSA) is employed with TR-57. Recall from previous discussions that the CSA separates a cable route into specific geographic areas called a CSA. The goal of the CSA concept is to provide every customer with a 56 kbit/s service over an unrepeatered facility when all the CSAs were activated. The requirement for the separation define any cable route beyond 12 kft from the CO to separated into CSAs. Figure E–1 provides a summary of the requirements from the remote terminal to the network interface on the customer premises.

ASPECTS OF TR-507

Most vendors products also adhere to Bellcore specification TR-NWT-000507, *LATA Switching Systems Generic Requirements* (LSSGR), hereafter referred to as TR-507. TR-507 is a module of a more expansive specification dealing with LSSGR and numbered FR-NWT-000064. We

Sets requirements for signal performance in the PSTN local loop (transmit loop loss [TLL], hybrid loss [HL], network loss [L], receive loop loss [RLL]):

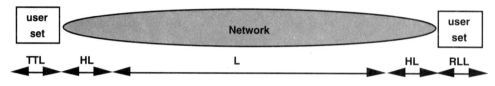

Figure E–2 TR-507.

concern ourselves with TR-507 because it is this specification that defines the performance in the network. Emphasis is placed on four principal transmission performance parameters: (1) end-to-end connection loss, (2) connection noise, (3) echo path loss, and (4) echo path delay.

Parts of the performance in the communications systems can be controlled, notably connection loss and echo path loss. However, echo path delay is a function of the length of the connection and process delays encountered in the network elements as well as the propagation speed of the signal itself. Connection noise also cannot be controlled precisely because it is a function of impairments introduced by the system itself, such as switches for example.

The challenge is to balance the fact that decreasing the magnitude of echo increases the connection loss. Also, increasing the connection loss to reduce echo in turn reduces the signal's noise ratio. Ideally, one would like to have a connection loss at 0 dB, but this is impossible to achieve because of the affect of echoes in the system (except with very short lengths). Therefore, a certain amount of loss must be tolerated to compensate against echo.

ASPECTS OF TR-08

TR-TSY-00008 (or simply TR-08) is titled *Digital Interface Between the SLC 96 Digital Loop Carrier System and a Local Digital Switch*. It is an old specification, first published by Bellcore in 1987, and it is based on the DLC system made by then AT&T.

TR-08 defines the operations of subscriber access lines running from a remote digital terminal (RDT) to a local digital switch (LDS). It supports up to 96 subscriber access lines running over three to five T1 lines.

The interface between the LDS and RT is a DSX-1 cross-connect, and TR-08 defines the following requirements for the system: (1) framing and signaling, (2) call control, (3) electrical specifications, (4) system maintenance, (5) testing , and (6) protection line switching.

The conventional T1 signals are employed, as well as the T1 framing conventions, and AB bits. The SLC 96 operates with a 4-shelf unit to support the 96 channels. Each shelf support 24 channels.

TR-08

- TR-08 is titled *Digital Interface Between the SLC 96 Digital Loop Carrier System and a Local Digital Switch.*
- It was first published by Bellcore in 1987, based on the DLC system made by then AT&T.
- It defines the operations of subscriber access lines running from a remote digital terminal (RDT) to a local digital switch (LDS).
- It supports up to 96 subscriber access lines running over three to five T1 lines.
- It defines the following requirements for the system:
  (a) framing and signaling
  (b) call control
  (c) electrical specifications
  (d) system maintenance
  (e) testing
  (f) protection line switching

Appendix F

GR-303 Requirements for ADSL, HFC, ATM, and Wireless-loop Distribution

GR-303-ILF REQUIREMENTS

GR-303-ILR is published by Bellcore with the title *Integrated Digital Loop Carrier System Generic Requirements, Objectives, and Interface.* This publication sets forth the requirements for the installation, operation, and maintenance of the ADSL, HFC, ATM, and wireless technologies on the local loop. GR-303-ILR also contains a description of the ongoing issues regarding the uses of these technologies, and the status of their resolution.

The document is divided into four sections, each dealing with one of the technologies. Bellcore acts as a coordinating body to assimilate the Regional Bell Operating Companies' views on the subject, and GR-303-ILR reflects a consensus on the issues. The results of these deliberations become required (R) or optional (O) provisions in the document.

Currently, 412 required or optional provisions are in the specification and are broken down as shown in Figure F–1. Final comments are due on these matters in late 1997.

ADSL/IDLC FUNCTIONAL REFERENCE ARCHITECTURE

Figure F–2 shows the reference architecture for the ADSL/IDLC scheme. Two modems are installed in a point-to-point configuration. The ADSL Terminal Unit-Central Office (ATU-C) is the closest to the Central

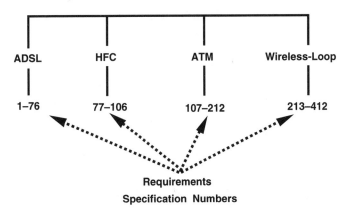

Figure F–1   GR-303-ILR requirements.

Office (CO), and the ADSL Terminal Unit-Remote (ADSL-R) is at the other end of the configuration. Its exact location depends on local conditions, and GR-303 stipulates that the ADSL system is subtending a GR-303 RDT.

The ATU-C and ATU-R terminate each other's signals, and the ATU-R has direct interfaces to the customer equipment through service modules (SM) (exact functions are being defined). It is likely that the ATU-R will be implemented as part of the CPE.

GR-303 ADSL/IDLC REQUIREMENTS (NOT ALL-INCLUSIVE)

Table F–1 provides some examples of the GR-303 requirements for ADSL. As noted in the table, these are not all-inclusive. Currently, provisions 1 to 76 are included (noted as R) or optional (noted as O) in GR-303-ILR, Issue 1D, December 1996.

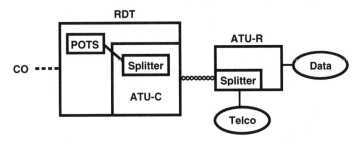

Figure F–2   ADSL/IDLC functional reference architecture.

Table F–1   GR-303 ADSL/IDLC Requirements (Not all-inclusive)

Requirement Number	Summary of Requirement
R-xDSL-1	ATU-C must support POTS and all CLASS services
R-xDSL-2	ATU-C must operate over twisted-pair IAW Bellcore TR-57
R-xDSL-3	Voice splitters must conform to T1E1.4 ADSL
R-xDSL-4/5	Power removal from ATU-C must not affect voice service
R-xDSL-6	Downstream: 6.144 Mbit/s, & 384, 160, 64 kbit/s Upstream: 384, 160, 64 kbit/s
R-xDSL-7	Within downstream: four 1.536 Mbit/s, three 2.048 Mbit/s, or up to two 3.072 Mbit/s within the 6.144 Mbit/s stream
O-xDSL-28	RDT should perform peak cell rate (PCR) policing
R-xDSL-33	OSI/CMIP shall be provided at the RDT/HDT interface
R-xDSL-44/46	System shall monitor for loss of signal (LOS), and loss of frame (LOF) in each direction
R-xDSL-70	Removal or unplugging ADSL CPE must not interrupt POTS
R-xDSL-71	POTS testing and ADSL testing must be transparent to each other
O-xDSL-74	Any new internal wiring for ADSL or Ethernet transport should be Category 5

GR-303 HFC REQUIREMENTS

Table F–2 provides some examples of the GR-303 requirements for HFC. As noted in the table, these are not all-inclusive. Currently, provisions 77 to 106 are included (noted as R) or optional (noted as O) in GR-303-ILR, Issue 1D, December 1996.

GR-303 WIRELESS-LOOP DISTRIBUTION SYSTEM (WLDS) REQUIREMENTS

Table F–3 provides some examples of the GR-303 requirements for ATM. As noted in the table, these are not all-inclusive. Currently, provisions 107 to 212 are included (noted as R) or optional (noted as O) in GR-303-ILR, Issue 1D, December 1996.

Table F–2   GR-303 HFC Requirements (Not all-inclusive)

Requirement Number	Summary of Requirement
R-HFC-77	System shall support loop-start signaling
O-HFC-78	Should support ISDN services and DS-1
R-HFC-79	Round trip delay (echo path delay) should not exceed 2.0 ms
R-HFC-82	BER for DS0 or equivalent signal shall not be less than 10^{-6} in the measurement period
R-HFC-83	BER for DS0 signal providing ISDN BRI shall not be less than 10^{-7} in the measurement period
R-HFC-84	BER for DS0 signal providing ISDN PRI shall not be less than 10^{-9} in the measurement period
R-HFC-85 through 88	Jitter generation and transfer must adhere to Bellcore GR-499-CORE
R-HFC-92	ATM cell loss rate shall be less than 10^{-9}
R-HFC-93	ATM cell insertion ratio shall be less than 10^{-9}
R-HFC-94 and 95	ATM bit error, jitter, wander, delay, delay variation, shall adhere to ongoing standards (GR-1110-CORE, and TA-NWT-001112)
R-HFC-96 through 98	Video signal quality must be at the FCC and NTSC standards
R-HFC-99	Audio quality is set for signal-to-noise ratio, harmonic distortion, gain, crosstalk
R-HFC-100 through 106	Sets minimum requirements for the optical part of the link, including wavelength range, transmitter/receiver requirements, permissible signal loss optical path penalty, and others

Table F–3   GR-303 ATM Requirements (Not all-inclusive)

Requirement Number	Summary of Requirement
R-ATM-107	If required, RDT shall support cell relay services
R-ATM-108 through 112	RDT must support (a) 1.544 Mbit/s DS1, (b) 155.52 Mbit/s SONET, (c) 44.736 Mbit/s DS3, (d) 25 Mbit/s UTP category 3 cable, (e) Frame Relay FUNI specifications
R-ATM-114 and 115	RDT shall support ATM peak cell rates, usage parameter control, sustained cell rate, and maximum burst size cited in industry standards
R-ATM-127 through 138	RDT bridges MAC frames at RDT to/from ATM cells. Supports 802.3, LLC/SNAP, Ethernet, Token Ring, and FDDI
R-ATM-147	For statistical multiplexing options, sum of peak cell rate allocations can exceed bandwidth of cell-based channel termination into which they are multiplexed
R-ATM-149 and 150	For management operations, RDT must support CMIP and run CMIP over one of these options: (a) TP4/CLNS, (b) ATM-CLNS, (c) TCP/IP over ATM, or (d) TCP/IP over non-ATM lower layers.
R-ATM-152 through 158	Configuration management is in accordance with ATM Forum standards and uses ILMI rules
R-ATM-159 through 175	Fault management operations are based on SONET standards, ITU-T ATM-based OAM
O-ATM-183 through 185	Congestion management measurements should be based on these options: (a) buffer occupancy, (b) utilization (number of cells transmitted), and/ or (c) percentage of dropped cells

GR-303 WIRELESS-LOOP DISTRIBUTION SYSTEM (WLDS)

Table F–4 provides some examples of the GR-303 requirements for wireless-loop access. As noted in the table, these are not all-inclusive. Currently, provisions 213 to 412 are included (noted as R) or optional (noted as O) in GR-303-ILR, Issue 1D, December 1996.

Table F–4   GR-303 Wireless-Loop Distribution System (WLDS) Requirements (Not all-inclusive)

Requirement Number	Summary of Requirement
R-FWA-213	Shall provide Message Telephone Service privacy equivalent to wire line
R-FWA-215 through 221	For optical fiber, SONET, and DS1 in the distribution plant, ongoing industry standards must be met
R-FWA-222	Loop-start signaling shall be supported[1]
O-FWA-223	Should support ISDN services
R-FWA-232	Interfaces shall be with conventional RJ-11 jacks, and CPE interface must be with conventional AWG cable
R-FWA-243 through 253	Signaling and ringing shall be in compliance with Bellcore practices
R-FWA-255 through 264	Transmission path, off-hook, loop closure, and other local loop signaling shall adhere to GR-303
R-FWA-265 through 275	Voice grade analog transmission requirements shall adhere to ongoing Bellcore and IEEE requirements (TR-57, IEEE 455)
O-FWA-281 through 285	Establishes optional guidelines for dealing with burst errors on a wireless loop
O-FWA-286 and 287	Provides guidance on speech clipping
O-FWA-289 through 291	Establishes requirements for transmission delay and the use of echo cancellers
O-FWA-292 through 294	Establishes bit error rate (BER) requirements in accordance with Bellcore GR-499

[1]Reverse loop signaling is also supported, under certain conditions. See citations 234–240 for more information.

SUMMARY

GR-303 requirements for the Residential Broadband technologies are now available. Requirements are published in GR-303-ILR (Integrated Loop Carrier). GR-303-ILR sets forth optional and required conditions for four technologies: ADSL, HFC, ATM, and wireless-loop distribution.

Additional References
and Acknowledgments

This book is one in a series of books in Prentice Hall's Advanced Communication Technologies which serves as a complement to the flagship book, "Emerging Communications Technologies."

In addition to the references cited in the book and those listed below, I would like to extend my appreciation and thanks to the following individuals and organizations who were most helpful to me during the preparation of this book.

Nortel provided me with information on their Internet gateway products (Chapter 6) and were always willing to answer questions and assist my analysis of their systems.

Lucent Technologies (Bell Labs) provided excellent descriptions of the ADAPt+ system (Chapter 7) and I am particularly indebted to Bharat T. Doshi, Subrahmanyam Dravida, Peter D. Magill, Curtis A. Siller, Jr., and Kotikalapudi Sriram for their views published in the Bell Labs Technical Journal, Summer 1996.

AT&T gave me excellent views on NEXT (near and crosstalk) and CAP (carrierless amplitude modulation) and I thank Richard L. Townsend, Jr., Jean-Jacques Werner, and Mai-Huong Nguyen for their research published in the AT&T Technical Journal, July/August 1995.

IBC Technical Services, London (as always) provided several avenues to learn about RBB in Europe, and those specific sources are cited in the book.

1. Fenton, Frank M. & Sipes, James D. (1996). "Architectural and Technological Trends in Access: An Overview," *Bell Labs Technical Journal.*

2. Lawrence, Victor B, Smithwick, Luke J., Werner, Jean-Jacques, & Zerros, Nickoloas A. (1996). "Broadband Access to the Home on Copper," *Bell Lab Technical Journal.*

3. Townsend, Richard L. Jr., Werner, Jean-Jacques, & Nguyen, Mai-Huong (1995). "Using Technology to Bring ATM to the Desktop," *AT&T Technical Journal.*

4. Nortel's "10 Gbit/s Transport Platform," *Telesis,* Issue 103.

5. Luther, William A. (1997). "Forces Shaping Spectrum into the Next Century." Conference on Spectrum Management sponsored by IBC Technical Services, LTD., London.

6. Brodsky, Ira (1996). "What will LMDS Hatch?" *Telephony.*

7. Palmer, Nate (1996). "The Wireless Local Loop: A Matter of Simple Economics," *Telephony.*

8. Titch, Steven (1997). "Blind Faith," *Telephony.*

Index